TWISTED RAILS, SUNKEN SHIPS
The Rhetoric of Nineteenth Century Steamboat and Railroad Accident Investigation Reports, 1833-1879

R. John Brockmann
University of Delaware

Baywood's Technical Communications Series
Series Editor: Charles H. Sides

Routledge
Taylor & Francis Group
LONDON AND NEW YORK

First published 2005 by Baywood Publishing Company, Inc

Published 2020 by Routledge
2 Park Square, Milton Park, Abingdon, Oxon OX14 4RN
52 Vanderbilt Avenue, New York, NY 10017

First issued in paperback 2020

Routledge is an imprint of the Taylor & Francis Group, an informa business

Library of Congress Catalog Number: 2004057394

Library of Congress Cataloging-in-Publication Data

Brockmann, R. John.
 Twisted rails, sunken ships : the rhetoric of nineteenth century steamboat and railroad accident investigation reports, 1833-1879 / R. John Brockmann.
 p. cm. - - (Baywood's technical communications series)
 Includes bibliographical references and index.
 ISBN 0-89503-291-0 (cloth)
 1. Railroads--United States--Accidents. 2. Steamboats--United States--Accidents. 3. Accident investigation--United States. I. Title. II. Baywood's technical communications series (Unnumbered)

 HE1780.B76 2004
 363.12'265'097309034--dc22
                                                    2004057394

ISBN 13: 978-0-415-78479-5 (pbk)
ISBN 13: 978-0-89503-291-1 (hbk)

Dedication

At the end of his 1879 book, *Notes on Railroad Accidents*, Charles Francis Adams, Jr. wrote:

> The worst of it is, too, that if the blood of the martyrs thus profusely spilled is at all the seed of the church, it is a seed terribly slow of germination. Each step in the slow progress is a Golgotha. In the case of railroad disasters, however, a striking exception is afforded to this rule. The victims of these, at least, do not lose their lives without great and immediate compensating benefits to mankind. After each new "horror," as it is called, the whole world travels with an appreciable increase of safety. Both by public opinion and the courts of law the companies are held to a most rigid responsibility. The causes which led to the disaster are anxiously investigated by ingenious men, new appliances are invented, new precautions are imposed, a greater and more watchful care is inculcated. And hence it has resulted that each year, and in obvious consequence of each fresh catastrophe, travel by rail has become safer and safer, until it has been said, and with no inconsiderable degree of truth too, that the very safest place into which a man can put himself is the inside of a first-class railroad carriage on a train in full motion [1, p. 276].

This book then is dedicated to the memory of those thousands who lost their lives on steamboats and railroads in the nineteenth century and whose lives allow us in the twenty-first century to travel safer.

I would specifically like to thank:

University of Delaware's Interlibrary Loan Program

My brother Paul and his children in St. Louis

Those at the Princeton Libraries

A variety of British historians of the Board of Trade's RR Inspectorate

The archives at the Railroad Museum of America

Hagley Museum and Library

Thomas Taber and the railroad historians in Reading, Penn.

Table of Contents

List of Figures and Tables

List of Figures

List of Tables

Acknowledgments

Figure 5. photograph courtesy Peabody Essex Museum, Salem, MA.

Figure 22, Mayor Samuel Davies of Cincinnati, and 23, Professor John Locke, with permission from the Cincinnati Museum.

Figure 36. Eyewitness Sketch of the Gasconade Wreck with permission from Professor Karl Roider.

Figure 45 with permission from the North Adams (MA) Public Library.

Introduction:
The Dance of Nineteenth Century Steamboat and Railroad Accident Investigation Reports

TWO 1911 ICC REPORTS

With the passage of the Accident Reports Act of May 6, 1910, the federal government became involved in railroad accident investigations. Many of these reports are now available online at

http://dotlibrary1.specialcollection.net/scripts/ws.dll?login&site=dot_railroads

Below are two of the railroad accident investigations collected at this site, and one can easily see their similarities.

Report 1		Report 2
May 23, 1911.		Washington, D.C.,
		June 6, 1911
REPORT OF INVESTIGATION RELATIVE OF CAUSE OF ACCIDENT TO BALTIMORE & OHIO RAILROAD PASSENGER TRAIN No. 14 ON THE WASHINGTON TERMINAL COMPANY'S TRACKS, MAY 30th, 1911.	*Both use the format of a letter.*	Honourable C. C. McChord, Commissioner, Interstate Commerce Commission. In re train accident near Martin's Creek Station on the Belvidere Division of the Pennsylvania railroad.
From a personal investigation and interviews had with the Baltimore & Ohio and Washington Terminal people we find as follows:	*Both address the ICC commissioner.*	Dear Sir: We have the honor to report to the Commission the result of our inquiry, held, jointly with the Board of Public Utility Commissioners for the State of New Jersey, at Trenton, New Jersey,
That train #14 left the Union Station bound for Baltimore, Md., at 10:54 p.m. and nosisted of B&G		May 31, into the causes leading to the

Locomotive #2121, one mail, one baggage, three coaches and one parlor, making a total of six cars. The crew was composed of S. Montgomery, Conductor; John Michael, Baggageman; B. Kimmell, flagman; C. H. Burch, Engineman; and Howard Cramblitt, Fireman.

Conductor Montgomery stated that the crew had not been on duty an excessive length of time, having left Cumberland, Md., at 6:52 p.m. after having had ten hours rest before leaving time of train.

At the frog [sic] is crossover track near bridge "L", about 3300 feet north from where the train started at Union Station train shed, the locomotive left the track and ran on the ground some two-hundred feet. The train did not break loose from the locomotive, neither did it leave the track, but continued on the rails of the crossover track. The locomotive when it stopped was nearly diagonally across the tracks to the east of crossover track and the tender cramped around towards the right-hand side of the locomotive. When the locomotive left the track the fireman was standing on the apron between the locomotive and tender, he jumped off from the right-hand side and stated that the train was running from eight to ten miles per hour, that he did not fall or get hurt and that when he jumped the engineman was getting off his seat in the cab but did not see him get off and did not see him again until his body was found between the rails and partially under the forward tracks of the mail car.

The body did not seem to have been run over by the wheels but had been crushed by the brake rigging under the trucks. The shock caused by the stopping of the train was so slight that it was hardly noticed by the passengers in the train. No one was injured in any was except the engineman.

Both begin with a recitation of the facts of the accident as provided by eyewitnesses.

Both have a high percentage of passive voice verbs (23% and 36%).

Both have similar readability scores: the Flesch reading indexes are 56.1 and 47.3, while the Flesch-Kincaid grade levels of the two are 11.6 and 12.0.

accident which occurred eight-tenths off a rile south of Martin's Creek Station on the Belvidere Division of the Pennsylvania Railroad, April 29, 1911.

Description

The second section of passenger train No. 573 consisted of Pennsylvania engine No. 3169, D.L.&N. combination car No. 706, D.L.&N. coaches Nos. 84, 100 and 85, and D.L.&N. dining car No. 458, in the order named. All of the cars were of wooden construction with vestibules and steel platforms. Coach No. 100 was lighted with acetylene gas, and dining car No. 458 was lighted with acetylene gas and equipped with an axle-generator for electric light. The other cars were lighted with Pintsch gas. Train enroute from Union, New York, to Washington, D. C., with 166 passengers and 2 tourist agents. Train left Manunka Chunk at 2:40 p.m. and was derailed at about 2: 56 p.m. April 29, 1911, eight-tenths off a mile south of Martin's Creek Station, about ten miles south of Naminka Chunk, resulting in the death of 12 persons and the injury of 101 persons, many seriously. The enginemen, conductor and baggageman received injuries from which they soon died, and the fireman was seriously injured.

The train was running at a speed of about 50 miles per hour when the forward trucks of the tank cars with the exception that the rear pair of wheels of the dining car was not derailed. None of the cars was telescoped. The train was thrown down an embankment on the east and outside side of a 3 1/2 degree curve, the engine, tender, and first car of the train turning over on their side, the remaining cars standing nearly upright.

The detailment was immediately followed by fire caused by the ignition of gas, evidently from a puncture in

The tower-man said the accident happened at 10:57 p.m. This being the case, in making the distance of 3300 feet in three minutes, would indicate that the train had not exceeded any average rate of speed of 121/2 miles per hour.

It is impossible to state whether the engineman was thrown off or jumped. The statements made by the fireman, with reference to observing the engineman getting off the seat and what transpired on the locomotive after he left the track, cannot be fully relied upon as it was stated that he was dazed and when interviewed later seemed excited and confused.

The steam on the locomotive was not shut off. The drivers continued to turn rapidly for some five minutes after having left the track and until the locomotive had damaged herself to such on extent that she had no power. It is though that the engineman did not apply the power brakes and those they more nor applied [sic] until some break occurred in the air connections by the derailment causing the brakes to apply automatically. If the engineman was thrown off that could account for his not shutting off the steam and applying the air.

From what we could observe and learned from others, the track, switches and signals were all in good condition. The curve to crossover track is 121/2 degrees. The wheelbase of the locomotive is 13 feet 2 inches.

It is our opinion that some obstruction may have been on the track or something may have fallen from the locomotive truck, derailing the same. The frog showed some irregular marks as if something scraped over it and a few feet north shows the first marks where the wheels left the rails. These marks were not very heavy and would indicate that the forward truck wheels made them. Where the drivers left the

Both draw conclusions at the end from the evidence provided.

the gas tank under the third coach (No. 100) as well as from the escaping gas from the gas tanks under the other cars, which has their connections broken and permitted gas to escape. All cars were totally consumed by fire. The gas tank under the dining car exploded several hours after the wreck, which was caused by heat from the burning cars.

The section foreman had been throwing, or shifting, about 1,000 feet of track on this curve the day of the accident, and was engaged, at the time of the accident, in lining up and surfacing that portion of the track in the immediate proximity to the spot where the accident occurred.

The track is laid with 85-pound standard, steel rails, which had been in service for nine years, and showed from 1/2 to 1/2 inch wear. There were from 1 to 2 bad ties in the track for each rail length, and tieplates were used on each rail. Track is ballasted with gravel and cinders.

On the morning of April 29, 1911, acting under the instructions of the Supervisor of the Belvidere Division of the Pennsylvania Railroad, the section foreman, with a force of seventeen men, was engaged on throwing, realigning and surfacing the curve south of the Ferry Crossing, about eight-tenths of a mile south of Martin's Greek Station, to the line stakes that had been set some months before.

The track at this point runs almost directly north and south with about 1/2 to 1% grade toward the south. The curve is about 21/2 degrees, and has a superelevation of about five inches for the east or outside rail.

The required work was to throw or shift the track from about two to nine inches at different points for a distance of about two or nine inches at different points for a distance of about track the rails were bent and torn up for some distance.

The fireman stated that he had fired for five years on freight and three locomotive #2121, also that the locomotive was in good condition, rode good, took all curves nicely and nothing wrong with it which would account for its leaving the track.

There was no damage done to the cars in the train. There was an excessive strain on the draw heads between the tender and mail car caused by the cramped condition in which the cars were, which made it impossible to uncouple them at that time and as there was only a small amount of mail in the car the mail was transferred to the baggage car and balance of train taken back to Union Station.

From the damaged condition in which we found the locomotive so many of its parts destroyed and missing, loose driving wheels, damaged trucks, broken bores and brake rigging, in fact the locomotive (as the saying is) had stripped herself - it would be difficult for us to say that there had been anything wrong with the locomotive which would have caused the accident.

Later we attended the Coroner's inquest but there was no information brought out that we had not previously obtained.

The officials and employees of both the Baltimore & Ohio Railroad and the Washington Terminal Company were very courteous and perfectly willing to render us all the assistance within their power in making the investigation, in fact, we received the thanks of the officials for our assistance in endeavoring to locate the cause of the accident.

We attach hereto copies of statements from the employees which were interviewed in regard to the matter.

Respectfully submitted,

In Report 1, the evidence was destroyed or missing, and so the conclusions are drawn by those writing the report.

We can read in Report 1 that there is a parallel and independent investigation being done by a coroner.

1000 feet. The ballast was removed from the ends of the ties on the outside of the curve for the distance necessary to permit of the throw or shift of the truck to the proper alignment. After throwing this track by the use of bare and by easy stages of from one to two inches at a time to the proper alignment as indicated by the line stakes, the ends of the ties were tamped up with shovels, the section foreman them lined up and surfaced the inside rail, and had partially lined up and surfaced the outside rail.

The track, both north and south of as well as at the point of derailment, had been thrown from two or nine inches on the day of the accident. Track jacks were used at different places on the curve in raising track to proper level, and the lining up and surfacing had not been completed.

At the time of the accident the men were engaged in filling up the center of the track and tamping up under the ties with shovels at a point just immediately north of the place where the derailment occurred. The truck gauge was not used at any time in doing this work but the level board was used for the purpose of arranging proper superelevation and the necessary run-off leading to the same.

During the forenoon flagman were used to protect this track in both directions, and after the noon hour a flagman was used to protect against trains from the north, until about 1:00 p.m., the time of the arrival of train 1st 573, after which time no flagman was used. Three trains passed over this track between 1:00 p.m. and 2:56 p.m., the time 2d 575 was wrecked. None of them, however, was running at the race of speed of the wrecked train.

Eyewitnesses of the accident say that the cars were derailed first. Some testified there was an explosion followed by the crash of derailment, others that the crash of derailment was immediately followed by an explosion, others say that the crash or derailment was all that they heard or saw. All agree as to the almost immediate presence of fire. Testimony as to the condition of the gas tank equipment disproves any theory of gas explosion on account of the fact that the gas tank under car No. 100, the one supposed to have exploded, had been punctured by some outside agency.

Two committees of experts selected by the Pennsylvania Railroad Company made careful inquiry and investigation as to the cause of the accident, and agree as to it being a derailment of the forward trucks of the tender and agree, practically, as to where these trucks left the rail. They disagreed as to the cause of the derailment. One committee reported the derailment as evidently caused by a combination of uneven and irregular track, the high speed of the wrecked train while passing over the track, and the probable failure of the section men to have proper superelevation on the curve, together with suitable run-off leading to same, and sufficient ballast against end of ties on high side of curve. The other committee reported that track condition was such as would warrant them expressing the opinion that it was not the cause of the derailment.

An outside expert, who was on the ground May 2d, gathering data and making measurements as to the condition of the track both at the point of the accident and at the curve just north of the accident, expresses the opinion that the cause of the derailment was the uneven and irregular condition of the track and the failure to have proper superelevation on the curve, and run-off leading to some, causing the forward trucks of the tender to mount the rail, followed by the derailment of the other cars in the train.

In Report 2, outside experts selected by the companies under investigation were allowed to offer their opinions.

In both cases, the companies seem to be looking to the ICC investigation to "locate the cause of the accident."

Finally, in both cases, the findings seem to be future-oriented in suggesting what might be done to prevent such accidents from recurring, and they do not include any legal indictments.

Conclusion

There can be no doubt from the evidence in this case, that the accident was a derailment, caused by an uneven, irregular, and insecure condition of track which would not permit a train to pass over it in safety at a speed of from 50 to 60 miles per hour, the rate at which this train was running.

It is our opinion that this piece of track should have been protected by flag, until the work was completed, that is, until the elevation of the high rail had been carried around the curve and properly run off at the same point the surfacing had been run off on the lower rail, and ballast replaced against the ends of the ties on the high side of the curve.

The rule, as interpreted by an official of the Pennsylvania Railroad Company, does not require flag protection in doing work of this character, and we believe such rule should be so amended as to leave no doubt as to the requirement of flag protection to all trains when the track is being shifted, railroad or thrown, or where such similar insecure condition of track exist.

The fact that the cars in this train were of wooden construction, and that the lighting system used was gas, are evidently responsible for the great loss of life and the total construction of the train by fire. Had the cars been of steel construction, or had electricity been used as the lighting system, it is certain the loss of life would not have been so great.

The similarities of these two 1911 ICC reports did not happen by chance, but were the result of an evolution of the discourse communities involved with investigating technological accidents. The relationships of private companies, coroners, outside experts, and government investigators all had to be developed and experimented with before a genre of investigation reports could exist. The position of science as a public investigation tool, evident in these two reports, was not so in the beginning. This discourse community began with the technology of the steamboat in the 1820s and the railroad in the 1830s. This book is the story of the evolution of these investigation discourse communities in published reports written between 1833 and 1879 [1]. Specifically, we look at the inter-actions among three different types of investigation reports: the findings of the coroner's jury, defensive explanations from involved companies, and reports by scientists. Using the reports generated by seven accidents on railroads and steam-boats between 1833 and 1876:

- The Explosion of the Steam Boat *New England* in the Connecticut River, 1833
- The Explosion of the Locomotive Engine *Richmond* near Reading Penn-sylvania, 1844
- The Explosion of the Steam Boat *Moselle* in Cincinatti, 1838
- The Camden and Amboy Railroad Collision in Burlington, New Jersey, 1855
- The Gasconade Bridge Collapse on the Pacific Railroad in Missouri, 1855
- The Eastern Railroad Collision in Revere, Massachusetts, 1871
- The Ashtabula Railroad Bridge Collapse in Ohio, 1876

we can observe the changes in how these reports interacted and changed over the course of the nineteenth century.

Four major changes took place in the country during these years that greatly affect the impact of one or another of the reports, and the roles of those involved in the investigations. Such accidents obviously involved American technology and corporate management structure, and the great increase in complexity of these two had a large effect on the rhetoric of the reports. Moreover, the geographic location of "cutting-edge" technology involved in the accidents moved from established communities in the East to the Western frontier with several effects on the rhetoric of the reports. Such accident investigations were also a legal matter, and the replacement of the supremacy of private property rights early in the century by the supremacy of governmental oversight later in the century had great effects on the rhetoric of the reports. Finally, these accidents involving the cutting-edge technology of the day did not just happen in the United States. Great Britain also experienced such disasters, and its creation of the Railroad Inspectorate of the British Board of Trade had a large effect on the final development of accident investigations in the United States.

The final chapter, Chapter Eight, goes beyond these reports to look at a book, *Notes on Railroad Accidents*, in which the leader of the Massachusetts Railroad Commission reviewed progress in accident investigations over the course of the nineteenth century, as well as his personal involvement in the investigations related to the collision on the Eastern Railroad at Revere, Massachusetts, in 1871, and the collapse of the railroad bridge in Ashtabula Ohio in 1876. This book closes with the publication of this key technical text, since one of the results of this book is that the federal government through the creation of the Interstate Commerce Commission (ICC) directed all subsequent investigations.

SHIFTS IN AMERICA AFFECTING ACCIDENT INVESTIGATION REPORTS

The Evolution in Accident Complexity

The power of the steamboat beginning in the 1820s and the locomotive in the 1830s introduced the world to more than technology; it changed the very definition of causation and accident. In Diderot's pre-industrial-world *Encyclopedia* (1772), he defined "accident" as a "grammatical or philosophical concept equivalent to coincidence" [2, p. 131]. In 1844, only seventy-two years later, the French *Encyclopedia of Fire and Steam* devoted a nine-page article to defining "accidents":

> All man-made things are subject to accidents. By a kind of compensation . . . , the more these things are perfected, the greater the gravity of the accidents that happen to them. That is why, without rigorous surveillance at all points, the most powerful and most perfect industrial means, that is, steam engines and railroad trains, can cause the most grave and fatal mishaps. The mass of objects they set in motion, the velocity they engender, their very power, once halted or turned from its proper objective, is transformed into a terrible agent of destruction. Steam power, while opening up new and hitherto unknown roads to man, also seems to continually put him in a position best compared to that of man who is walking along the edge of the precipice and cannot afford a single false step. It is a situation analogous to the one engineers term an unstable equilibrium, which can be upset by the least little effort [3, pp. 2-3].

"Accidents" of this latter sort were new in antebellum America, and thus the initial step in the investigation of an accident fatality was still the traditional convening of a coroner's jury. Such juries predated the *Magna Carta* and were a "tribunal of record" composed of twelve citizens meeting to collect evidence shortly after an accident and usually at the scene of an accident.

However, such venerable methods of collecting evidence became problematic with the increasingly complex technology of steamboats and railroads. The *Railroad Gazette* was scathing in its judgment of coroner's juries in 1877:

> Coroner's juries are proverbial for their stupidity, and, when the subject to be investigated involves some of the most abstruse facts involved, or drawing correct conclusions from premises involving profound mathematical and scientific questions, it is very rare that either coroners or coroners' juries have

any special training which would qualify them for investigating intelligently the causes of ordinary railroad accidents, and, when such inquiries involve some of the most profound questions of engineering science, the average coroner and his jury are as helpless and imbecilic as so many children would be in dealing with the facts or in drawing conclusions therefrom [4, p. 6].

Combined with this increase in technological complexity, the venerable coroner's jury was also confronted with a rise in organizational complexity, most especially in the organization of railroads. Alfred Chandler demonstrated in *Strategy and Structure* that prior to 1850, organizations had little need for administrative structure because their small size allowed owners to manage personally. However, as organizations grew in size, so did their organizational complexity, giving coroner's juries great difficulties in designating wrongdoers:

What is more, wrongs were occurring that it was increasingly difficult (expensive, unfeasible) to lay at the feet of any particular human wrongdoer: When a bridge collapsed, for example, who was at fault? More complicating still, even where the wrongful act could be traced to some particular tangible human, he was increasingly not, as in some of the early cases, a well-to-do (read sue-able) executive, but a railroad porter or a dock worker. When one looked behind this complex network of authority and communication, who—what particular individual—was his principal? The question was to become increasingly exasperating and meaningless, as the organization grew more complex [1, p. 23].

Figure 1. Coroner's jury in the investigation of the sinking of the steamboat *General Slocum* in 1904.

Interestingly, even if the leading lights of the legal and scientific establishment were able to look behind the proximate cause and participants, the general American public, as reflected in its popular culture, did not. As late as 1887, when Artie Kellogg wrote "The Railway Wreck" song, the fault was assigned to human error but not anything systemic in the technology or organization [5, pp. 83-84]. Corporate managers and superintendents also found it convenient to assign blame to the proximate actors in an accident. Lt. Col. Wynne of the British Railway Inspectorate in the investigation of a February 8, 1858, boiler explosion at Caterham Junction, wrote in his report:

> I desire to take the opportunity of stating that all my experience goes to confirm the view I have for many years taken, that the majority of these explosions occur under ordinary working pressure of the steam, and can be traced to the boiler being worked out or to some marked defect in its construction, and not to steam of extreme tension generated by the willfulness of the driver loading the safety-valves, and which is a favorite theory of locomotive superintendents to relieve themselves from blame [6, p. 52].

The Evolution in Liability Leads to Blamelessness

Once the coroner's jury accomplished the rough collection of evidence and causation, the victims and defendants began their debate over legal responsibility in liability and negligence litigation. Initially such debate was argued at a quite primitive level, since the courts simply asked: Did the defendant perform the physical act that injured the plaintiff? [8, p. 5]. Considerations of blameworthiness or carelessness did not arise in the early part of the nineteenth century at this time of this "strict liability" [9, p. 85].

Overwhelmed by such complexity of causation and complexity of organizational responsibility, a sense of inevitability began to emerge in the courts and be embodied in the law. The model for such inevitability was the blamelessness of a captain or pilot of a vessel that collided with another vessel during a natural disaster despite the best efforts of that captain or pilot to prevent the accident [8, p. 6]. This new notion of inevitability transformed the earlier simple notions of "strict liability" into a concern for "ordinary care." Now the courts began to ask: Did the defendant use all means of "ordinary care" to prevent the accident from occurring? If the answer was "Yes," the defendant would not be liable to the victim for negligence. This new legal notion of causation came to be called "universal liability," in which the whole world, as Supreme Court Judge Oliver Wendell Holmes stated, was liable for the "ordinary care" of the rest of the world [8, p. 6].

Soon it became clear that such universal liability could be an obstacle to the risk taking of technological entrepreneurs with cutting-edge technology. In response,

PUNCH, OR THE LONDON CHARIVARI—September 26, 1874.

RAILWAY RESPONSIBILITY.

Mr. Punch. "NO, NO, MR. DIRECTOR, *THEY'RE* NOT SO MUCH TO BLAME. IT'S *YOUR* PRECIOUS FALSE ECONOMY, UNPUNCTUALITY, AND GENERAL WANT OF SYSTEM THAT DOES ALL THE MISCHIEF."

Figure 2. *Punch*'s cartoon about relative responsibility for railroad wrecks (1874) [7].

legal buffers on the notion of universal liability began to be developed, so that entrepreneurs soon looked to the following liability defenses:

- Assumption of risk—Employees took their own chances and assumed the risks involved with working. When an employee "hired out," he was expected to know, for example, that railroad work was dangerous and that there was a good chance that severe or fatal injuries could occur at some point in time. Thus, employees could not sue an employer for negligence.
- Negligence of a fellow employee—A company was not liable when an injury to an employee was the result of the carelessness of a fellow employee.
- Contributory negligence—When a victim contributed to his or her own injury or death, the courts viewed such a contribution as a complete bar to assigning negligence to another.
- Proximate cause of injury—An injured party had to prove that negligence was the most likely cause of an injury, or the cause without which his or her injuries would not have occurred.

The railroads applied these legal concepts very successfully, and many who suffered disabling injuries, or were the survivors of fatally injured persons, were left to rely upon family resources or welfare to survive [11]. In short,

> a pattern of practice emerged in which the courts increasingly found the behavior of industrialists—factory, steamship, and railroad owners, primarily—to be within the parameters of 'ordinary care,' even when the facts suggested an absence of care or an adequate attention to safety [8, p. 8].

Since a court could find a defendant negligent only after overcoming each of these legal buffers, blamelessness in technical accidents became an increasingly common finding:

> Whatever natural philosophers may think of this, the elements which combine to create the power of steam, are entirely within the reach of accident, and are no more subject to fixed laws than the elements which propel the ship at sea. Whatever may be the theories on the subject, universal experience is that no human skill can entirely guard against accidents, either in the one case or in the other [12, p. 290].

By 1840, the "principle that one could not be held liable for socially useful activity exercised with due care became a commonplace of American law" [9, p. 99]. From the point of view of the defendant risk-taking entrepreneurs, after the coroner's jury had collected its evidence, the second step in the dance of accident investigations was production of a report that would protect the entrepreneurs from accusations of negligence by demonstrating that "due care" and "common practice" had been followed.

However, a general feeling of helplessness in the face of "the mighty despotism of steam" began to emerge in American society. Blamelessness in accidents, though legally sufficient to protect entrepreneurs, was insufficient to quiet society's emotional need to find a culprit. Here, for example, is an 1851 editorial entitled, "Killing of No Consequence," in which the *New York Times* argued, "such accidents have been too long suffered to pass without blame to anyone":

> Killing men by Railroad trains seems to be all in the way of business—a thing to be looked for, and no more to be punished by hanging than killing by physicians in regular practice or killing by inches in a County poorhouse. We have no faith in these accidents. Accident has very little to do in this world's affairs. Everything that happens has an adequate cause, and that cause can be foreseen. . . . When a train of cars goes off the track, something throws it off. It was made expressly to stay on—and it will stay on, unless something interferes with it [13, p. 12].

Moreover, in the investigation into the Gasconade bridge disaster of 1855 (the subject of Chapter Five), here is what the *Scientific American* anticipated would be found:

> The Committee appointed by the citizens of St. Louis to investigate the affair of the bridge over the Gasconade River, on the Pacific Railroad, after taking and destroying so many lives, have reported that it was caused by the speed at which the train was going, the bridge being unable to sustain loaded trains running at more than five miles per hour. One of the Committee, Henry Kosier [sic], presented a minority report declaring that the bridge was totally incapable of bearing even its own weight.
>
> What a trifling there was in this instance with human life.
>
> But who is to blame?
>
> Nobody, we suppose [14, p. 1].

Blamelessness, helplessness, and an inability to find effective redress in the traditional channels of jurisprudence found its nadir in the polemical duel played out in the newspapers of New York and New Jersey during the 1855 case of the Camden and Amboy railroad accident.

The Evolution of an Alternative to Coroner's Juries and Liability—Disinterested Scientific Investigations

In the face of such blamelessness and helplessness, many wanted accident investigations to move beyond simply proving that actions causing injuries were "common practice" to examining the procedures themselves, the technology itself, and to bring in questions of a systemic nature. In the majority of cases during the Antebellum Era, the people who wanted to look at root causes and systemic problems of technology were the very same "objective judges" appealed to during consideration of the Steamboat Bill of 1838: the scientists of the Franklin Institute who were, by 1840, organized into the Committee of Science and the Arts [10, 15].

Composed of strictly volunteer scientists and mechanicians, the Committee of Science and the Arts had at its disposal unique, strength-of-material, testing instruments and a body of knowledge developed during the 1830s and the institute's original, federally funded investigations into steamboat explosions. Whereas the coroner's jury and company investigative reports focused on assigning liability for a past event, the institute's "disinterested" reports had the following as their typical goal:

> . . . it is not our intention to dwell upon anything which relates merely to the disaster itself; that is past, and if retribution is to be exacted, it must be in due course of law, which we have no desire to forestall by prejudging the case either to condemnation or acquittal of my one concerned. Nor shall we dwell upon the tone of the report in question, which has been complained of as cold and unfeeling: but we desire to advert to parts of it, in which opinions are expressed as to the possibility of lessening the liability to accidents upon this and other roads, and the means to be used for such a purpose [16, p. 347].

In the first two accident investigations, all before the Civil War and all in the East, where the power of courts and the adversarial approach was fully established, the results of these "disinterested" scientific investigations were presented long after the accident and had only peripheral impact. The time required for scientific investigations meant that the application of disinterested scientific findings from the Committee of Science and the Arts had no specific effect on the investigations. The "disinterested scientific" answers usually arrived too late and were usually published only in small-circulation, scientifically sophisticated journals, such as the *Journal of the Franklin Institute*.

However, as technology moved toward the Western frontier where the power of the courts and the adversarial approach was only just being established, and as scientific know-how was disseminated throughout society, other "disinterested" judges entered the investigations and their findings began to take more and more of a central role. Some of these "disinterested" judges were pioneer scientists and civil engineers, while later government commissions such as those of the Massachusetts Railroad Commission under Charles Francis Adams, Jr. took center stage in the 1870s, leading eventually to the creation of the Interstate Commerce Commission in the mid-1880s.

The reports of these later "disinterested" investigators came out more quickly and were often part and parcel of the coroner's report or even of the defendant company's report. Reaching the general public quickly, they hoped to mold public opinion to secure a future solution to steamboat and railroad accidents. In his 1879 valedictory letter, Chairman Charles Francis Adams Jr. wrote about the crucial role of communicating to the public about the accidents:

> The Commissioners have no power except to recommend and report. Their only appeal is to publicity. The Board is at once prosecuting officer, judge, and jury, but with no sheriff to enforce its process. This method of railroad

supervision is peculiar to Massachusetts; but I do not hesitate to say that I believe that it is the best and the most effective method which has ever been devised,—the best for the community, and the best for the corporations.

...

Where, as in this case, a board depends for its power almost exclusively on the way it is able to present facts to the public, it can accomplish nothing unless it contains someone specially trained to do this effectively and understandingly.

...

The idea as respects railroads which this Board originated and now represents—the supervisory regulation through publicity and intelligent discussion—has just begun to be developed [17, pp. 3-4; 5-6; 6].

THREE SHIFTS IN THE DISCOURSE COMMUNITY

The changes in these reports and their interactions in the temporary discourse communities responding to disasters move through roughly three stages:

1. Part 1 (Chapters 1 and 2) describes the investigation arrangements that prevailed in the earliest steamboat and railroad accident investigations. In these earliest investigations, the corporate defensive report used science on its behalf and carried the weight of the explanation for the public.

2. Part 2 (Chapters 3, 4, and 5) describes a transition time in the design and interaction of the investigation reports brought about by increased publicity, political involvement, and the emotional engagement of the authors. Earlier arrangements and interactions were overturned in this era of transformation.

3. Part 3 (Chapter 6, 7, and 8) describes the new standard investigation arrangements in which the public investigations used science on its behalf and carried the weight of the explanation. This new standard was heavily influenced by the chair of the Massachusetts Railroad Commission, Charles Francis Adams, Jr.

ENDNOTES

1. Christopher D. Stone, *Where the Law Ends: The Social Control of Corporate Behavior*, New York: Harper & Row, 1975.
2. Wolfgang Schivelbusch, *The Railway Journey: The Industrialization of Time and Space in the 19th Century*, Berkeley, Calif.: University of California Press, 1986.
3. Felix Tourneux, *Encyclopedia of Fire and Steam* (Paris, 1844) [Cited in 1, pp. 131-132].
4. "The Ashtabula Accident," *Railway Gazette*, 1/5/1877.
5. Jon W. Finson, *The Voices that Are Gone: Themes in Nineteenth-Century American Popular Song*, New York: Oxford University Press, 1994.

6. Christian H. Hewison, *Locomotive Boiler Explosions*, North Pomfret, Vt.: David & Charles, 1983.
7. *Punch, or the London Charivari*, September 26, 1874.
8. Nan Goodman, *Shifting the Blame: Literature, Law, and the Theory of Accidents in Nineteenth-Century America*, Princeton, N.J.: Princeton University Press, 1998.
9. Morton Horwitz, *The Transformation of American Law, 1780-1860*, Oxford: Oxford University Press, 1992,
10. R. John Brockmann, *Exploding Steamboats, Senate Debates, and Technical Reports: The Convergence of Technology, Politics and Rhetoric in the Steamboat Bill of 1838*, Amityville, N.Y.: Baywood, 2002.
11. Crow Law Firm, California, 1998 Website, www.crowlaw.com.
12. Citizens Insurance Company of Missouri v. Glasgow, Shaw and Larkin, 9 Missouri Reports, 246. [Cited in Louis C. Hunter, *Steamboats on the Western Rivers: An Economic and Technological History*, Cambridge, Mass.: Harvard University Press, 1949.]
13. Wu Jie, "The Public Reaction to Railroad Accidents in the United States: 1850-1900," Master of Arts Thesis, History Department, University of Massachusetts, Boston, 1982.
14. *Scientific American* 9 (13), December 8, 1855.
15. Stephanie Morris, "For the Promotion of Technology: An Historical and Archival Essay on the Franklin Institute's Committee on Science and the Arts," in A. Michael McMahon and Stephanie Morris (eds.), *Technology in Industrial America*, Wilmington, Del.: Scholarly Resources, 1977, xiii–xxxix.
16. "Railroad Accidents," *Journal of the Franklin Institute*, 30(5), November 1855.
17. *Massachusetts House of Representatives Document Number 225*, (March 1879), Boston, n.p.

PART ONE

Using Science as a
Corporate Defense

CHAPTER 1

The Collaboration of Science and the Corporations Takes Center Stage While the Coroner's Jury is Befuddled by Complexity

THE ACCIDENT—THE EXPLOSION OF THE STEAM BOAT *NEW ENGLAND*, OCTOBER 9, 1833

In 1830, Professor Benjamin Silliman turned his attention from editing his *American Journal of Science and the Arts* to composing an article suggesting alternative designs to increase the safety of steamboats. He despaired that the engines would ever be completely free of boiler explosions because the pressure of the steam created in the boilers was so high, while the quality of metallurgy for the boilers was so low [1, pp. 353-355; 2, pp. 49, 98]. However, Silliman also felt that "[t]he boat which is first ascertained to afford absolute security will be a fortune to its proprietors" [1, p. 353]. He offered two design approaches.

One was the creation of "safety barges" (also called "lady boats" [4, p. 54]), in which boats with engines aboard would tow barges without engines, and the passengers would be carried on these engine-less barges [1, p. 354]. Such safety barges were already being successfully operated by William Redfield between New York and Albany as the Swiftsure Line [5, p. 19; 6, p. 317]. Newspaper advertisements for the line asked, "Why sleep over a volcano?" [7, p. 59]. Others advertisements for the line claimed, "Passengers on board the Safety Barges will not be in the least exposed to any accident by reason of the fire or steam on board the steamboats" [8, p. 38].

The second design option Silliman advocated was to move the boilers from their customary placement in the middle of the vessel below the deck to over the paddle-wheel's "guards" (housing) outside the hull and deck. Shifting the placement of the boilers in this way would not correct any inherent problems [10], but it would minimize any effects of an accidental boiler explosion by allowing the explosive force to blow out freely overboard to the port and starboard and away from the passengers and hull. Such a design was much like that of the gunpowder

Figure 3. Professor Benjamin Silliman, editor of *American Journal of Science and the Arts* and Chair of Board of Examiners appointed by the Connecticut River Steam Boat Company to inquire into the causes of the explosion of the steamboat *New England* [3, p. 77].

works of the time, in which gunpowder manufacturing buildings had three stone walls and one wooden wall. The wooden wall could blow out, and thus the force of the accidental explosion could be expended outward saving some lives and equipment [1, p. 355].

When Lawrence and Sneden designed the steamboat *New England* for the Connecticut River Steam Boat Company in 1833, they capitalized on Silliman's second suggestion, placing the steam boilers on the guards. Moreover, the boilers were made of copper rather than the customary cast iron in response to the public clamor concerning an earlier ship of the Connecticut River Steam Boat Company, the *Oliver Ellsworth*, whose boilers had exploded partly because the corrosive effects of the salt water had weakened her cast iron boilers [11, p. 432].

Figure 4. William Redfield, member of Board of Examiners and
steamboat entrepreneur [9].

The *New England*'s 250 tons enabled her to weather the swells of Long Island
Sound while offering accommodations unique in her class [4, p. 52]. Of this,
the proprietors crowed, "the convenience and comfort of passengers has not
been lost sight of, in providing for their safety," [4, p. 52; 12, p. 3] and there was
". . . no danger of explosions as now the boiler was no longer on the vessel itself
at all" [4, p. 54].

Beginning in September 1833, the *New England* commenced her route between
New York and Hartford, soon settling into her role as the night boat on this circuit
[4, p. 52]. As was customary, therefore, on Tuesday, October 8, Captain Waterman
eased the *New England* out of her berth in New York City at 4 P.M. Isaac Potter,
the usual engineer of the vessel, had a substitute on this run, Alexander Marshall,
an engineer from the West Point Foundry Association, the company that had
built the engine and boilers. Captain Waterman had requested Marshall's presence

Figure 5. The *New England* as launched in 1833 with boilers safely
placed on the outboard guards (boxed).

aboard to "remedy a defect in the machinery" [13, p. 2]. The rest of her voyage
that night is in this account:

> She started in company with the Providence steamboat, *Boston*, but gradually
> gained on the latter through the [Long Island] Sound. A degree of anxiety was
> felt by some of the passengers on account of the competition between the two
> boats. But we have no evidence that this anxiety was warranted by any
> unusual press of steam on board the *New England*. The boat reached the river
> about 1 o'clock, when, of course, all competition was at an end. At Saybrook,
> some difficulty occurred with the engine, which rendered it necessary to
> throw out an anchor to prevent the boat from drifting ashore. After a detention
> of twenty or thirty minutes at Saybrook, the boat proceeded on her way up the
> [Connecticut] river about eight miles, and arrived opposite Essex about 3
> o'clock. Her engine was stopped, the small boat was let down to land a
> passenger, and had just reached the shore, when both the boilers exploded,
> almost simultaneously, with a dreadful noise like heavy cannon. The shock
> was dreadful; and the scene which followed is represented by those who
> were present as awful and heart-rending beyond description. The morning
> was excessively dark; the rain poured in torrents; the lights on deck and in
> the cabin were suddenly extinguished; and all was desolation and harrow
> on board. Those only who witnessed the havoc which was made, and heard
> the shrieks and groans of the wounded and dying, can form an adequate
> conception of the scene.
>
> There were upward of seventy passengers on board and others, belonging to
> the boat, for the number of about twenty, —making, in all, nearly one hundred

persons. Most of the passengers were fortunately in their berths. Those who were in the gentleman's cabin escaped without any serious injury. The most destructive effects of the explosion were felt on the deck, and in the ladies' cabin. The ladies who were in their berths and remained there, we believe, were not much injured; but those who were on cots opposite the cabin doors, and others, who on the first alarm, sprang from their berths, were more or less scalded. All who were on deck abaft [sic.] the boilers, we believe, were either killed or wounded. Had the accident occurred in the daytime, when the passengers are generally scattered about the deck and promenade, the destruction of lives would, in all probability, have been much greater.

Captain Waterman was on the wheelhouse at the time of the explosion, attending to the landing of passengers from the small boat. He noticed a movement over the boilers, and immediately jumped, or was thrown upon the forward deck. He was somewhat bruised, but not seriously injured.

From the inhabitants of Essex the sufferers experienced the most kind and hospitable attentions. Their houses were thrown open for their reception and every thing which could contribute to their relief and comfort promptly afforded.

As soon as the melancholy intelligence reached Hartford, on Wednesday morning, the proprietors dispatched the steamboat *Massachusetts* for the surviving passengers, and several of our physicians repaired to the scene of suffering. The *Massachusetts* returned the same night, bringing a number of passengers, some of the wounded, and one dead body. Two or three bodies were also brought up on the next day by the *Chief Justice Marshall* [itself the victim of a steam-boiler explosion and 11 deaths three years earlier on the Hudson] [14, pp. 118-120].

The *New England* exploded after only one month in service within moments of disembarking passengers requiring that the engine be stopped. At this time, the boiler powered both the engine propelling the boat as well as the pump bringing water into the boiler [15]. In this double-duty situation, turning off the power to propel the boat also disengaged the pump and stopped water from replacing that already evaporated in the boiler. Theoretically, this should not have been a problem except that in the frequent, short, stop-and-go of steamboats coming in to pick up and deliver passengers or cargo, standard practice kept the fire stoked so that the vessel could quickly build up propulsive power to pull away and continue on its journey. If there was little water in the boiler, the iron would be superheated, so that when the engine was restarted and cold water pumped into the boiler, it would instantly create a large volume of steam, possibly explosively shattering the boiler. Two-thirds of all steam boiler explosions at this time occurred after stopping the engines and thus stopping the water-replacement pumps [16, p. 295].

Figure 6. The wreck of the *New England* on the shore of the
Connecticut River opposite Essex, Connecticut.

THE CORONER'S JURY INVESTIGATION

Two days after the explosion, a jury of inquest was convened near the site to
hear testimony regarding the cause of death for one of the passengers, who was
used as the focus of their investigation [13, p. 2]. Eleven witnesses were called in
the case. However, the jury's verdict after receiving such testimony was only the
most obvious:

> ... the deceased, _____, came to his death in consequence of the bursting
> of the boilers of the Steam Boat *New England* near Essex, in the town of
> Saybrook, on the morning of the 9 of October 1833 [13, p. 2].

Moreover, the jury did not want to assign any blame for the bursting of the
boilers: "The Jury do not deem it either necessary or expedient to express any
opinion upon it . . ." [13, p. 2]. The record of the jury's examination was published
in Hartford's *Connecticut Courant* on October 28, 1833, and simply listed the
witnesses in hierarchical order, following the line of responsibility aboard the
New England from Captain Waterman to John Mack, a passenger. Thus presented
by novel complex technology beyond their abilities to understand, the coroner's
jury report failed to draw any conclusions, and imposed no order on the witness
testimony other than that of hierarchical order aboard the ship.

THE COMPANY INVESTIGATION REPORT EXONERATES ITS ACTIONS USING SCIENCE

Soon after the publication of the jury's investigation, T. B. Wakeman, corresponding secretary of the institute, received the company's investigation report at the American Institute of New York, drawing this comment:

> This board [the Board of Examiners] compiled and published the best account which has been given to the public of any explosion which has occurred in this country; the facts of the case were carefully collected and distinctly stated, and the conclusions which they drew from a consideration of them appear to me irresistible [17, p. 658].

Within a month of the coroner's jury report, the Connecticut River Steam Boat Company, owners of the *New England*, appointed some of the top scientists and mechanicians of the time to a "Board of Examiners"—Professor Benjamin Silliman, as chairman and Mr. William Redfield as a member—the same Silliman who had proposed the alternative safety design method employed on the *New England* and the same Redfield who had earlier followed the "lady boat" design option of Silliman on his Swiftsure Line [18; 19; 20, Reel 1, 2; 21, p. 427; 22]. Silliman and Redfield were joined on the Board by three others: another Yale professor, Denison Olmsted; the engineer of the sister ship to the *New England*; and an engineer and manufacturer of engines in Hartford.

Silliman and Olmsted traveled up from their posts at Yale University in New Haven to Essex, and Redfield from his New York City steamboat company. Neither these three nor any of the other members of the board were first-hand witnesses to the explosion or the casualties. They did examine the wreck and some of its torn fragments, but relied mostly on witness testimony.

After a single meeting on November 7, the Board of Examiners came to its conclusions, and on November 27, the Board produced its report exonerating the crew, the builders, and the management of the company:

> As regards the bearing of our conclusion, we do not feel it necessary to attach any high degree of blame to those who were in charge of the boat and engine at the time of the accident; and they may be justly exonerated from any charge of voluntary or willful misconduct. . . . The board of examiners are fully and unanimously of the opinion, that in the construction and management of this boat, the steamboat company, used their best endeavors, for the accommodation of the public, and committed the navigation of it to persons of established reputation for prudence and skill in their profession [23, p. 21].

The report, largely written by Silliman, revealed an emotional disengagement from the accident that gave him the emotional distance to be able to write, "Many interesting and important considerations, connected with Steam boat navigation, have presented themselves, during our discussion . . . [23, p. 2].

In his memoir, Silliman nonchalantly recorded that as a consequence of his participation in the investigation, he was invited to lecture "gratuitously" a month later, December 10, on steam and steamboats in Hartford, the destination of the *New England*'s passengers and the location of many mourners. Silliman wrote in his memoir that 400 to 500 people attended the lecture in which he offered drawings and plans for about one and a half hours [20, Reel 1]. However, when his information about steam and steamboats failed to fill out the appointed time of his lecture, he simply added material on his forté, geology.

ESTABLISHING A SCIENTIFIC ETHOS FOR THE INVESTIGATION REPORT

Not only was Silliman personally distant and emotionally unruffled by the explosion that killed or injured twenty-five people, but also, when the report was finally publicly distributed, the *Connecticut Courant* described it rather summarily as "impartial" [25, p. 3]. The report was rapidly distributed within the scientific community, as illustrated by the fact that within a remarkably short time for the era, one month, Silliman's report found its way into Philadelphia's *Journal of the Franklin Institute* [26, pp. 55, 126, 289], into the *Boston Mechanics Magazine* [27, p. 55], and into both New York City's *Mechanic's Magazine* [28, pp. 11-16] and the journal of the American Institute, as illustrated by T. B. Wakeman's earlier glowing assessment of the report [17].

Silliman and Redfield evidently also impressed the government with their report, because five years later they were commissioned along with a few others to investigate and report on national steamboat safety, and Silliman and Redfield's *New England* investigation report was reprinted in this commission's *Report 21* as the final piece in a 450-page document [19, pp. 451-452; 20, Reel 8, Reminiscences, and Reel 2]. Redfield wrote at length in this government report, but failed to note in his prefatory report that he had been on the committee, and instead noted in a self-congratulatory observation:

> [The proprietors of the *New England*] procured the attendance of a board of examiners, comprised of persons from different parts of the country, deemed competent to the investigation; and ever facility was afforded for the most full examination, as given in the report of the board, has been already published; but its importance, as connected with the history of steamboat explosions, and its bearing on the future safety of steamboats induces me to annex a copy of the this same communication. . . . It appears remarkable, therefore, that this inquiry, instituted by the owners of the *New England*, should be the only attempt at careful and thorough investigation, for the benefit of the profession and of the public, which has yet been, made in our country [29].

In that same *Report 21*, a critic of Silliman and Redfield's report felt compelled to begin his remarks by acknowledging their very effective ethos:

I am aware that three very learned gentleman (two of them, in fact professors in an institution which is the pride of our country [Silliman and Olmsted from New Haven's Yale] have gone before me, and perhaps have settled the matter beyond a possibility of dispute . . . [19, p. 76].

Thus the company enlisted the persuasive ethos of Silliman, Redfield, and others on the board to produce a corporate report which few questioned, and which effectively defended the company from any liability exposure.

DISPOSITIO (ARRANGEMENT) AS A MEANS
OF PERSUASION IN THE INVESTIGATION REPORT

The report's arrangement also played a large role in its persuasiveness. In its twenty-four pages and appended illustrations, the Board of Examiner's report had six parts, conforming to the classical parts of rhetoric's dispositio:

1. A single-page, introductory cover letter described the purpose of the report and limited it to an investigation of the single *New England* explosion—not steam explosions in general—and fulfilled all the purposes of an exordium.
2. Four pages described the physical evidence of the explosion, fulfilling the purposes of a narratio.

The next four parts comprised the reports conformatio—

3. The testimony of ten witnesses to the actual explosion, with headings noting the name and role aboard the *New England* at the time of the explosion and an illustration (below) is also included.
4. A discussion of the four possible theoretical explanations for the explosion that were then in current scientific debate: 1) hydrogen gas produced by "decomposition" of the water during the boiling process; 2) superheating of a part of the boiler (the water legs), causing a rapid increase in the steam pressure; 3) a lack of water resulting in an event much like a superheating of a part of the boiler, causing a rapid increase in the steam pressure; and 4) the normal pressures of the boiler, producing a stress on the boiler metal and joints beyond its capacity to hold. This fourth cause was the one chosen by the committee as most likely.
5. The physical evidence and summary of the witnesses' testimonies from parts (2) and (3) are reviewed in order to explain the likelihood of the fourth explanation.
6. Finally, the report suggested corrective measures to safeguard the future applications of steam engines, and to reassure the public that steam engines were not inherently flawed. Thus, the Connecticut River Steam Boat Company wanted to reassure its investors and its customers in the normal way a peroratio would:

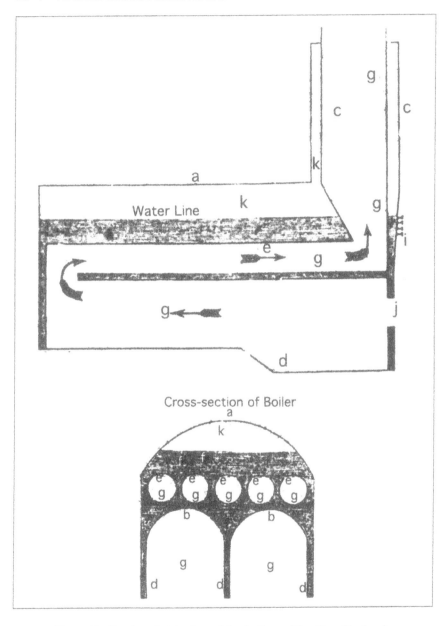

Figure 7. Front and side view of the boilers of the *New England*.
Legend: (a) Outer wall of the boiler; (b) Arches or tops of the main or furnace flues; (c) Steam Chimney; (d) Water Legs; (e) Upper or return flues; (f) Water in the boilers; (g) Passage for the fire through the flues to the chimney; (h) Iron chimney pipe cut off above its junction with the steam chimney; (i) Water cocks; (j) Furnace door; (k) Steam chamber.

It is now known, that circular flues can be constructed of a very small size with increasing safety and advantage, and we confidently expect that a combination of parts can be made upon the principles here recommended, which shall furnish steam sufficient for the supply of the largest engines; while the degree of safety shall be so much increased, as will reduce the hazard of traveling in steamboats to an almost inappreciable ratio; and while our rivers shall be navigated by these wonderful vessels, one of the highest gifts of art and civilization, and our plains be traversed by the unrivalled speed of the locomotive, it is hoped that we never may have occasion to lament such a melancholy disaster as that which has occasioned our present labors [23, p. 22].

An interesting element of Silliman's report is its "finished" quality. For example, in the second part of his conformatio, he offered the reader four alternative methods for explaining the accident, and he progressed from, according to the Board, the most incorrect explanations to the most correct explanation. In doing this, the Board smoothly transitioned the reader into the explanation of the correctness of this choice in Part 5. The finesse and seamless design of the conformatio suggested, to the reader, that the choice of four explanations was as inexorable as the scientific laws of the universe. It must have seemed inexorable to the board also, since its decision was made "on the spot," and "was unanimous."

Comparing the Order of Witnesses in the Corporate Report to the Coroner's Report

Despite this projection of an inexorable conclusion, Silliman subtly changed the order of presenting witnesses in Part 3 from that of the coroner's jury [13, p. 22], and, in doing so, implicitly shifted the onus for the accident from the captain to the West Point Foundry Association, the company that made the boiler and engine. For example, the order of witnesses testifying before the coroner's jury strictly followed the hierarchical order of responsibility aboard ship from captain to passenger:

• Captain Waterman
• Seymour, first mate
• Potter, the usual engineer but not aboard on this trip
• Vail, the river pilot
• Wilcox, a deckhand
• Farnham, Bell, Chapell, and Goodrich, the firemen who stoked the fire
• Palmer, an Assistant Engineer, and
• Mack, a passenger

This order in the coroner jury's report strictly followed the hierarchical order of responsibility aboard ship and may have led to its inability to later draw any conclusions; the jurors simply took an order for their own presentation from a preexisting order aboard the steamboat. This "pre-set" order caused the jurors to ignore whether a particular witness was aboard the vessel or not at the time of the accident (e.g., Potter was the usual engineer and was not aboard, but he was still interviewed). This pre-set order used by the jury also tended to highlight the captain and his actions, since his recitation as the first witness set out the general narrative direction of the accident and the important points of the investigation. Such an organization thus tended to highlight his responsibility in the explosion.

In the Board of Examiner's report, however, Silliman did not follow the pre-set hierarchical order of responsibility aboard ship. Now the captain's testimony was positioned in last place of the witnesses, was only half as long, and was much less specific on speeds, steam levels, time, etc. Much of the testimony previously assigned by the coroner's jury's organization to the captain—the general narrative direction and the important points of the investigation—was instead offered by the engineers from the West Point Foundry Association, Marshall and Younger, who were only substitute engineers on this voyage, and thus had no position at all in the usual hierarchy of the boat. This then is Silliman's order of witness testimony:

- Marshall, substitute engineer
- Younger, substitute engineer
- Vail, the river pilot
- Farnham and Bell, the firemen who stoked the fire
- Seymour, first mate
- Potter, the usual engineer but not aboard on this trip
- Hall, engineer at West Point Foundry Association but not aboard on this trip
- Captain Waterman

Marshall and Younger's responsibilities as substitute engineers were highlighted by Silliman's positioning them as the first and second witnesses. That Silliman included evidence from Marshall and Younger, who were aboard the vessel at the time of the accident, does, in fact, make more sense than the coroner jury's interview of the engineers Potter and Palmer who were *not* aboard during the incident. However, Adam Hall, another engineer at the West Point Foundry, but not aboard on the trip, was included in Silliman's report. Thus, whether a witness was present or absent aboard the vessel during the incident was not a deciding organizational factor for either Silliman or the coroner's jury.

It is also interesting to find in the report's appendix, the final text in the report, a "certificate" from a coppersmith (the boilers on the *New England* were made by the West Point Foundry of copper—not iron—to withstand the corrosive effects of salt water of Long Island Sound). This certificate was appended to the report three days *after* Silliman dated the transfer of the report from his hands into those of the company, and this last piece of text in the report again tends to throw culpability for the accident on the West Point Foundry Association.

John Hannah, the coppersmith issuing the certificate, assured readers that the operators had sufficient water in the boilers:

> The present appearance of the aforesaid sooty deposit, of the flues and other metals of said boilers, is entirely incompatible with the supposition, that the metal has been heated in consequence of the absence of water in the boilers. I am fully convinced by the appearances of the metal as aforesaid, that the boilers were fully supplied with water at the time of the explosion [23, p. 23].

The net effect on readers of Silliman's alterations in the order of witness's testimony subtly shifted blame from the report's sponsor, the Connecticut River Steam Boat Company, owners of the *New England*, to the West Point Foundry Association.

"OUTSIDE EXPERTS" GIVE THEIR FINDINGS . . . BUT NOT VERY PERSUASIVELY

Within six months of the completion of the report, and the month after Silliman and Redfield's report was serialized in three separate issues of the *Journal of the Franklin Institute*, Thomas Ewbank published a challenge to Silliman's report [30 pp. 289-294]. Ewbank was uniquely qualified to make this challenge as an inventor and manufacturer of tin and copper tubing, and having obtained two patents for improvements in steam-boiler safety valves. His investigation of the *New England* explosion was the first in a series of four articles between 1832 and 1837 on steam-boiler explosions in the *Journal of the Franklin Institute* [30, p. 289] (Ewbank became U.S. Commissioner of Patents in 1849.) Thus, where Silliman's and Redfield's credibility with the scientific community was already established, Ewbank's was, in many ways, yet to come, and that placed his outside evaluation immediately at a disadvantage.

Although Ewbank agreed with Silliman's general conclusion that the explosion occurred due to excessive pressure in the boilers, he observed some special problems unique to the copper used in the boilers of the *New England*, an aspect not commented upon in Silliman and Redfield's report. With his own special experience regarding copper, Ewbank sent parts of the *New England's* boiler to the committee of the Franklin Institute on boiler explosions for strength of materials' analysis. Ewbank wrote that some of the causes of the problems caused by the copper could have been:

1. If the copper used in the boilers had been overheated during its fabrication by the West Point Foundry, it would have been more brittle than expected and thus its "tenacity" would have been injured [30, p. 290].
2. An inferior or variable quality of copper used in the boilers that made its ability to contain steam pressures unpredictable. Hall from the West Point Foundry declared that the boiler should have borne fifty pounds to the

square inch. Yet, when the pressure rose to only twenty-four pounds, the boilers gave way [30, p. 290].
3. Copper boilers, no matter how good or of consistent a quality, can handle no more than fifteen pounds to the square inch.
4. Because of the arrangements of the pipes in the boilers and the water legs, water may have been present and sufficient in the boilers, but it was not uniformly distributed.
5. The placement of the gauge-cocks in an unusual location near the steam pipes confounded their ability to accurately convey the water level in the boilers.

Much of what Ewbank described could only come from an expert in the scientific analysis of copper and its problematic manufacturing. However, Ewbank's outside scientific insights were published five months after Silliman and Redfield's report, or excerpts from it, were reprinted throughout the scientific community in journals and in the local Hartford newspaper. Moreover, it was not only the lack of timeliness that undercut any effects from Ewbank's work, but also that he initiated his short article by saying "there is room to suppose that one remote source of the calamity can be found . . ." [30, p. 289]. A *remote* source probably suggested to the reader that his report was of marginal importance.

Where Silliman and Redfield imposed an effective rhetorical order on the material, Ewbank seemed to be less effective. Like their earlier report, Ewbank's article uses:

1. Six lines that announce that the manufacturing or quality of the copper could be a remote cause of the boiler explosion, fulfilling the purpose of an exordium.
2. Twenty-four lines describing the physical evidence of the explosion that he collected and submitted to the Franklin Institute for analysis, fulfilling the purposes of an narratio [30, p. 289].

The next four-and-a-half pages comprising the report's conformatio and offering the alternative problems with copper do not have the strong delineation of Silliman's and Redfield points, so Ewbank's points are not developed in any kind of progression but seem to proceed serendipitously [30].

He also has no clear ending, refutatio, or peroratio, but just stops writing. There is no call to action or ringing summation such as the one that completed Silliman's and Redfield's report:

> . . . safety shall be so much increased, as will reduce the hazard of traveling in steamboats to an almost inappreciable ratio; and while our rivers shall be navigated by these wonderful vessels, one of the highest gifts of art and civilization, and our plains be traversed by the unrivalled speed of the locomotive . . . [23, p. 22].

OTHER "OUTSIDE EXPERTS" OFFER THEIR CRITICAL COMMENTS, BUT MUCH LATER

Recall that Silliman and Redfield were employed by the government as commissioners on a national steamboat safety board in 1838, and that Redfield managed to get the *New England* report reprinted in *Report 21* to the Senate. However, *Report 21* also included the observations of two customs collectors, Elihu Bunker (New York City) and N. A. Phelps (Middletown, Conn.), who both considered Silliman's report and its failure to conclusively assign responsibility unsatisfactory [19, p. 102]. Charles Hinman, an agent of the rival New Haven Steamboat Company, even offered an alternative explanation to that in the *New England* report [31].

In questioning the well-received board of examiner's report, Hinman knew he was directly confronting two of the examiners directing the government investigation, two powerful figures in the steamboat community, and two powerful figures in his own hometown of New Haven, Conn.:

> I am aware that three very learned gentleman (two of them, in fact professors in an institution which is the pride of our country [Silliman and Olmsted from New Haven's Yale] have gone before me, and perhaps have settled the matter beyond a possibility of dispute, that her boilers were burst under an ordinary pressure, with a sufficiency of water; that it was the fault of the boilers, not the engineer; yet notwithstanding all that, I may be permitted, as humble an individual as I am, to defend the boilers of the steamboat *New England* from all unjust aspersions which have been heaped upon their remains. In doing it, I shall humbly cross the wake of the learned gentlemen at a respectful distance astern, and, standing over to the shore of practical knowledge, carefully avoid the tide of theory entirely [19, p. 76].

Thus, Hinman's use of nautical figures of speech in this passage, such as "cross the wake," "a respectful distance astern," "standing over to the shore," and "the tide," may be his method of establishing rapport with his audience either by anticipating them to be nautical men, or, more likely, he may have employed such obvious figures of speech marking him as a mariner who doesn't know when to turn off his salty dog talk. In any case, he began his rebuttal by soliciting audience sympathy by projecting a humble nautical bumpkin persona [31].

Continuing his criticism of the board's report—hitherto accepted as the only true report of the accident—Hinman restated its conclusions:

> The gentlemen decided that her boilers burst with a sufficiency of water, under a gradually-increased pressure of steam; or, in other words, that a pressure of one-half pound or one pound of steam more to every superficial inch of surface of the boilers than they were capable of sustaining, caused the explosion and all the damage resulting from it.

According to the evidence of the engineer and firemen, (say they) the steam was up to thirty inches—and so said some of the passengers; and the boilers were not capable of sustaining a much greater pressure. Granted.

But let me inquire into the facts; they are these: she left New York in the afternoon on her second or third trip bound to Hartford, and had proceeded as far as Lyme, on the Connecticut River, where she was stopped to land some passengers; some eight or ten minutes time was occupied in landing; the engine was started, and had performed one or two revolutions when the explosion took place; both boilers were torn asunder at the same instant, and portions of the flues and shell were thrown in different directions; the boilers were on the guards [32], and so tremendous was the concussion, that the guard-beams, planks, braces, and knees [33] were taken off close to the hull, leaving the boat almost a wreck; and all this done, in the opinion of the gentlemen who were appointed as a committee to inquire into the causes, by a gradually-increased pressure of steam, with a sufficiency of water.

The boilers were so nearly of equal strength, each as a whole, and each in its parts, that the different parts of each, and the whole of both, must be torn asunder, and thrown from their position on the guards—some portions of them on shore, and other portions into the middle of the river, leaving the boat almost a wreck; . . . [19, p. 77].

Having established the Board's case, and complimenting them as gentlemen, Hinman began to wonder aloud how both boilers could explode at the same instant, and yet maintain the mercury in the pressure gauge:

. . . and that both boilers should go at the same instant, and the mercury should all be found in the gauge in the engine-room, where it would have been blown out long before the bursting of the boilers. If there was a sufficiency of water, and the steam was gradually increased to a point beyond what the boilers were capable of bearing, why did not the mercury take French leave [34] of the gauge? [4, p. 57]. And why is it that the steam could not find some weak point in the shell, flues, or legs, to escape, and relieve the boilers? Is it because there was not one foot or inch of surface of either of the boilers, but that was equal in strength to the remainder? If so, then her boilers were constructed by something more than human, or it was one of the most remarkable coincidences that has ever taken place [19, pp. 76-77; 35].

Having piqued his audience's curiosity with these two simple details, especially since these details seem obvious with only a country bumpkin curious about them, Hinman moved to the heart of his rebuttal:

The truth is, there was not a sufficiency of water; the engineer was deceived; the water foamed badly [36], as is generally the case in new boilers; and the water, when foaming, will deceive the engineer, unless he has had a good deal of experience on board of a steamboat; and the tendency of the water to rise when the engine is in motion, so as to take the appearance of solid water on the gauge-cock [37], would deceive the engineer unless he was an experienced one. The engineer for the *New England*, for that trip [Marshall], was not experienced; he came from an engine establishment, where he had assisted in putting up steam-engines for years; still he was inexperienced, it being his first trip as engineer of a boat. The true cause of the explosion, therefore was want of water. The water had so far decreased as to leave the tops of the return-flues bare after the engine was stopped at the landing; that, while lying there, they were exposed to a hot fire, and would, in ten minutes, become red with heat; that, immediately after opening the cylinder-receiving-valves [38], millions of fine particles of water followed the first rush of steam, and, coming in contact with the hot metal, were made into steam instantly; and the pressure no man can calculate. We can only judge of the pressure by its effects: we can safely say that it is not possible to burst two boilers on board the same ship, at the instant, under a gradually-increased pressure of steam with a sufficiency of water; but where there is a want of water, and the steam is generated in the manner described above, no man on board such a boat is safe, even if the boilers were a half foot thick [19, p. 77].

Thus, Hinman's rebuttal four years after the explosion pointed out that it was operator error by Marshall, and not design or forging problems by the engine manufacturer as the original report insinuated. However, he made his criticism by letting the facts, as much as possible, speak for themselves, "We can only judge of the pressure by its effects" [19, p. 77], thus maintaining a disinterested scientific ethos.

IN THE END

Real culpability for the accident was never established; no court case followed up the observations of Ewbank, Hinman, Bunker, or Phelps. Silliman and Redfield's attempt to shift the responsibility to the West Point Foundry Association also did not succeed, for the association soon began building artillery and locomotives—in fact, the West Point Foundry Association built the first locomotive in the United States and was a major supplier of sophisticated artillery in the Civil War [8, pp. 387-388; 38, p. 152]. The Connecticut River Steamboat Company also continued to do well financially although hard-pressed by competition from the Vanderbilts and railroads. The Connecticut River Steamboat Company was finally bought out by the Vanderbilts in 1841 [8, p. 142].

Silliman continued for many years as editor of the *American Journal of Science and Arts* and offering public lectures across the nation on science. Twenty-two years later, in 1855, Silliman was still traveling and giving lectures across the United States and just happened to appear in St. Louis in November 1855 within a week of a railroad bridge collapse on the Pacific Railroad of Missouri (the subject of Chapter 5):

At the appointed hour, the Professor was introduced by Mr. Douglas, and without delay proceeded to his task. He referred in words of tender endearment to the late Railroad catastrophe, which had spoken—especially to the aged—of the brevity of life and the certainty of death. He then proceeded to define Geology . . . [39, p. 2].

Once refitted and refurbished to the tune of $17,500 [19], the *New England* returned in the spring of 1834 as the night boat on her New York–Hartford circuit. In 1837, she was shifted to a Boston–Portland circuit, and sank in 1839 after a collision [8, p. 133].

Redfield moved from his very practical orientation in steamboats as director of the Swiftsure Line to a disinterested scientist in meteorology. For his work in this latter area, he was elected as the first president of the American Association for the Advancement of Science [22].

What were presented as inexorable, unanimous conclusions in Silliman and Redfield's report made "on the spot" and presented in a "thorough and impartial" style could have been questioned and found wanting, as indeed they were by Ewbank and Hinman. But by then Silliman and Redfield's report had been accepted by the scientific community, the local Hartford community, and the federal government as the "report of record."

The company-issued report employing "outside, objective" investigators with a very high scientific ethos who exonerated the company and tended to shift the blame to the engine manufacturer was the report of record because of its effective rhetoric. It also became the report of record because the coroner's jury report drew no conclusions at all, and Ewbanks and later scientific analyses focused on "remote" causes.

ENDNOTES

1. Benjamin Silliman, "The Safety of Steam Boats," *Journal of the Franklin Institute,*6, No. 5, 1830. It is interesting to note that in contrast to boilers causing huge injuries to passengers aboard steamboats, it was very rare aboard railroads. "In fact, the only known case of a passenger death owing to such a cause on the general public railroad system occurred on the Main Central, near Ayers Junction, in 1915," and, in general, "the perils of steamship travel were many times greater than those of the railroads" p. 7.

2. Robert B. Shaw, *A History of Railroad Accidents, Safety Precautions and Operating Practices,* Binghamton, NY: Vail-Ballou Press, Inc., 1978.

3. Lillian C. Buttre, *The American Portrait Gallery,* New York: J. C. Buttre, Vol. 1, 1877.

4. Melanchthon W. Jacobus, *The Connecticut River Steamboat Story,* Hartford, Conn.: The Connecticut Historical Society, 1956.

5. "Report No. 478, Steamboats, May 18, 1832," in *Reports of Committees of the House of Representatives at the First Session of the Twenty-Second Congress, Begun and*

Held at the City of Washington, December 7, 1831, Washington, D.C.: Duff Green, 1831.

6. William Redfield, "Notices of American Steam Boats," *Journal of American Science* 23 (2), 1833: "These barges which were run during the summer season from 1825 to 1829, had attained a speed of eight to nine miles per hour; but the increase which, during the same period, was given to speed and size of the steam boats, tended to discourage this mode of conveyance, and it has since been discontinued, to the regret of those who love quiet enjoyment, and whose nerves have not been inured to composure by frequent proximity with the moving power" [p. 190].

7. C. R. Roseberry, *Steamboats and Steamboat Men,* New York: G. P. Putnam's Sons, 1966.

8. Fred Irving Dayton and John Wolcott Adams (illustrator), *Steamboat Days,* New York: Fredrick A. Stokes Co., 1928.

9. *Popular Science Monthly,* 50, 1896.

10. R. John Brockmann, *Exploding Steamboats, Senate Debates, and Technical Reports: The Convergence of Technology, Politics and Rhetoric in the Steamboat Bill of 1838,* Amityville, N.Y.: Baywood, 2002.

11. Secretary of the Treasury, *Information Collected on Accidents on Board Steam Boats*: 25th Congress, 3rd Sess, Doc. 21, Serial Set #345, Washington, D.C., 1838.

12. "Steam Boat *New England, " The Connecticut Courant* 69 (3580), September 2, 1833.

13. "Steam Boat *New England:* Examination Before a Jury of Inquest," *The Connecticut Courant,* 69 (3588), October 28, 1833.

14. S. A. Howland, *Steamboat Disasters and Railroad Accidents in the United States,* Worcester, Mass.: Dorr, Howland & Co., 1846.

15. This would be solved in the future by a Pittsburgh inventor, Cadwallader Evans, who invented a secondary engine called a "doctor," which would pump replacement water into the boilers and not propel the boat.

16. Louis C. Hunter, *Steamboats on the Western Rivers: An Economic and Technological History,* Cambridge, Mass.: Harvard University Press, 1949.

17. T. B. Wakeman, Second Response to W. H. Hale in correspondence regarding the causes of steam boiler explosions, *Journal of the American Institute* 3 (10) July 1838.

18. It is interesting to observe that Silliman had termed Redfield a "valued correspondent" in his journal two years earlier [20 (2) July 1831, p. 336], and Redfield later collaborated on a report for the Federal Government in 1838, [19].

19. Secretary of the Treasury, *Information Collected on Accidents on Board Steam Boats* (1838), 25th Congress, 3rd Sess, Doc. 21, Follow Up to House Resolution of Previous 29th of June—Serial #345), Washington, D.C., 1838.

20. Silliman Family Papers (1792-1862), Journals of Benjamin Silliman. M. Film No. 3615. Later that winter, Silliman gave a lecture on steam and boilers explosions in Hartford. It also appears that Olmsted may have been the one who introduced Redfield to Silliman because Olmsted was the one who first suggested to Redfield that he publish in Silliman's *American Journal of Science.*

21. Denison Olmsted, *Men of the Time or Sketches of Living Notables*, New York: Redfield, 1856. He also wrote Redfield's epitaph [22].

22. Denison Olmsted, *Address on the Scientific Life and Labors of William C. Redfield, A.M. First President of the American Association for the Advancement of Science*, Cambridge, Mass.: Allen and Farnham, Printers, 1858.

23. *Report of the Board of Examiners Appointed by the Connecticut River Steam Boat Company to Inquire into the Causes of the Explosion of the Steam Boat New England Which Occurred at Essex, October 9, 1833*, New Haven, Conn.: Connecticut River Steam Boat Company, 1833.

24. Or January 10, 1834, as he noted in another part of his memoirs.

25. *Connecticut Courant*, 69 (3594), December 9, 1833.

26. *Journal of the Franklin Institute*, Vol. 13, 1834.

27. *Boston Mechanics' Magazine*, Vol. 3, 1834.

28. *Mechanic's Magazine*, 3 (1), January 1834.

29. Mind you, this is after Redfield himself later says that "of the experimental investigations which have been made public, none have a higher claim to consideration than those which have been made at Philadelphia by a committee of the Franklin Institute; and the elaborate report of this committee must be considered as a document of high value and great practical utility" [19, p. 432].

30. T. Ewbank, *Journal of the Franklin Institute*, Vol. 13, 1834.

31. Charles Hinman, in [19], pp. 76-77.

32. The paddlewheel housing on the port and starboard sides of the boat.

33. *Oxford English Dictionary*: A piece of timber naturally bent, or a piece of iron used to secure parts of a ship together, especially one with an angular bend used to connect the beams and the timbers.

34. *Oxford English Dictionary*: "Originally, the custom (in the 18th c. prevalent in France and sometimes imitated in England) of going away from a reception, etc. without taking leave of the host or hostess. Hence, jocularly, to take French leave is to go away, or do anything, without permission or notice."

35. "Curiously enough the Board also found that the safety valve was 'unimpaired' and was 'large and apparently well constructed'; and that a mercury steam gauge 'remained in good order after the accident.' These may have been mere flukes of the explosion, but I rather suspect they simply showed the inaccuracy and ineffectiveness of such devices at the time. Surely a safety valve or steam gauge in working order would never have allowed three million pounds of pressure to build up [as the board calculated], and an engineer who relied on his instruments cannot, I think, be held too much to blame" [19, p. 433].

36. Bubbles created by the boiling of the water in a boiler, which would cause water to issue from a stop-cock—seeming to indicate that there was water at or above the stop-cock—even though it was foam carrying the water up to the stop-cock from several inches below.

37. A safety apparatus in which two spigots on the side of a boiler, one above the other by some few inches, which would directly measure the level of the water and steam in the boiler because water or steam issuing from them when they were opened would indicate the level of steam or water inside the boiler, e.g., if water issued then the valve was below or at the water line; if only steam issued then the

water was below that stop-cock. This apparatus was confounded by the problem of foaming [36].

38. Albert Fishlow, *American Railroads and the Transformation of the Ante-bellum Economy*, Cambridge, Mass.: Harvard University Press, 1965. It is interesting to note that a boiler made by the West Point Foundry Association also exploded and caused the first train accident in U.S. history. The *Best Friend of Charleston* exploded on June 17, 1831.

39. "Prof. Silliman in St. Louis," *St. Louis Missouri Republican*, November 8, 1855.

CHAPTER 2

Science for Sale

THE ACCIDENT—EXPLOSION OF THE LOCOMOTIVE
ENGINE *RICHMOND* NEAR READING, PENNA.
ON THE 2nd OF SEPTEMBER 1844

In 1844, William Norris was in a tight spot. The general business depression affecting the whole country also affected his locomotive works in Philadelphia. However, his company's financial problems were magnified by the fact that when his company sold its locomotives, it often took stock rather than cash in payment, and now many of his customers were going bankrupt, making their stocks worthless. Hoping that overseas marketing would prove a solution, William left for Europe, while his brother Richard took over as chief executive officer. However, the creditors would not wait for the materialization of overseas orders, and they took over the company in such a fashion that the Norris brothers wound up managing their business for the benefit of the creditors [1, pp. 17-56].

The only bright spot that year was brother Septimus's patent for a locomotive frame employed on a new engine just delivered to the Philadelphia and Reading Railroad [1]. Septimus's uniquely designed locomotive was needed to aid with opening of the Pennsylvania coal mines and their quick shipment to markets via the Delaware and Raritan Canal in New Jersey—the topic of Chapter Four [2; 3, p. 88; 4, p. 264]. This 18.5 ton freight engine, the *Richmond*—designated by Norris Brothers as a third-class, six-wheel, combined locomotive [1, p. 302]—was delivered August 14 [5, pp. 16–31], and by September 2nd had run 997 miles, hauling 368,631 tons of coal [6, p. 17].

On September 2nd the *Richmond* was hauling eighty-eight empty coal cars when:

> ... the engine started from the company's coal depot at Richmond, at eleven o'clock in the forenoon, taking a train of 88 wagons, the engine being driven by Joseph Ward, attended by Franklin Tye and Peter Mahon, as firemen, accompanied by James M'Cabe, as conductor, and Matthew Smith and Patrick Nugent, as brakesmen. At Norristown, about sixteen miles from Philadelphia, two additional brakesmen, Thomas Cowden and John Webster Powell, were taken up. The train arrived at Reading at a quarter past seven o'clock the same evening. It was detained there until ten minutes past eight

Figure 8. Ad for Norris Locomotive Works with 0-6-0 Locomotive, like the *Richmond*, shown at top. *American Railroad Journal*, 1845.

o'clock, when it started for Pottsville, but before leaving the town, was again stopped and delayed about quarter of an hour, and finally left the crossing of the main street, Reading, at twenty-five minutes past eight precisely.

A storm of thunder, lightning and rain had commenced about sunset, and continued with unusual violence till a late hour at night. The lightning was frequent and vivid, and of the kind called zigzag lightning. The peals of thunder were loud and hard, the sound being observed to follow the flash almost immediately. The danger was considered so great, that individuals who had been accustomed to the climate, feared to venture out, and it was said that such a thunder-burst had not been witnessed at Reading for twelve months past. It was in the midst of this storm that the train started from Reading. On arriving at *a* point of the road situated on a low embankment, two miles from Reading, a terrific explosion was heard from the head of the train; the cars were suddenly stopped; and the brakesmen on proceeding to the place of the engine, found the working part of the machine scattered in fragments about the road and on the slopes of the embankment; the tender was thrown over upon the wheels and broken carriage of the engine, and the boiler and its appendages had totally disappeared. The bodies of the firemen, Franklyn Tye and Peter Mahon, were found under the wagons killed by fractures of the head and body, and after further search, the body of the engineer was found in an

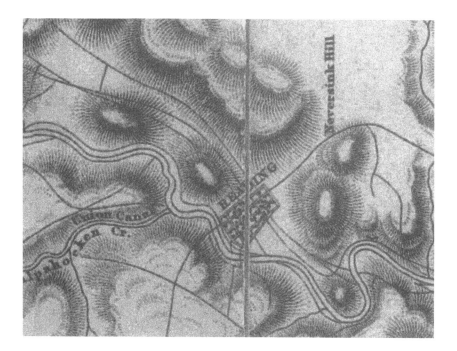

Figure 9. 1838 topographical map of Reading showing the Philadelphia and Reading Railroad [7].

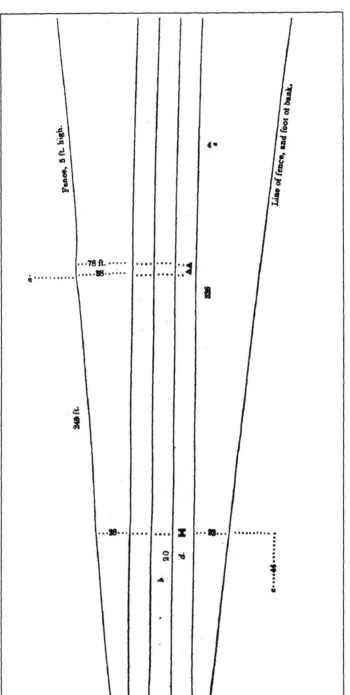

Figure 10. Lardner's plan of ground on the Philadelphia and Reading Railroad where the *Richmond* engine exploded, September 2, 1844 [6, p. 24]. **Legend:** (H) Spot where Engine Exploded (a) Position where Engine Lodged (b) body of fireman (c) body of engineer (d) body of engineer (e) body of conductor. Embankment at (a) 11 ft. high, Embankment at (H), 5 ft. high. A rise of 6 ft. per mile ascending left to right.

adjacent field, about twenty yards on to the right of the place of the tender, with the head cut across the forehead and the leg crushed, being quite dead. The body of Mr. M'Cabe, the conductor, was found, also dead, on the embankment at a point three hundred and thirty feet ahead of the tender, and the boiler, with the fire-box, smoke-box, chimney, and the two cylinders and pistons, was discovered lying in a field to the left of the road, at a distance of 250 feet from the place where the wheels and carriage of the engine lay. At a point in the field, about thirty feet nearer to the engine, a deep cavity was left, produced by the end of the boiler striking there, and rebounding from it to the place where it was found. The mass, which was thus projected to the distance of 250 feet from the spot where the explosion took place, weighed about ten tons.

The cylindrical part of the boiler and the smoke-box were uninjured. The funnel was lying near the boiler, and partly beneath it. The round end of the fire-box next the stand of the engine-man was flattened, so as to be crushed in and brought near the flue plate; the roof or crown piece of the fire-box was torn from the walls, the rent being generally above the angle, but in some places upon the angle at which it joins the walls or upright sides of the fire-box. The crown piece was found jammed in the fire-box between the part beaten in and the flue plate. The grate bars and ash pan were driven down upon the road with such force, that the latter took a very distinct print of the transverse wooden sleeper upon which it fell. The proper form of the crown piece is slightly concave at the lower surface, and it is secured by a series of strong cast iron stays, bolted to the upper surface so as to aid in resisting the downward pressure of the steam. Its form, when found after the catastrophe, was at three of its four sides concave at the top, but at the fourth side concave at the bottom, the edge being curled downwards in a considerable degree. In the steam-casing surrounding the fire box were found three holes, about three inches diameter, the edges of which were turned inwards, *i. e.* towards the steam.

The working parts of the boiler, except the steam cylinders and pistons, which still remained attached to it, were broken into an extraordinary number of small fragments. The rods and other parts which had any considerable length, were twisted in the most irregular and capricious manner, and were scattered in every direction around the place where the event occurred [6, pp. 6-8].

THE CORONER'S JURY VERDICT—
ACT OF GOD OR AN ACT OF MAN

As with the *New England* explosion, the assembly of a coroner's jury (or coroner's "inquisition" in Pennsylvania parlance) was the first group to attempt to make sense of the accident. From comments in other reports and from newspaper articles [8], Dr. Nagle, physician to the coroner, visited the scene and reported on the cause of death for each of the four victims as well as the positions of their bodies at the scene [6, p. 22]. Six witnesses then gave testimony at the inquisition [5, pp. 28-29], but over the next several days the cause of the accident changed:

> *Pennsylvania Inquirer* and *Reading Democratic Press* September 4—At the time of the accident, the train was under full headway, and the explosion must have been instantaneous, as it was fatal. It was raining in abundance and vivid flashes of lightning were play in the heavens, and it is supposed that a heavy bolt of electricity struck the engine. It must have been caused by the lightning, as all circumstances prove that to no other cause can it be attributed [9, p. 2; 10].

> *Berks & Schuylkill Journal* September 7—It was at first computed that the engine was struck by lightning, but on investigation the conjecture was found to be erroneous [11, p. 2; 12, p. 3].

> *Reading Gazette* September 7–The cause of this accident is attributed principally to the fact that the cast iron stays across the crown of the fire-box were too light to bear the pressure of steam required. The boiler iron forming the top of the [fire]box was also of bad iron, and hammered too thin at the angle, where it was riveted to the sides of the box [5, p. 25; 13, p. 2; 14, pp. 43-44].

These later findings that the cast iron stays—not lightning—caused the explosion received verification from a distant source, Professor Olmsted of Yale, one of the members of the board of examiners in the *New England* investigation.

These alternative explanations for the *Richmond* explosion in the local press must have piqued Olmsted's interest because the *Richmond*'s boiler explosion was quite similar to the *New England* accident he had investigated eleven years earlier with Silliman and Redfield. However, the possible role of lightning in this accident was something quite novel to Olmsted, who also lectured on meteorology and later published a book on the subject [16]. The *New Haven Palladium* reported that Olmsted, having examined the reports of the coroner, said that lightning did not cause the explosion because of the grounding effect of the locomotive's metal on the metal rails, and that the entire explosion could best be explained by steam alone:

> What the facts were which led to the inference, that the explosion was caused by lightning (except that "vivid flashes of lightning were playing in the heavens" at the time) we are not informed, and until these are stated, we may be permitted to doubt the correctness of the conclusion, and to incline to the opinion that the accident was caused by the violence of the steam alone, under some mismanagement, occasioned probably by the darkness and confusion incident to such a time [16, p. 2; 17, p. 2].

The same alternative explanations of lightning strike versus design and materials problems also found its way into the *New York Tribune,* which reported that letters to a local New York City director of the railroad had assured him that "the engine which exploded was not struck by lightning" [18, p. 3].

Figure 11. Denison Olmsted of Yale, investigator of the
New England and the *Richmond*.

Local notices in the Reading newspapers of the explosion of a nearly new
locomotive was bad enough for Norris Brothers Locomotives, but now national
news concerning the explosion with Olmsted's comments could be fatal if not
rebutted. This was especially true for, as the *New York Tribune* observed, if the
locomotive explosion was not caused by a lightning strike, then "the loss does not
fall on the Company [the Philadelphia and Reading Railroad] but on Mr. Norris,
the maker, who guaranteed the engine for sixty days" [18, p. 3].

Yet, as luck would have it, The Rev. Dionysus Lardner from England, who had
an international scientific reputation in the area of steam engines and meteorology,
was then visiting Philadelphia on his American lecture tour. At the behest of
Norris Brothers Locomotives, and with their financing, Lardner detoured to
Reading on the 21st of that month to begin his own investigation of the explosion.

Norris Brothers probably reasoned that if Olmsted, Silliman, and Redfield, with
purely domestic reputations as scientists, could offer an unimpeachable scientific

ethos in their investigative report on the *New England* in 1833, helping it become the report of record and exonerating the company, wouldn't an internationally acclaimed scientist like Lardner do even better in keeping them from having to make good on their guarantee for the locomotive?

THE SHAKY SCIENTIFIC ETHOS OF DIONYSUS LARDNER

By 1840, at the age of 47, Lardner epitomized the scientific and technological amateur at a time when amateurs could claim to understand a wide variety of subjects without embarking on a rigorous, systematic study [19, pp. 531-532]. He had already published forty-three books in English, as well as being translated into French and German. Moreover, he had published four books on steam engines:

• *Popular Lectures on The Steam Engine, in which its Construction and Operation are Familiarly Explained; with an Historical Sketch of Its Invention and Progressive Improvement*—three editions.
• *The Steam Engine Familiarly Explained and Illustrated*—four editions
• *Steam and Its Uses: Including the Steam Engine, the Locomotive, and Steam Navigation*
• *Steam Communication with India by the Red Sea*

In 1840, Lardner came to America to begin a lecture tour much like Silliman's [21, pp. 602-626]. Lardner later summarized this tour in two volumes entitled, *Popular Lectures on Science and Art; Delivered in the Principal Cities and Towns of the United States* [22]. In 1843, halfway through his American tour, the *New York Herald* observed:

> Dr. Lardner is a very remarkable man. During the last year, he has traveled 10,000 miles, given 114 lectures, spoken nearly ten weeks, has been heard by 50,000 persons, has been several times nearly blown up or burnt up in steam-boats, has been attacked by 116 newspapers, but has at length got into smooth water with plenty of cash, a great reputation . . . [23, p. 3, col. E].

When these lectures were published in 1845, the *American Whig* review praised them:

> The usual books on Science and Art are altogether unsuited to impress the mass, even of intelligent people. We do not ask that a scientific work shall amuse; but certainly, if a book does not interest, it can make no impression on the general reader. The best treatises, however, that we have been accustomed to see on these subjects—those really freighted with knowledge—have commonly been set forth so much in abstract and technical terms, as to render them readable, often understandable, only by the few; while those apparently designed for very popular use . . . have been as commonly found quite free, from abstractions not only, but in truth, of any information. It is the singular merit of these essays for they now, in fact, appear under that form that

Figure 12. The Rev. Dionysus Lardner [20, p. 696].

they really present, not in general the processes, but the whole immense results of all science and practical art, from the ages of the intellectual old Greek philosophers down to the amazing discoveries of modern times, and that in a form and guise which cannot fail to make them both intelligible and deeply interesting to any class of readers. Dr. Lardner's style for such subjects is incomparable. We do not, at least, conceive it to be surpassed by that of any other English writer. It is wonderfully concise and exact, yet so flowing and luminous as of itself to lead the readers mind through many pages before he becomes aware of the excellence to which the original presentation of the subjects in public lectures has, no doubt, greatly contributed. Besides this remarkable merit, there is a constant employment of illustration, by anecdotes and references to distinguished inventors and scientific men in different ages, that adds exceedingly to the attractiveness of the work [24, p. 217].

Lardner's lectures were, as the *American Whig* noted, "incomparable" in their scientific approach because, on one hand, though Lardner rarely used mathematical demonstrations, he emphasized that "[c]learness and order must be conspicuous in his reasoning, and his illustrations must not only be apposite, but adapted to the character, capacity, and acquirements of his audience" [25, p. 16].

Lardner's lectures were very popular: he earned over $200,000 for his four years of lecturing, and spoke to nearly 5 percent of the urban population of the United States [34, p. 214; 28]. Yet, such "incomparable" science was not welcomed by the established American scientists of the age such as Joseph Henry, secretary of the Smithsonian. Henry wrote to a colleague that Lardner "met with no encouragement from scientific men of any standing in our country" [29, pp. 244-245]. The British magazine, *The Athenaeum,* described this paradox of Lardner's popularity and limitations in the following way:

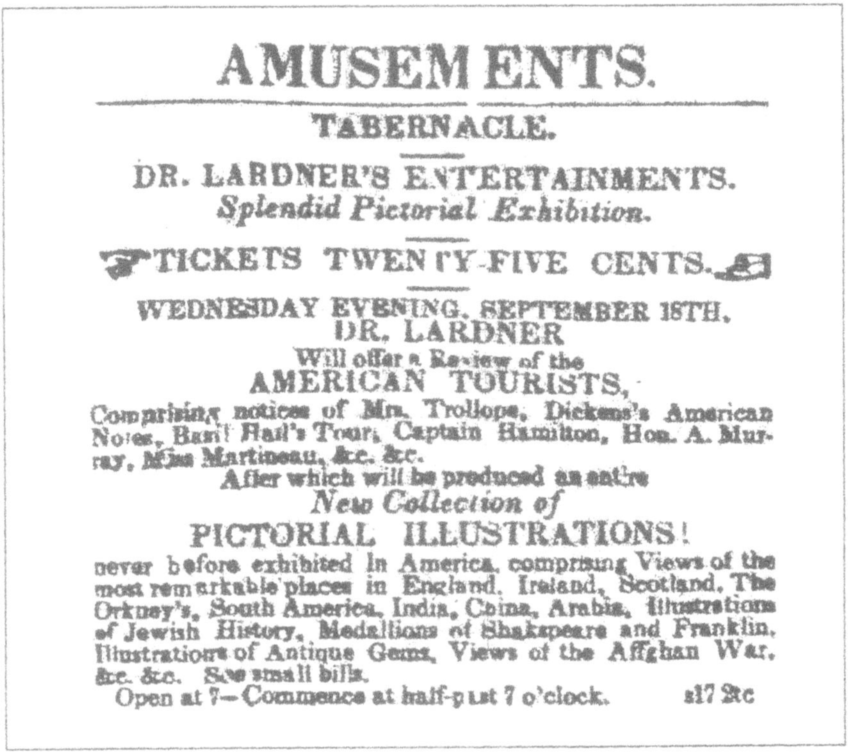

AMUSEMENTS.

TABERNACLE.

DR. LARDNER'S ENTERTAINMENTS.
Splendid Pictorial Exhibition.

TICKETS TWENTY-FIVE CENTS.

WEDNESDAY EVENING, SEPTEMBER 18TH,
DR. LARDNER
Will offer a Review of the
AMERICAN TOURISTS,
Comprising notices of Mrs. Trollope, Dickens's American Notes, Basil Hall's Tour, Captain Hamilton, Hon. A. Murray, Miss Martineau, &c. &c.
After which will be produced an entire
New Collection of
PICTORIAL ILLUSTRATIONS!
never before exhibited in America, comprising Views of the most remarkable places in England, Ireland, Scotland, The Orkney's, South America, India, China, Arabia, Illustrations of Jewish History, Medallions of Shakspeare and Franklin, Illustrations of Antique Gems, Views of the Affghan War, &c. &c. See small bills.
Open at 7—Commence at half-past 7 o'clock. s17 2tc

Figure 13. *New York Tribune* advertisement for the last New York Lardner lecture before he went to Philadelphia to consult with Norris Brothers [26, p. 3; 27, p. 2].

It was curious to examine at this moment into the secret of Dr. Lardner's great popularity as an author. It is probable, that had he lived either twenty years later or earlier, he would not have been so distinguished as he has been. He was floated into popularity on the very crest of the tide of diffusion-of-knowledge treatises, popular universities, and popular libraries; of popular institutions, and lectures of all kinds; and he was, we think, decidedly the most popular, and the most deservedly popular, of all the popular writers of his day. As a lecturer in the London University, no man gave better attended lectures on the elementary parts of science, and no one could have addressed a greater number of empty benches when the profounder abstractions of mathematics were to be developed [30, p. 962].

In 1869, Lardner was termed "a popular lecturer, very much overrated" [31, p. 33], and one hundred and fifty years later, when Rolt considered Lardner in his history of British railroads, Rolt also observed this dual edge to Lardner's popularity:

> That he enjoyed for a time a great reputation as a railway expert was due to the fact that he was one of the first masters of the art of blinding the layman with science . . . [32, p. 23].

Beyond the peculiar combination of strengths and weaknesses that were uniquely Lardner's, he shared another weakness with all touring lecturers of this period; his public lectures took time and effort away from research and study. "Public lecturing was an evil keeping men of science from research and leading to charlatanism" [21, p. 625; 33]. These were the words of Alexander Dallas Bache, head of the U.S. Coastal Survey, and originally the leader of the Franklin Institute's Committee on Steam Boiler Explosions (the precursor to the Committee on Science and the Arts and the committee to which Ewbank had sent his samples of the *New England*). This warning was apropos in the case of Lardner, for he spent little time staying abreast of scientific information even when he claimed that his U.S. lectures were prepared fresh for the tour [25, Vol. 1, p. 18]. Later researchers have pointed out that his 1840s' lectures on "electricity never mentioned any material dating past 1800; for galvanism, not past 1820; and for electromagnetism, not past 1830" [34, p. 234]. More specifically, even though Lardner spent extensive time in Philadelphia, and even though he did discuss such Philadelphia technological breakthroughs as the Ericsson propeller on the steam frigate *Princeton* being built at the time in the Philadelphia Navy Yard [25, Vol. 1, pp. 274-282], Lardner never mentioned any of the steam boiler explosion investigations done by Bache and his colleagues at the Franklin Institute of Philadelphia a decade earlier—work that Locke found so crucial in his 1838 discussion of the *Moselle* steamboat tragedy, the subject of the next chapter [33].

There also is more evidence of Lardner's lack of time spent on preparing his materials. When he lectured in New York in 1841, Henry J. Raymond, as associate editor on the *New York Tribune*, was so proficient at transcribing the lectures that they were frequently run on the front page of the paper each day during the entire month of December, and sometimes ran the full page. Later, the articles were collected into a pamphlet printed by the *New York Tribune: Course of Lectures Delivered by Dionysus Lardner* [35]. When it came time for Lardner to publish his own record of these lectures, *Popular Lectures on Science and Art; Delivered in the Principal Cities and Towns of the United States* [25] in 1846, he largely adapted Raymond's transcriptions with only slight revisions [31, p. 33].

Lardner noted in his preface to these published lectures that when he was in Philadelphia his audiences sometimes exceeded two thousand [25, pp. 12-13]. Based on such local and international popularity, is it any wonder then why Norris Brothers Locomotives would want to retain such a celebrated British scientific lecturer to write an investigation report about a local locomotive explosion [36, p. 48]? Moreover, in the financial situation that the Norris Locomotive Works was in in 1844, any damage to its reputation, let alone the replacement of a $10,000 guaranteed locomotive, might be financially fatal.

Within eighteen days of being retained by Norris Brothers, Lardner began his investigation and completed his report within a week [6, pp. 5, 28]—much like the speed of Silliman's and Redfield's investigation of the *New England* explosion. Lardner's report was privately published as a pamphlet by Norris Brothers and excerpted in *American Railroad Journal* and *Journal of the Franklin Institute* [37, pp. 30–31].

NEEDING TO PRESENT BOTH SIDES WHEN LARDNER DECLAIMS

After the Franklin Institute had demonstrated its national preeminence in the area of steam boiler investigations with the federally-funded Committee on Steam Boiler Explosions in the 1830s [33], the Committee on Science and the Arts had begun to investigate all steam boiler explosion within the vicinity of Philadelphia. Thus, at precisely the same time Lardner was performing his commissioned investigation, this committee of the Institute was also investigating it, sometimes using identical witnesses. The committee generated a report within twelve days of Lardner's, and *Report 408* [37] was published in the *Journal of the Franklin Institute* [5, pp. 16-31; 38, p. 50] and excerpted in the *American Railroad Journal* a month after Lardner's [39, pp. 91-92].

The *American Railroad Journal* felt the need to publish the Franklin Institute article contradicting Lardner in a number of ways so as to "give our readers both sides of the question" [39, pp. 91-92]. Such a publication circumstance echoed the earlier publication of Lardner's only other original research done up to this time (1839 and 1841) on "railroad constants" published in the *Reports of the 8th Meeting of the British Association for the Advancement of Science* [40, pp. 197-252].

In the "railroad constants" research, Lardner and a Mr. E. Wood produced separate reports, both of which the Association published because:

> The report of Mr. E. Woods, while it agrees in many important particulars, differs in others from the reports of Dr. Lardner, and, when viewed as a whole, is somewhat different both in its structure and in the manner in which the conclusions are arrived at, deduced, and reasoned upon.

> Under these circumstances, the Committee of the Mechanical Section of the British Association at Plymouth were of opinion that the objects of the Association would be best fulfilled by the publication of both; the results which both agree will be looked upon as extremely valuable both by the theoretical and practical man, while those in which they differ will form subjects of great interest for future inquiry [41, p. 205].

The Association might have done this because, in this "railroad constants" research, Lardner correctly deduced that resistance would increase as locomotives attained higher and higher speeds due to air resistance and friction along the rails. However, as a remedy, Lardner advocated laying track on inclines:

> In laying our lines of railway, therefore, intended exclusively or chiefly for rapid passenger-traffic, instead of obtaining by a large outlay of capital a road nearly level, steeper gradients would be adopted, and the resistance to the moving power rendered sufficiently uniform by variation of speed [40, p. 252].

Wood retorted in his report that:

> The experiments described in this and the former Report show the fallacy of erecting theories and establishing formulae on too slender a basis of facts. In a department of science, whose principles and laws are not yet fully developed, it behooves us to proceed upon a plan of the most cautious and rigid induction. Formulae derived from mere theoretical considerations are of little value in reference to such a subject . . . [41, p. 254; 42; 43; 44; 45, p. xviii].

Lardner also did not aid his reputation with the British Association for the Advancement of Science when he proclaimed to this association that "to cross the Atlantic by steam was mathematically impossible." He made this statement while the large steamboat, *Great Western,* was about to be launched, and prove, rather resoundingly on a monthly basis, that he was quite incorrect [46].

Thus, where Silliman, Denison, and Redfield had unimpeachable scientific credentials to offer in bolstering the persuasiveness of the Connecticut River Steam Boat Company investigation, Lardner offered popular, but questionable, scientific credential to bolster the persuasiveness of a report blaming lightning for the explosion of the *Richmond.* Moreover, such questionable credential caused the two publications which reprinted Lardner's pamphlet also to print reports that disagreed with his results just as the British Association for the Advancement of Science had done five years earlier.

Lardner's 1844 Report for Norris Brothers Locomotives

The very qualities Lardner was at the time approaching in his oral and written versions of his lectures were very much applied to his investigation report:

* There are no mathematical demonstrations.
* Clearness and order is conspicuous.
* Illustrations are not only be apposite, but were adapted to the character, capacity, and acquirements of his audience.

The closest that Lardner gets in his report to any mathematics was a diagram of the positions of the bodies and locomotive after the accident, Figure 10. His diagram was Appendix Q. Compare it to the same information diagramed by the Franklin Institute's Committee on Science and the Arts in Figure 14.

Lardner's diagram was on the last page of his report, in an appendix, and was not analyzed or even used in his discussion; the Committee's diagram was in the middle of its report and was discussed at length. Lardner's distances in the diagram were all done on straight lines, i.e., the distance from where the engine was when it exploded (X) to where it landed (a) cannot be ascertained with Lardner's diagram, which fails to give (h) the hypotenuse of the a-f-g triangle present in the committee's diagram and the probable line of flight of the engine. Also, the distance at which the body of the engineer was found at (c) was not directly reckoned by Lardner because he had left out the hypotenuse of the a-c-k triangle present in the Committee's diagram and the probable line of flight of the body. There also seems to be a major contradiction in the position of the body of the fireman (d), which is a-d, 155 ft. forward of the explosion in contrast to where Lardner positions the body of the fireman (d), behind the point of the explosion—no distance given.

Despite these semimathematical or geometrical mistakes, Lardner's report does have an overall clearness and order. His arrangement was a classic Ciceronian dispositio arrangement as laid out in the *Encyclopaedia Britannica* [47; 48; 49, pp. 83-124].

1. an *introduction* whose purpose is to make the readers receptive to the author's message.
2. a *narration* or a statement of background facts that lays the foundation of understanding for the central message.
3. a *partition* that quickly previews the parts of the confirmation to come.
4. the *confirmation* is the central statement of the author's argument for the point or subject.
5. the *confutation* where the author would seek to discredit any opposing views in a kind of preemptive strike.

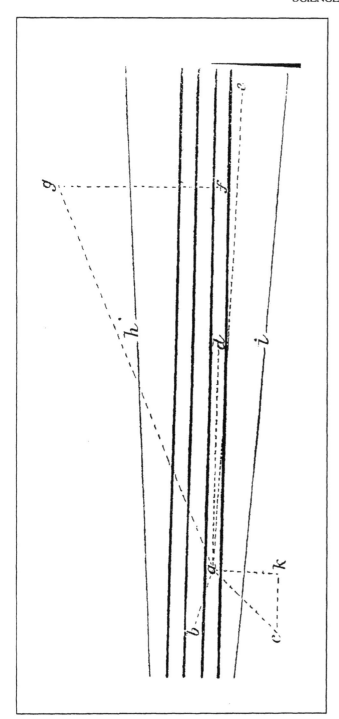

Figure 14. Committee on Science and the Arts's diagram of the relative positions of the bodies [5, p. 18].

Legend: The road at this point runs nearly north and south; the boiler itself, with its cylinders, dome, and fire-box, was thrown to the northwest, a distance of 249 feet; its distance in a perpendicular direction west of the center of the track 78 feet. (a) Spot where the engine exploded (b) body of fireman (c) body of engineer (d) body of conductor (e) body of fireman (g) Spot where the engine lodged (h) foot of embankment (i) foot of embankment. ab, 20 ft; ac, 54 ft; ak, 32 ft; ad, 155 ft; ae, 326 ft; ag, 249 ft; kc, 44 ft; fg, 78 ft; e to the rail is about 4 ft. The embankment is 5 ft high at (a) and 11 ft high at (f). The line is straight, and rises from a, towards f, at the rate of six feet per mile.

6. the *conclusion* that can sum up the argument as a whole, move the audience to action, and often amplify the conclusions to a more important plane of significance.

Lardner's introduction to the report would certainly have captured the reader's interest by alluding to the "recent destruction of the engine" and "loss of four lives and property amounting in value to nearly ten thousand dollars" [6, p. 4]. His "general outline of the history of this catastrophe" [6, p. 8] proceeds from page 4 to page 8. His partition on pages 8 and 9 states four different suppositions that could explain the accident:

- That the fire generated steam faster than it was discharged through the cylinders or valves, and that an accumulation of elastic vapor was thereby collected in the boiler, having a pressure which augmented in the ratio of its accumulation, until at length this pressure became greater than the resisting power of the crown piece, which bursting downwards, caused the catastrophe.
- That water was not supplied to the boiler as fast as it was consumed by the evaporation, and that thereby the crown piece and upper flues became uncovered; that, as a necessary consequence, these parts became overheated, and possibly even were rendered incandescent; that in this condition, water being thrown upon them, flashed suddenly into steam of enormous pressure and caused the catastrophe.
- That the engine was stricken by lightning that broke it, tore the crown piece from the sides of the fire-box, and caused the catastrophe.
- That lightning striking on the boiler raised some part of it to a high temperature; that the water taking up the heat was rapidly evaporated, as it would have been by contact with highly heated or incandescent metal; that steam of great volume and very extreme pressure being thus suddenly produced, the boiler yielded to the force, and the catastrophe took place [6, pp. 8-9].

Each of these suppositions is clearly separated by small headings and italicized. He then suggested that "I shall examine them successively, and state distinctly the circumstances and reasonings which have led me to their rejection or adoption, as the case may be" [6, p. 9].

Lardner proceeded through each of these suppositions in the body of the report, the confirmation, separating each with a heading and a restatement of the question, and proceeding to the fourth and final supposition, which is the one he advocated. The evidence for or against each of the possible explanations is contained at length in the appendix, where the content of the interviews with witnesses was printed. The fourth solution he advocates is that lightning struck the iron boiler of the *Richmond,* abruptly heating a portion of the boiler and causing the water to produce more steam than could be quickly let out through the safety valves.

This four-part conformation follows exactly the discussion of the four possible theoretical explanations for the explosion done by the Silliman/Redfield committee a decade earlier in the *New England* steamboat explosion. Also like the *New England* committee, the fourth and final cause was the explanation advocated by the authors. The net effect of this conformatio design by both the *New England* committee and Lardner was that it implied to the reader that the choice of four explanations was inexorable, and that, like the scientific laws of the universe, pointed to the final supposition as the culprit.

Lardner's confutation is in two parts, the first being somewhat of a scientific straw man. Early on in the investigations into boiler explosions there had been a theory that the water in the boiler decomposed into its constituent parts of hydrogen and oxygen, and that one of these gases, after accumulating, would explode—this had been dismissed by investigations of the Franklin Institute six years earlier [50, p. 292; 51; 52, Fiche #149-151, p. 61; 53]. However, this was the counterargument he chose to refute in his confutation. (Another explanation for the presence of such a strawman argument is that Lardner was perhaps unaware of the finality in which *Part 1 Report* of the Franklin Institute six years earlier had laid to rest this hypothesis—another example of his inability to keep up with the scientific literature.)

However, in the second confutation, Lardner directly confronted the earlier explanation Olmsted had given to the newspapers ("the accident was caused by the violence of the steam alone, under some mismanagement," [17, p. 2]). Lardner stated that

> I do not forget that it may be urged that the boiler and its appendages were in metallic communication with the earth, and that during heavy rain, the soil itself was in a favorable condition for the escape of the electricity; but I know that in the structure of the boiler and appendages, there were interruptions of the metallic continuity greater both in number and degree, than between the links of a chain, and, in other cases, in which it is proved that masses of iron have been rendered incandescent by lightning [6, p. 16].

Notice, however, that even in this most specific rebuttal situation, no names are used, and the scientific disinterested ethos is maintained. Lardner's conclusion was that the accident was an act of God, and, therefore, no liability could be assigned to the Norris Brothers, the builders of the *Richmond,* or its operators, the Reading Railroad [6].

In a nutshell, Lardner's report on the *Richmond* explosion was quite similar to the earlier one on the *New England* in its adherence to arrangement, and in having the same number of parts to the conformatio. It also was quite similar to Lardner's own lectures in the quality of organization and illustration, the dearth of disciplined analysis, and the scientific ethos.

COMMITTEE ON SCIENCE AND THE ARTS REPORT

Where Lardner did not include much mathematical analysis, Frazer and the Franklin Institute's Committee on Science and the Arts did [38, p. 50; 54]. To complete his investigations in 1837 leading to the *Report of the Strength of Materials Employed in the Construction of Steam Boilers,* Professor Walter Johnson not only invented the science of materials testing at the Institute, but also created the testing apparatus to put such testing into practical effect [55, 56]. After the conclusion of the steam boiler investigations in the mid-1830s, the Committee on Science and the Arts used its knowledge and instruments in a number of technical investigations [57]. In five months, Frazer was able to bring the science of testing and this apparatus to bear on the *Richmond,* discussing the breaking points in pounds per square inch to the third decimal point. The result of such testing found that "the workmanship of the boiler was such as to sustain the reputation which the Messrs. Norris have acquired in their business" [5, pp. 20-21].

Both the institute's committee and Lardner came to a similar estimate of Joseph Ward, the engineer in charge of the *Richmond* on this particular trip:

> . . . reputed one of the most capable and trustworthy upon the road, and his character for carefulness and sobriety was such as to forbid the suspicion of any improper tampering with the valves [5, p. 21].

But the institute's committee and Lardner dramatically disagreed on two facts:

- That there was lightning present at the time of the accident.
- That the pumps were correctly operating at the time of the accident.

Was Lightning Present?

The presence of lightning was a key point for Lardner, and he described its presence in the following way:

> It appears by the general evidence of the entire population around the vicinity of the catastrophe, as well as by the special evidence of the individuals who have been personally examined, that, at the time of this occurrence, a terrific storm of thunder and lightning raged; two of the men upon the train who survived, prove that the flashes of lightning were incessant, both before and after the explosion, and that the lightning was of the species called "zig-zag lightning." It is proper here to observe that, of the different species of lightning, this is the kind by which terrestrial objects are generally stricken; . . . There seems to be then present all the conditions necessary for the production of such a phenomenon; the lightning is in continual play; it is of the kind necessary to produce the effect; 18 tons of iron, in the shape of the boiler and machinery, are present to attract it; there are abundance of disjunctions in this machinery . . . by which conduction may be sufficiently broken to give full effect to the heating power of the electricity; finally this mass is broken to pieces, its parts scattered about in all directions, broken, bent, and twisted, and

projected in considerable masses to distances analogous to those recorded in similar cases [5, p. 15].

The Institute Committee, however, found:

. . . two other brakesmen, McGuire and Smith, declare that they saw no lightning, and heard no thunder, which is scarcely reconcilable with the supposition of lightning striking the boiler. Messrs. Weber and Shipp, persons residing near the place of accident, both of whom saw the explosion, agree likewise in the statement that there was no lightning at the time. In the testimony collected by the Committee, it will be found that the storm . . . had passed off to the south-east, and was almost entirely over before the *Richmond* had left Reading, so that Mr. Ward had laid aside his outer coat. Mr. Spayd [of Reading] asserts with confidence, that for some hours previous to, and after, the explosion, there was no lightning to the north of Reading; he heard the explosion, and is sure there was no flash at the same moment. Messrs. Heister, Herbst, Richardson, and Gruber [all farmers in the area of the explosion], all testify to the same absence of lightning. The evidence, therefore, alone is perfectly conclusive, that the explosion was not due to the fact of the engine being struck with lightning [5, p. 22].

At the moment the committee could be most combatively critical of Lardner, it was not. The members maintained their scientific ethos by writing: "The evidence, therefore, alone is perfectly conclusive, that the explosion was not due to the fact of the engine being struck with lightning" [5, p. 22]. Moreover, even if lightning was present, the members of the institute committee were unaware of any experiments or observations

. . . tending to show the power of electricity to produce such effects in a good continuous conductor, as a locomotive engine, running too, be it observed, upon a wet rail, the Committee are in ignorance of them; and independently of this, the evidence to the contrary is as plain as could be desired [5, p. 21].

Thus, there was basic disagreement between the reports as to the presence of lightning and its ability to cause such a freakish accident.

Were the Pumps Correctly Operating?

If lightning was not present, and, if it could not have affected what Lardner asserts even if it were, then what caused the explosion? Ward, the engineer, knew what he was doing, and the boiler had sufficient strength and integrity of workmanship. The Committee suggested that the explosion might have occurred if evaporation caused by the work of the locomotive was not replenished with water from the pumps. If the water level was not replenished, the level could have receded leaving a part of the heated boiler uncovered and making it liable to superheating. If a quantity of water were then suddenly introduced and covered this superheated portion of the boiler, a sudden increase of steam could have produced sufficient quantity of steam to cause the explosion [5, pp. 22-23].

Were there any reports of the pumps not working properly? According to the Institute, there were plenty:

- "Mr. Kirk, foreman of the Reading workshops, and Mr. Loser, a clerk at the depot, both testified that Mr. Ward had several times told them that the pumps did not work well, and that they had given him much trouble" [5, p. 23].
- "Mr. Yeager, the engineer of the freight train, which was immediately behind the *Richmond* when she exploded, testified to Mr. McCabe's (the conductor's) statement, as to the cause of delay on the Saturday preceding, at the Manayunk tunnel, to which Patrick Nugent, a brakesman upon the train also testified; this is, moreover, confirmed by the statement of Mr. Simpson, at the time foreman of the workshops to one of the committee, that he did not see Mr. Ward upon Saturday evening, but that upon inquiring of another engineer, whose train had been behind, as to the cause of the detention, was told that the pumps of the *Richmond* had given out, and that Ward had to take them to pieces" [5, p. 23].
- "Mr. Day, also an engineer upon the road, testified that Mr. Ward told him some day of the week preceding the accident, that 'his pumps worked badly, and that he never could start them without first unscrewing them, and lifting the caps.' He also testified that he passed the *Richmond* at Pottsville, upon the day of the accident, that Ward was then just starting, and was engaged in unscrewing the cap of his pump in order to make it work" [5, p. 23].

While Lardner also interviewed Kirk and Nugent, he failed to include any of the above information. Oddly, Lardner did, however, include a preemptive rebuttal of the faulty pumps as the cause of the explosion:

> . . . a rumor was prevalent that the explosion was produced by the imperfect action of the feed pumps. I traced this rumor to one of the brakesmen [Matthew Smith, not interviewed by the Franklin Institute Committee] who was accordingly examined. It appeared that he was so unacquainted with the structure of a locomotive, that he was unable to point out the place of the feed pump on such a machine, and that when he saw the engineer, Joseph Ward, on Saturday, 30th September, repairing the pin of the half-stroke, he mistook that for the feed pump, and thereupon circulated the rumor that the pumps were imperfect, and hence the reported cause of the catastrophe [6, p. 13].

However, in the Franklin Institute Committee report, those giving evidence regarding the faulty pumps did not include Smith, but did include the sworn statements of four others giving evidence that Ward—considered by both Lardner and the Franklin Institute Committee to be competent and careful—thought the pumps were faulty [5]. Moreover, all of these give evidence of words spoken by Ward rather than depending upon the "rumors" of Smith.

Not only is Lardner's explanation for the accident unprecedented, but even the presence of lightning is questioned. At the same time, an explanation with much more precedent in steam engine operation and calling for fewer freakish acts of nature was explicitly discounted by Lardner, who termed it a "rumor" and questioned the capability of one witness while ignoring the evidence of four others.

Why Did Lardner's Conclusion Differ So Greatly from the Committee on Science and the Arts?

One possible explanation for the different conclusions may be that Lardner's scientific approach was characterized by wonder, amazement, and child-like delight:

> Rational calculation could only work on facts, but discovery was presented as a dramatic result in which happenstance governed. . . . Happenstance, wonder, and amazement provided a dramatic frame for Lardner's presentation. Yet they also posed problems . . . [they] were in sharp contrast to the calm rationality otherwise ascribed to legitimate scientists [34, p. 225].

Is it not possible that the dramatic happenstance of lightning striking a locomotive for the first time in history and causing it to explode contained much more wonder and amazement than the rather mundane problems of a fire-box bridge-bar?

Lardner's errors could also have been a function of the limited time given to the investigation by a man in the midst of a nationwide lecture tour, as well as his overreliance on witness testimony. The relative proportions Lardner and the Committee on Science and the Arts gave to the various parts of their dispositio can imply these problems. Lardner gave 27 percent (three of eleven total pages) to a statement of the facts involved in the case, whereas the Committee dedicated 13 percent more of its report to the statement of facts (four of ten pages). Lardner spent much more time on his conformation, his four-part argument, 72 percent, and 5 percent on his refutatio, whereas the Committee spent 50 percent of all its pages on its statement of the argument, and only 3 percent on its refutatio. Lardner saw his primary objective as persuasion, whereas the Committee on Science and the Arts saw its objective primarily as description.

Also indicative of Lardner's limited time for analysis is that his conformatio goes through the four suppositions based solely on testimony from witnesses who had appeared before the coroner's jury. The Franklin Committee also used testimony from witnesses who had appeared before the coroner's jury, but then they also conducted their own separate and more extensive interviews. Also, the Committee in its conformatio, described the deformation of the boiler parts, Figure 15, the tensile strengths of boiler fragments, Figure 16, and even evidence of a competitor's very similar cast-iron bridge-bar failure, Figure 17.

Finally, when Lardner gave his conclusion, it was succinct and cast in legal parlance befitting the very limited goal of his patron, Norris Locomotive Works,

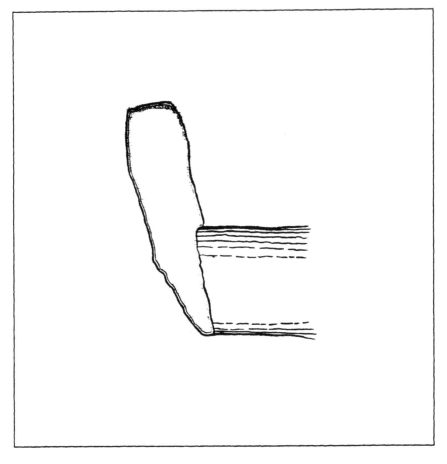

Figure 15. The fire-box and part of the boiler surrounding it
were driven to the left and flattened [5, p. 19].

which had guaranteed the engine for sixty days [18, p. 3] and needed to have
Lardner blame the lightning rather than their workmanship:

> In fine, if my evidence were required on this point, in a case where rights
> or liabilities of individuals rendered a positive decision of the question
> indispensable, I should not hesitate a moment to affirm that that decision must
> be made on the last of the above suppositions [6, p. 16].

On the other hand, nearly a tenth of the committee's report was dedicated to
the conclusions drawn from its investigation, and some were quite far ranging
in their import. The first conclusion of the Committee was critical of the work
of the coroner's jury:

No. 1, No. 2, } Across the grain,	{ Breaking weight 51.120 lbs. pr. sq. in.		
No. 3, No. 4, } With the grain,	{ " 55.320 " "		
	" 50.280 " "		
	" 51.120 " "		
Average of No. 1, and No. 2,	" 53.220 " "		
" No. 3, and No. 4,	" 50.700 " "		
" the four pieces,	" 51.860 " "		

Figure 16. Committee on Science and the Arts' table of the tensile strength of various samples taken of the *Richmond's* boiler [5, p. 20].

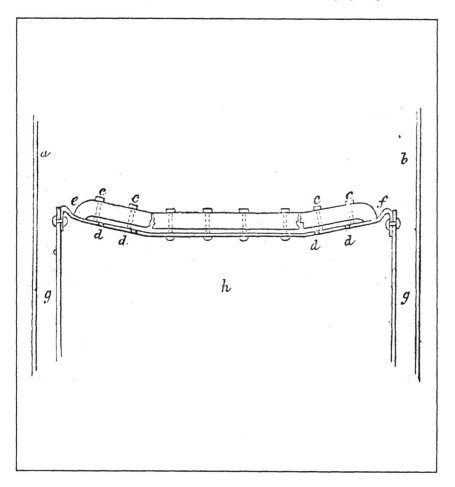

Figure 17. Fractures in cast-iron bridge-bar over the boiler's fire-box [5, p. 18].
Legend: (ab)Interior of the Steam Dome (cc) Bolts of which the Lower Parts Were Sheared Off (dd) Holes Left Open by the Shearing Off Referred To (ef) Cast-Iron Bridge-bars As Broken (ff) Water legs on sides of the Fire-box (h) Fire-box.

> In the first place, permit us to draw attention to the total inefficiency of our
> present system of coroner's inquests. There can be no doubt that had the
> examination, in this case, been properly and efficiently conducted, much
> important information upon the subject would have been elicited, which is
> now forever lost, and much trouble labor saved in the endeavor to investigate
> the causes of the explosion [5, p. 25].

In fact, the committee used this accident and another aboard a Delaware River
steamboat [58, p. 31] to argue that America should change its procedure of
conducting coroner's inquests:

> . . . how deplorable the remissness of juries, and the apathy of an injured, a
> defenseless, but too patient, and long suffering public, whom the newspapers
> almost invariably endeavor to assure that no blame can possibly be attributed
> to any of the parties concerned [59, p. 34].

The institute at large took up changing the process of coroner's jury investigations, and a set of resolutions was sent to the Pennsylvania state capital in
Harrisburg for legislative enactment. The Institute reminded the legislators of
Pennsylvania that the institute had carried out extensive research in steam-boiler
problems and that it had examined most of the explosions occurring in the
vicinity of Philadelphia. Coroner's inquests, the Institute noted, might be the
source of valuable information, but "are usually conducted with a carelessness
which exceeds belief, and leave no trace behind them, except a verdict of *accidental death* when in many cases the most culpable negligence has existed"
[59, p. 34]. The Institute proposed to the legislature that coroners be required
to call before inquests "the nearest scientific and practical men"; that the causes
of explosions be "minutely" examined; that the results of the inquests be published in one Philadelphia newspaper, as well as in the local paper of the town
in which the accident occurred; and finally, that coroners be directed to furnish
the Institute with a printed record of the inquest [60]. This legislation was never
passed, but Professor Locke, an associate of the Institute who lived in Cincinnati,
did, in fact, fulfill this prescription in his 1838 investigation report that we will
examine in the next chapter.

A second conclusion the Franklin Committee offered was more particular to the
engine. The Committee noted that the positioning of stop-cock gauges used to
measure the amount of water in the boiler could provide faulty information.
Stop-cock gauges directly indicated the level of steam or water in the boiler by
allowing the engineer to observe whether water or steam issued from them when
they were opened, e.g., if water issued when opened, then the stop-cock was below
or at the water line; if only steam issued when opened, then the water was below
that stop-cock. Note, however, the position of the "stop-cock" gauges on right of
the *New England* boiler in Figure 7(i) in a very small part of the space given over
to water in the boiler, the water legs. Foaming of the water in such small confines
could easily make these gauges yield faulty information because foam created by

the boiling of the water could carry some water up to the stop-cock from several inches below—seeming to indicate that there was water at or above the stop-cock—even though it was actually several inches below.

A third conclusion the Franklin Committee reached can be seen by referring to Figure 17. The bridge-bar made of cast-iron by Norris Brothers was insufficient to withstand the temperatures in the fire-box below and the steam pressures in the boiler above, and should be replaced with wrought-iron bridge-bars of greater strength. This was one of the original suggested causes for the explosion as reported by the *Reading Gazette* on September 7 [13, p. 2; 15]. A month after Lardner wrote his report, on October 26, the *Gazette* reported that another explosion had taken place on the Reading and Philadelphia Railroad, and that this time the exploded locomotive was built by Baldwin & Whitney Locomotives, a competitor to Norris Brothers Locomotives. The article went on to explain: "An examination of the cause attributes the explosion to the weakness of the stays across the fire box, being too light to bear the pressure of the steam required." The result was that the Reading and Philadelphia Railroad examined all such locomotive, cast-iron bridge-bars, and took "measures to guard against future accidents from the same cause [61, p. 2]. The committee also noted that Baldwin & Whitney Locomotives were changing from cast-iron to wrought-iron bridge-bars.

Thus, other than Norris Locomotive Works, the only other companies most affected by these conflicting reports decided to spend money to implement the Franklin Institute Committee solution rather than resting on the freakish act of God suggested by Lardner. Later, even Norris Locomotive Works, Lardner's patrons, heeded the Committee's recommendations rather than his act of God. Septimus Norris, the designer of the *Richmond,* was undoubtedly referring to this fact when in his 1852 book, *Norris's Hand book for Locomotive Engineers,* he wrote:

> The roofs of all fire-boxes require to be stayed by cross-bars; but the bars are required to be both stronger and more numerous for the square fireboxes, and should always be carefully made of wrought-iron, and very carefully fitted before being bolted on. Stay-bars of cast-iron have been employed, on account of their cheapness; but, having led several times to accidents from explosion, they are now discarded [62, p. 245].

Beyond his lacking the calm rationality ascribed to legitimate scientists, his lack of time to spend on analysis, and an overreliance on others (e.g., Raymond's transcriptions of his lectures and the witness testimony from the coroner's jury), there may have been another reason why Lardner's conclusions could be so different. Lardner could also have been partial to offering an explanation pleasing to his patron, Norris Locomotive Works, since Norris had contacted him, authorized him to investigate, and was paying him.

IN THE END

Within a month, the *Richmond* was rebuilt and renamed the *Philadelphia* by the Philadelphia and Reading Railroad [63, p. 305]. Norris Brothers did not have to honor its guarantee, since the accident was an "act of God." So, Lardner's report was successful. Later Norris Locomotive Works was able to move out of receivership when the U.S. economy grew in the following decade of the 1850s, and, in January 1853, the new company of Richard Norris & Son was announced. At the time, it was the largest national, if not international, manufacturer of locomotives [1, p. 27].

Lardner left the United States with a $200,000 profit from his lectures [25, pp. 12-13; 34, p. 211; 64, p. 2] and settled with his wife in Paris, where he died in 1859. He published the record of his American tour in his *Lectures on Science and the Arts* in 1846, and it was phenomenally successful, with fifteen editions [34, p. 215]. The *Lectures* were subsequently reworked into a twelve-volume set, *The Museum of Science and Art*, and published between 1853 and 1856 by Walton & Maberly (London).

Lardner also produced his most mathematically complex work, *Railway Economy*, in 1855:

> His *Steam Engine*, published in 1836, was a popular manual of applied science; his *Cabinet Cyclopaedia* (1849) in 133 volumes, was a compendium of knowledge of many kinds; but *Railway Economy*, published in 1850, was a different sort of work. It was an original investigation of railway management, based on the limited statistical information then available [65, p. 153; 66, 67, 68].

In none of these later books, whether under the heading of "lightning," "explosion," or "locomotive," did Lardner ever refer to his report on the *Richmond* locomotive in 1844. The only reference is one implied in Chapter 14 of *Railway Economy*, when he tabulates a list of causes for accidents on railroads, and it is the last one:

Accidents from collision	56
Accidents from broken wheel or axle	18
Accidents from defective rail	14
Accidents by switches	5
Accidents from impediments laying on the road	3
Accidents off rails by cattle on line	3
Accidents from bursting boiler	1
	100 [69, p. 276; 70].

If Norris Brothers Locomotives hoped that Lardner's report would help prevent liability lawsuits and bolster the confidence of customers in the safety of their locomotives, they were successful. However, if they or Lardner hoped that his report would become the "report of record," like the Silliman/Redfield/Olmsted report, they were sadly mistaken. Yes, Lardner had scientific credentials to imbue

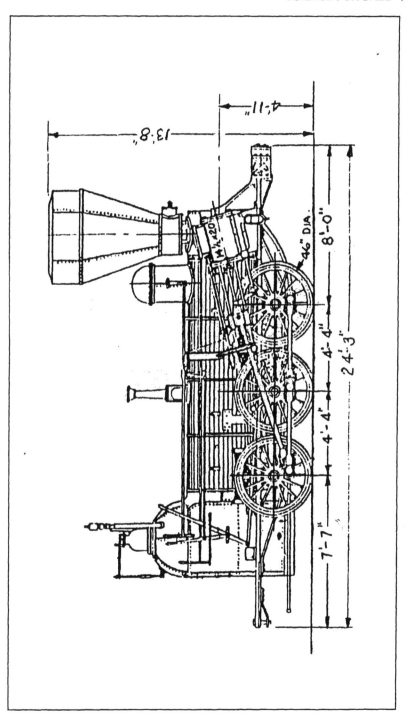

Figure 18. Rebuilt *Philadelphia* after *Richmond* explosion.

the report with authority, but only for the masses that filled his lecture halls. The leading scientists of the day gave him no encouragement [18, p. 540; 29, Vol. 5, pp. 244-245], and Benjamin Silliman, leader of the *New England* investigation and editor of the *American Journal of Science and Arts,* never mentioned Lardner's lectures while he was in the United States. Moreover, where Silliman's investigation report was lauded by the American Institute of New York [71, p. 658] and quickly found publication in the *Journal of the Franklin Institute* [72, pp. 55, 126, 289], New York City's *Mechanic's Magazine* [73, pp. 11-16], and five years later in a report to the U.S. Senate, Lardner's was reprinted only in the *Journal of the Franklin Institute* [5, pp. 16-31; 38, p. 50] and excerpted only in the *American Railroad Journal* [74, pp. 91-92].

Moreover, both journals felt compelled to "give our readers both sides of the question" [74, pp. 91-92] and thus published the Committee on Science and the Arts investigation in subsequent issues. Many at the time quickly challenged Lardner's findings. Thus, the persuasive effectiveness of the investigation on the *New England* explosion drew much from the unimpeachable reputations of the Silliman, Redfield, and Olmsted, while Lardner's questionable scientific reputation drew questions and challenges from the moment it was published in 1844. As Charles Hood wrote in *Herapath's Journal:* "The conclusion of Dr. Lardner's does not appear to me to be warranted by the facts . . ." [75, p. 158]. Never again in railroad history would there ever be a instance in which lightning caused a locomotive to explode, and, for the rest of his life, Lardner himself never referred to this report.

ENDNOTES

1. John H. White, "Once the Greatest of Builders: The Norris Locomotive Works," *Railroad History,* Bulletin 150 (Spring 1984).
2. *Report of the President and Managers of the Philadelphia and Reading Rail Road Company to the Stockholders, January 13, 1845,* Philadelphia, Penna.: I. M. Voss, 1845.
3. Albert Fishlow, *American Railroads and the Transformation of the Ante-bellum Economy,* Cambridge, Mass.: Harvard University Press, 1965, "The tonnage of the Reading Railroad in 1859 far exceeded that of any other single line and was comparable to the freight moved by the entire New York canal system." . . . They succeeded in a traffic composed almost exclusively of coal. . . .
4. J. Lane Wheaton, *From Indian Trail to Iron Horse: Travel and Transportation in New Jersey, 1620-1860,* Princeton, N.J.: Princeton University Press, 1939.
5. Robert Frazer, "Explosion of the Locomotive Engine 'Richmond'," *Journal of the Franklin Institute* 3rd Series, Vol. 9, January 1845. Diagram furnished by railroad's superintendent.
6. Dionysus Lardner, *Investigation of the Causes of the Explosion of the Locomotive Engine "Richmond" Near Reading, PA on the 2nd of September 1844,* New York: Herald Book and Job Printing Office, 1844.

7. R. B. Osborne, Philadelphia, Penna., 1838. Library of Congress Map 527.

8. Sadly, the actual record of the coroner's jury findings was discarded by the Berks County Coroner's Office.

9. *Pennsylvania Inquirer*, September 4, 1844.

10. *Reading Democratic Press* stated, "It is evident that it was struck by lightning," cited in *United States Gazette*, 9/4/1844, p. 2.

11. *Berks & Schuylkill Journal*, 26 (9), September 7, 1844.

12. *Ledger & Transcript*, Wednesday, September 4, 1844.

13. *Reading Gazette*, 5 (18) September 7, 1844. This explanation seems to be the one taken by most to be the real problem. For example, in a short time both Norris Brothers and their local competitor, Baldwin & Whitney, returned to using wrought iron in the bridge-bars rather than the cast-iron ones used in the *Richmond*.

14. Christian H. Hewison, *Locomotive Boiler Explosions*, North Pomfret, Vt.: David & Charles, 1983. This problem and solution were independently discovered by the Lt-Col. Wynne of the British Railway Inspectorate in the investigation of an April 7th 1856 boiler explosion on the Caledonian Railway.

15. *Outlines of a Course of Lectures on Meteorology and Astronomy*, New Haven, Conn.: T. J. Stafford, 1858.

16. *Reading Gazette*, 5 (18), September 14, 1844.

17. "Locomotive Struck by Lightning," *New Haven Palladium*, 4 (210) September 6, 1844.

18. *New York Tribune*, 4 (129), September 5, 1844.

19. J. N. Hays, "The Rise and Fall of Dionysus Lardner," *Annals of Science*, 38, 1981.

20. "Reverend Doctor Lardner," *Fraser's Magazine for Town and Country*, 30 (5) July 1832, "Lardner, called at his baptism by the name of Dennis, amplified by his own classical taste to that of Dionysus, but by his compatriots generally pronounced as Dinnish, stands before you, gentle reader, cloaked and hatted in his usual guise. His chin is perked up *a' l'ordinaire*, and his spectacled eyes beam forth wisdom. In order, we suppose, to illustrate some of the principles of his own treatise on mechanics, as published in the *Cab.*, he generally takes the position of standing toes in, heels out, according to the cavalry regulations; and therefore so is he depicted in the opposite engraving. What hulk it is he carries under his cloak we know not, nor have we any grounds whereon to offer a conjecture" [p. 42].

21. Margaret W. Rossiter, "Benjamin Silliman and the Lowell Institute: The Popularization of Science in Nineteenth-Century America," *The New England Quarterly*, 44 (1971), Silliman had developed a similar lecture tour on a smaller scale in Boston at the Lowell Institute.

22. He had, in fact, eloped with the wife of a British army officer and had a verdict of 8,000 pounds entered against him should he return.

23. *London Times*, 12/12/1843, p. 3.

24. *American Whig*, 2(2), August 1845.

25. Dionysus Lardner, *Popular Lectures on Science and Art; Delivered in the Principal Cities and Towns of the United States*, New York: Greenley & McElrath, 1849.

26. *New York Tribune*, September 17, 1844, p. 3. The following day the *Tribune* commented: "Those who have no interest in scientific matters will have an opportunity of enjoying Dr. Lardner's entertainment this evening, as he will give his personal recollections of London and Paris, in which cities he maintained for so many years

a prominent public position. He has been personally acquainted with nearly all the eminent public men in every department who have flourished in his time, and intimately so with many of them. His recollections must be rich with anecdote and sketches of character. After the discourse, a beautiful series of pictorial illustrations of various countries shown as dissolving scenes on an immense scale will follow. To afford every possible facility for the attendance of families, the admission will be only twenty-five cents." Evidently the title of the talk had been changed to "Personal Recollections of London and Paris" [27, p. 2].

27. *New York Tribune,* September 18, 1844, p. 2.
28. It could also be for the reason that he turned them more in the direction of entertainment rather than science, as can be inferred by this notice in the *Brooklyn Eagle:* "Dr. Lardner is playing with great success in New Orleans. His Lectures seem to have been completely turned into theatrical performances, as we see them advertised with the announcement that 'The entertainments will conclude with the admired petite comedy of the Youthful Queen in which Mrs. Stuart and J. M. Field appear" *Brooklyn Eagle,* April 4, 1843, p. 2.
29. Joseph Henry to John Stevens Henslow, July 5, 1842, in *The Papers of Joseph Henry,* Nathan Reingold, Marc Rothenberg, et al. (eds.), Washington, D.C.: Smithsonian Institution Press, 1972, Vol. 5. Silliman's *American Journal of Science and Arts* took no notice whatever of Lardner's lectures [19, p. 540].
30. *The Athenaeum,* December 5, 1840, No. 684.
31. Augustus Maverick, *Henry J. Raymond and the New York Press for Thirty Years,* Hartford, Conn.: A. S. Hale & Co., 1870.
32. L. T. C. Rolt, *Red for Danger: The Classic History of British Railway Disaster,* Phoenix Mill, Stroud, Gloucestershire, U.K.: Sutton Publishing, 1998.
33. R. John Brockmann, *Exploding Steamboats, Senate Debates, and Technical Reports: The Convergence of Technology, Politics and Rhetoric in the Steamboat Bill of 1838,* Amityville, N.Y.: Baywood, 2002. Offers a lengthy analysis of Bache's work.
34. Paul H. Theerman, "Dionysus Lardner's American Tour: A Case Study in Antebellum American Interest in Science, Technology, and Nature," in *Experiencing Nature: Proceeding of a Conference in Honor of Allen G. Debus,* Paul H. Theerman and Karen Hunger Parshall (eds.), The Netherlands: Dordrecht, 1997.
35. *Revised and Corrected from the Reports as They Originally Appeared in the New-York Tribune,* New York: Greeley & McElrath, 1842.
36. Robert B. Shaw, *A History of Railroad Accidents, Safety Precautions and Operating Practices,* Binghamton, NY: Vail-Ballou Press, Inc., 1978.
37. Percy A. Bivins, *Index to the Reports of the Committee on Science and the Arts of the Franklin Institute,* Philadelphia, Penna.: Franklin Institute, 1890.
38. Michael McMahon and Stephanie Morris, *Technology in Industrial America,* Wilmington, Del.: Scholarly Resources, 1977.
39. *American Railroad Journal,* 2 (6) 2nd Quarter Series, February 6, 1845.
40. Dionysus Lardner, "First Report on the Determination of the Mean Numerical Values of Railway Constants," in *Report of the 8th Meeting of the British Association for the Advancement of Science,* London: John Murray, 1839.
41. Dionysus Lardner, and Edward Woods, *Reports on the Determination of the Mean Value of Railway Constants (from the Report of the British Association for the Advancement of Science for 1841),* London: Richard and John Taylor, 1842.

42. It is interesting to note that when Lardner again offers some original scientific analysis of railways in his *Railway Economy, A Treatise on the New Art of Transportation* [New York: Harper & Brothers, 1850], no mention of the railway constants or resistance is included. Moreover, the report with its analysis of locomotives and lightning does not get included in the lectures in either place where locomotives or lightning are discussed. However, Lardner does seem in this last book-length project to answer the criticisms of being a mathematical lightweight. Later political economists claimed that this last work "is filled with factual information . . . and his algebraic equations are applied to the 'case of the Belgium railroads' as an example of their applicability to practical situations" and "He carefully distinguished between fixed and variable costs, and . . . developed the profit maximizing rule, marginal cost equals marginal revenue, all of which he illustrated with a geometric diagram" [43, p. 207].

43. James P. Henderson, "The Whewell Group of Mathematical Economists," in *William Whewell, Dionysus Lardner, and Charles Babbage*, Mark Blaug (ed.), Brookfield, Vt.: Edward Elgar Publishing Company, 1991.

44. Donald Hooks, "Monopoly Price Discrimination in 1850: Dionysus Lardner," in *William Whewell, Dionysus Lardner, and Charles Babbage*, Mark Blaug (ed.), Brookfield, Vt.: Edward Elgar Publishing Company, 1991.

45. Earlier, in Stanley W. Jevons's *The Theory of Political Economy*, London: Macmillian and Company, 1871, Jevons noted in a similar way: "Lardner's book has always struck me as containing a very able investigation the scientific value of which has not been sufficiently estimated; and . . . we find the Laws of Supply and Demand treated mathematically and illustrated graphically," p. xviii.

46. There were a number of reports and statements made by Lardner that he spent the rest of his life denying. Consider the following from Letter to the Editor, "The Prophet Dionysus," *London Times*, October 25, 1845, p. 4, col. B: "Sir, I perceive by your paper of October 20, that Dr. Lardner denies that he ever said before the House of Lords, that 'to cross the Atlantic by steam was mathematically impossible.' He also remarks on 'the impossibility' of his having made such an assertion. This, to say the least of it, is an uncommonly courageous asseveration, The truth is, that though the Doctor did not make the prophecy of non-steam transit of the Atlantic before the House of Lords, he did make it before the British Association for the so-called 'Advancement' of Science, at Bristol, while the *Great Western* was on the stocks; unless; indeed the report of his prophecy in the ninth volume of the *Athenaeum* (p. 656) be an entire fabrication. In his paper read before the association he computed that for each horsepower of steam one ton of coals would be required every 1,425 miles. 'Taking this as a basis of the calculation,' said he, 'and allowing one-fourth of a ton of coals per horse power as spare fuel, the tonnage necessary for the fuel and machinery in a voyage from England to New York would be 3.70 tons per horse-power, which, for a vessel with engines of 400 horse-power, would be 1,450 tons. Now as the *Great Western* was only to be 1,200 tons burden, the voyage according to the prophetic mathematician, was impossible. Since that time, as we all know, this 'impossibility' has happened pretty regularly about once a month; but the other 'impossibility' mentioned by the Doctor is not of such frequent occurrence; namely, that of a gentleman in equivocally denying 'having made such and such an assertion,' because it was entirely erroneous, and when it is to be produced in record against him. I am, yours &c., W.H.W. Edinburgh, October 22, 1845."

47. Douglas Ehninger, "John Ward and His Rhetoric," *Speech Monographs*, 17, March 1951. In the third edition of the *Encyclopaedia Britannica*, the *Encyclopaedia* largely reprinted John Wards's 1759 series of lectures at Gresham College called *A System of Oratory* ("the most extensive restatement of ancient rhetorical theory in English up to 1759" [50]). Ward tended to follow the hallowed conventions of Cicero's disposition rather than some of the new simpler Aristotelian formulas coming into vogue at the time and such as were used in the composition of the Declaration of Independence.

48. John Ward, Vol. 1, Lecture 12.

49. Wilbur Samuel Howell, *Eighteenth-Century British Logic and Rhetoric*, Princeton, N.J.: Princeton University Press, 1971: "John Ward's Lectures at Gresham College."

50. Louis C. Hunter, *Steamboats on the Western Rivers: An Economic and Technological History*, Cambridge, Mass.: Harvard University Press, 1949.

51. *Report of the Committee of the Franklin Institute of the State of Pennsylvania for the Promotion of the Mechanic Arts, on the Explosions of Steam-Boilers, Part 1, Containing the First Report of Experiments Made by the Committee for the Treasury Department of the U. States*, Philadelphia, Penna: John C. Clarke, 1836.

52. Franklin Institute and the Making of Industrial America, Stephanie Morris (ed.), (Microfiche Collection) 1987: Committee on Boiler Explosions, Franklin Institute, Philadelphia, Penna.: John C. Clarke. Locke also used Part I in his report to discuss this point.

53. *Report of the Committee Appointed by the Citizens of Cincinnati, April 26, 1838, to Inquire into the Causes of the Explosion of the Moselle, and to Suggest such Preventive Measures as May Best Be Calculated to Guard Hereafter Against Such Occurrences*, Cincinnati, Ohio: Alexander Flash, 1838.

54. George W. Smith, "Explosion of the Boiler and Steam Chimney of the Portsmouth," *Journal of the Franklin Institute*, 3rd Series (Vol. 9), January 1845.

55. Bruce Sinclair, *Early Research at the Franklin Institute: The Investigation into the Causes of Steam Boiler Explosions, 1830-1837*, Philadelphia, Penna.: The Franklin Institute, 1966.

56. Bruce Sinclair, *Philadelphia's Philosopher Mechanics; a History of the Franklin Institute, 1824-1865*, Baltimore, Md.: Johns Hopkins University Press, 1974.

57. The rest of the committee was composed of George W. Smith, Edward Miller, John C. Cresson, John Agnew, Isaiah Lukens, and Samuel V. Merrick.

58. "Another Locomotive Explosion," *Reading Gazette*, October 26, 1844.

59. Frederick Farley, "Address Delivered by Frederick Fraley, Esq., at the Close of the Fourteenth Exhibition of American Manufactures Held by the Franklin Institute of the State of Pennsylvania, for the Promotion of the Mechanic Arts, October 1844," *Journal of the Franklin Institute*, 39, January 1845.

60. Minutes of Meetings, January 16, 1845, cited in [59, p. 247].

61. This problem and solution were independently discovered by the Lt-Col. Wynne of the British Railway Inspectorate in the investigation of an April 7th 1856 boiler explosion on the Caledonian Railway [14, pp. 43-44].

62. Septimus Norris, *Norris's Hand book for Locomotive Engineers*, Philadelphia, Penna.: Henry Carey, Baird & Co., 1852.

63. John H. White, Jr., *American Locomotives: An Engineering History, 1830-1880*, Baltimore, Md.: Johns Hopkins Press, 1997.

64. Lardner, however, did not get to keep all the profits from this work for the Norris Brothers. Lardner noted in his preface to his published lectures that he was in Philadelphia in December 1843 and January 1844 and that his audiences sometimes exceeded two thousand. However, before he presented these lectures in December in Philadelphia, Lardner needed to replace a large amount of his theatrical apparatus that was lost in a fire on October 28: "Among them, a superior gas lantern, splendid Drummond Lights, a superior microscope, etc., etc. The principle loss of Dr. L. consisted of his immense collection of astronomical illustrations, including the Panorama of the Heavens. But these will be replaced as speedily as possible, and exhibited in this city [Philadelphia], at a course of lectures which is to be given at the Assembly Buildings" [65, p. 2].

65. "City Items: Lectures," *Pennsylvania Inquirer and National Gazette*, October 29, 1844. On the following page, "The Fire at Providence," it was estimated that the loss for Lardner was $8000.

66. Michael Robbins, "Dr. Lardner's Railway Economy," *Railway Magazine*, 96, March 1950.

67. Robbins does observe the following: "The dryness of style, and tendency to write as though figures from reports and books were being given life with difficulty, is a key to something that might be otherwise puzzling. Why was it that Lardner wrote with warmth, and even with enthusiasm, about the United States, to a smaller degree about France and Belgium, and yet with such rigidity about English railroad, to whose stockholders and management the work was presumably addressed? The conclusion is inescapable from the internal evidence of the book that Lardner wrote it at a distance from England." However, if he did write it only shortly after he departed from the United States, and, if he was warm and enthusiastic about the U.S. railroads, why did he not include the most specific accident and investigation he performed? [p. 155].

68. "The Wonders of Modern Locomotion," *The Dublin University Magazine*, 210 (35), June 1850, pp. 2, 664-673. This article excerpts from *Railroad Economy*.

69. D. Lardner, *Railway Economy, A Treatise on the New Art of Transportation*, London: Taylor, Walton & Maberly, 1850.

70. See also Laurence Turnbull and William McRea's *Railroad Accidents and the Means by Which They May Be Prevented*, Philadelphia, Penna.: Parry and M'Millan, 1854. This 1854 book quotes extensively from Lardner for fifteen pages on safety procedures, "Plain Rules for Railway Travellers."

71. T. B. Wakeman, Second Response to W. H. Hale in correspondence regarding the causes of steam boiler explosions, *Journal of the American Institute*, 3 (10), July 1838.

72. *Journal of the Franklin Institute*, Vol. 13, 1834.

73. *Mechanic's Magazine*, 3 (1), January 1834.

74. *American Railroad Journal*, 2 (6) 2nd Quarter Series, February 6, 1845.

75. Cited in *American Railroad Journal*, 1 (10), March 6, 1845.

PART TWO

Publicity, Political Pressure, and Emotional Involvement by Authors Transform Disaster Investigations

> If a railroad or steamboat disaster causes the slaughter of a score or two of people, we Americans fall into spasms of indignation, and threaten all sorts of frightful visitations on the reckless offenders. But it generally turns out that the preservation of life is, with us, more of a passion than a principle.
>
> "How We Exhaust Life," [1, p. 123]

The investigations in Part One of the *New England* and the *Richmond* disasters took place in relative calm, out of the influence of publicity or politics. In the case of the *New England* in 1833, only the local papers reported the disaster, and their reports were printed only as far as Boston, a hundred miles away [2, p. 72]. It took a month before Silliman, Redfield, and Olmsted arrived at the scene to begin their investigation, and their report establishing the collaboration of science and corporate interests was characterized by a diffident, abstract tone: "Many interesting and important considerations, connected with Steam boat navigation, have presented themselves, during our discussion . . ." [2, p. 2].

The local paper, *The Connecticut Courant,* duly reported the conclusions of the investigation [3, p. 3], but only on page three. Moreover, that article promised more details in subsequent issues of the paper, but nothing further was ever printed. Only the journals of mechanics' institutes in Philadelphia, New York, and Boston reprinted the report of the investigation, but they did so without any critical comment. This disaster did not tug at the emotional strings of the public, and there were no political interests involved.

In the explosion of the *Richmond* in 1844, only four people died, and all were company employees. Considering concepts of employee liability at the time, it was felt that the victims were implicated in their own deaths making the story less newsworthy. True, the local papers in Reading, Penna., and papers as far away as New Haven, Conn., announced the explosion of the locomotive and debated the role of lightening in the explosion, but only the *Journal of the Franklin Institute* critiqued Lardner's report, and only the *American Railroad Journal* excerpted Lardner's report and the Franklin Institute's discussion of it. Thus, this disaster too did not engender much public interest.

The Committee on Science and the Arts of the Franklin Institute, however, did try to awaken political pressure for changing the investigation procedures of coroners. The Committee tried to use the *Richmond* accident [4, p. 31] to argue that the traditional procedures used in coroner's inquests needed improvements to cope with the new technologies:

> . . . how deplorable the remissness of juries, and the apathy of an injured, a defenseless, but too patient, and long suffering public, whom the newspapers almost invariably endeavor to assure that no blame can possibly be attributed to any of the parties concerned [5, p. 34].

The Institute proposed to the Pennsylvania legislature that

- coroners call "the nearest scientific and practical men" as expert witnesses;
- the causes of explosions be "minutely" examined;
- the results of the inquests be published in one Philadelphia newspaper, as well as in the local paper of the town in which the accident occurred; and finally,
- coroners be directed to furnish the institute with a printed record of the inquest [6].

But the proposed legislation was never enacted. Blamelessness in both the *New England* and the *Richmond* accidents was found, and the public apparently had no difficulty accommodating to these findings for, as a judge wrote in an 1845 verdict a year after the *Richmond* explosion:

> Whatever natural philosophers may think of this, the elements which combine to create the power of steam are entirely within the reach of accident, and are no more subject to fixed laws than the elements which propel the ship at sea. Whatever may be the theories on the subject, universal experience is that no human skill can entirely guard against accidents, either in the one case or in the other [7, p. 246].

However, in the three investigations of Part Two, the 1838 *Moselle* steamboat explosion in Cincinnati, the 1855 Camden and Amboy Railroad collision in Burlington, N.J., and the 1855 Pacific Railroad of Missouri bridge collapse over the Gasconade River, everything changed. First, as the *Harper's Magazine* quote at the beginning of this chapter noted, "If a railroad or steamboat disaster causes the slaughter of a score or two of people, we Americans fall into spasms of indignation . . ." [1, p. 123]. Political and publicity pressure now entered into the investigations and transformed the roles of the investigators and the rhetoric of the reports. Moreover, public opinion that could not be aroused in the case of the *Richmond* was specifically appealed to in each of these new cases as illustrated by the words of a Cincinnati committee investigating the *Moselle* disaster in 1838:

> It may not be improper, however, to advert to the remote and moral causes which operate to increase steam boat disasters, especially on the western waters; causes which it is very possible to obviate, and especially by drawing public opinion to the subject [8, pp. 27-28].

Now there was publicity drawn to the investigations. Twenty thousand people participated in the funerals for the victims of the *Moselle* disaster, and Cincinnati shut down [9, p. 342]. Five months after this 1838 disaster, a span of time after which both the *New England* and the *Richmond* explosions had disappeared from public interest, the Cincinnati mayor and 200 others petitioned the city council demanding the investigation report be published. In response to the 1855 Camden and Amboy Railroad disaster, sermons were written, the New York papers were up in arms for weeks, and even the professional press weighed in for comment and critique for months after the disaster. In the New *England* disaster, only the journals of the mechanics' institutes reprinted the company report without critique or comment. In the 1855 accident, *Harper's New Monthly Magazine, American Railroad Journal, Colburn's Railroad Advocate, The New York Times, North American Review, American Railroad Times,* and *The Journal of the Franklin Institute* all joined in critically commenting on the company report. These articles helped generate great public interest in this 1855 case.

Some of this interest had to do with the specifics of the case, in that the dead and injured were not employees, but "innocent passengers," but also because a key figure in the accident was in the midst of running for president of the United States, and the railroad had been under statewide and regionwide scrutiny for a decade because of its monopoly status in New Jersey and its disregard of passenger safety.

However, the increased interest in the accidents also had to do with the rise of the professional press that focused on railroads. Consider Figure 19, and the list of periodicals debuts beneath the figure. When the *New England* disaster occurred in 1833, there were only three periodicals other than newspapers that focused on railroad issues. By 1855 when the Camden and Amboy and the Gasconade disasters occur, there were ten journals, with many more specializing in railroad topics. Thus, by the time of the disasters here in Part Two, there was a medium available to affect public opinion.

The *American Railroad Journal* saw the 1855 accident not just as a techno-logical problem, but also politically as "the commencement of a new sentiment on the part of the State":

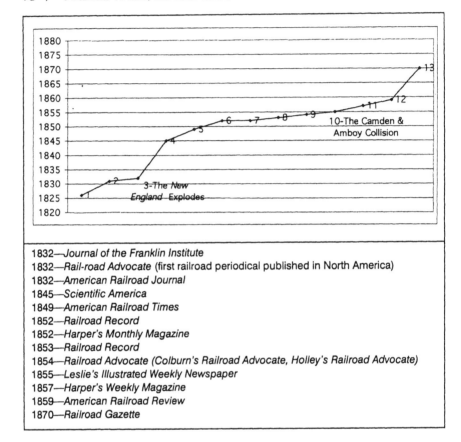

1832—Journal of the Franklin Institute
1832—Rail-road Advocate (first railroad periodical published in North America)
1832—American Railroad Journal
1845—Scientific America
1849—American Railroad Times
1852—Railroad Record
1852—Harper's Monthly Magazine
1853—Railroad Record
1854—Railroad Advocate (Colburn's Railroad Advocate, Holley's Railroad Advocate)
1855—Leslie's Illustrated Weekly Newspaper
1857—Harper's Weekly Magazine
1859—American Railroad Review
1870—Railroad Gazette

Figure 19. Debut of American journals commenting on railroads:
Specialized and general audience journals 1831–1880 [10].

We hope this accident may mark the commencement of a new sentiment on the part of the State—that it will be the signal for a successful outbreak against a despotism which has so long held it enslaved, Some flagrant illustration of its evils was needed as a rallying point. If the spirit and temper of the people are not utterly broken, we shall date this accident as the commencement of a new era in their history; one In which a generous competition may be allowed to correct the abuses of railway management in which the burdens imposed upon the traveling public shall be only a fair equivalent for services rendered, and one in which the territory of the State shall be thrown open, a free, field for the development of what is the great characteristic and improvement of modern times, instead of selling this, with the right and capacity for future progress for a mess of pottage [11, pp. 570-571].

It is also in these cases of Part Two that the public, or the newspapers and journals speaking for the public, began to refuse to accept blamelessness as an adequate verdict in the investigations. For example, the *American Railroad Journal* wrote in regard to the report of this 1855 investigation:

> The Camden and Amboy Company have published a report prepared by their Executive Committee regarding the late disaster on their road, at Burlington. The report takes issue with the verdict of the Coroner's Jury, extols the Company's regulations, exculpates its servants in charge of the ill-fated train, throws the entire blame upon Dr. Heineken, and winds up with various reflections and suggestions. It is quite natural that the Company or its Executive Committee, should put the best face on the matter, on their own side; and they are entitled to be heard in their own defense. But there is little probability that the public will accept their conclusion or consider their defense complete [12, p. 785].

The front page of the *Colburn's Railroad Advocate* declared:

> But seriously,—here is a road, denying all responsibility to public opinion,—and which openly and daringly violates the very first and essential rules of safety,—killing two dozen or more human beings one day, and the next, recklessly and defiantly backing its trains at full speed,—without signal, without flagmen, without thought, without care. [In fact, not two weeks after the first accident, there was another, and another death, and for the year, in addition to the Burlington deaths and injuries, there were another three deaths and four injuries.] [13, p. 3; 14, p. 196].

The large-scale publicity and political pressures certainly came to bear in the last of the three accidents of Part Two, the Pacific Railroad of Missouri bridge collapse over the Gasconade River in 1855. In this accident more than just four employees were killed, but rather, among others, two state legislators, two former mayors of St. Louis, two ministers, a justice of the peace, and the president of the St. Louis City Council. In response to the accident and these deaths, the presiding mayor of St. Louis proclaimed a day of mourning and the closure of all businesses for the day. In addition, this road had just been under scrutiny by the state legislature for profiteering, and the entire state legislature would, within weeks, be taking up the possibility of further funding to the railroad. As a result of this publicity and political ramifications, not only was the story of the disaster carried on the front pages of the St. Louis papers, but also thousands of miles away by, among others, the *Brooklyn Eagle, The New York Times*, the *National Observer* [15], and *Scientific American* magazine [16, p. 78; 17, p. 97].

The final aspect that separates these three cases from those in Part One is that the authors of the investigation reports or their critics were emotionally involved, and this emotional involvement was clearly visible in their rhetoric. Where Silliman could be emotionally disengaged from the *New England* accident and write "Many interesting and important considerations, connected with Steam boat navigation, have presented themselves, during our discussion . . . [18, p. 2], and Lardner could sum up his report as a lawyer would:

In fine, if my evidence were required on this point, in a case where rights or liabilities of individuals rendered a positive decision of the question indispensable, I should not hesitate a moment to affirm that that decision must be made on the last of the above suppositions [19, p. 16].

Locke would sum up his investigation on the *Moselle* with:

These causes are only an excess of those things which are in themselves laudable. They have their foundation in the present mammoth evil of our country, the inordinate love of gain. We are not satisfied with getting rich, but we must get rich in a day. We are not satisfied with traveling with a speed of ten miles per hour, but must fly. Such is the effect of competition that every thing must be done cheap; boiler iron must be made cheap, traveling must be done cheap, freight must be cheap and yet every thing must be speedy. A steam boat must establish a reputation of a few minutes "swifter" in a hundred miles than others, before she can make fortunes fast enough to satisfy owners. All this seems to be demanded by the blind tyranny of custom, and the common consent of the community. And while this is so, is it strange that ambitious young men should run the same risk they would run for the post of honor in the battle field? That they should jeopard [sic] every thing, even life itself, for that which has become a very deity, and should occasionally encounter a fate at which legislation, with all its terrors at its elbows, stand aghast and powerless? [8, pp. 27-28].

Newspaper dialogue concerning the Camden and Amboy disaster was characterized by the following emotional point and counterpoint:

These suggestions in regard to the defective management of this great railroad will, I doubt not, commend themselves to the great mass of intelligent and observing persons. The Amboy Company, however, show in their late Report a tenacity of preconceived rules, and an obstinacy of opinion, rarely to be encountered.... Oh, gentlemen, do you point in proof the wisdom of your rules, to your bleeding and dying victims? Do you add insult to injury and mockery to massacre? So it seems to me. Well that corporations have no souls, if such are their specimens of rationality and evidences of existence [22, p. 7].

...

You make it a matter of enormous crime that, in the Report of the Executive Committee, "sympathy is not expressed for the unfortunate sufferers." You call it a *"painful feature"* of the Report; *"unnatural indifference,"* and multiply epithets of reproach for this omission. . . . You, sir, who make this accusation, are a professional sympathizer general; it may be natural, therefore, for you to insist on its public and ostentatious manifestation on all occasions, without regard to the proprieties of time and place. And it ought, perhaps, to be considered as equally natural for you to magnify your own merit as a sympathizer, by contrasting your profuseness in that particular, with the deficiency of others [23, p. 2].

And a critical report of the company's actions in the Gasconade disaster would emotionally address the reader in these words:

> And, do you wonder, if such frail "false works," evidently erected without plumb or squared, which as a whole, or in their different sections, or in their component parts, present to the eye not one continuous horizontal or perpendicular line, and resemble more a field of corn-stalks after corn gathering, than anything in the way of building, —I ask, do you wonder if such frail "false works," under the pressure of a heavy weight moving on them, sink, give way or break? particularly when I have to add that, already at the time of the inspection by the Commission, two of said bents in one of the middle bays were entirely gone, and others had so much settled, sunk and inclined under the weight of the bare superstructure that the railway thereon presented wave-lines, more than two feet out of grade and out of line, while the testimony attests that but ten days before it had been laid pretty fair and true?
>
> Or, is it necessary to make any further investigation as to the strength of the superstructure with its floor beams, 7 by 13 Inches, laid from 4 1/2 to 6 feet apart over a span of 15 feet, when borne by such "false-work?'' Or, is it essential, which of the timbers broke first, or whether the pile and post-rows in these "false-works" suddenly slipped, or broke in their doweled knee-joints? Or, is it material, whether the speed of the locomotive to the attempt of carrying six hundred human lives over these "false-works" was at the rate of five, ten, fifteen or twenty miles per hour? Or, is it of avail to calculate, whether, in case the locomotive had run at a less speed over those "false- works," the train might have been carried safely over to the other side of the Gasconade? Or, whether the gravel train which runs over these "false-works" weighed more or less than the train freighted with six hundred passengers? Or, in short, is it compatible with common sense to resort to any scientific or mathematical calculations to prove a mere *scaffolding* a *Railroad bridge?*
>
> I say, No! [24, p. 14].

These investigations under the pressure of publicity and politics moved the writers emotionally; they were not disinterested. They cared deeply about what happened because, in a number of cases, they knew the victims or those lower-echelon workers being blamed.

This new publicity, political scrutiny, and emotions seized the customary roles and process of investigating technical disasters and transformed them. This period of transformation caused a number of different provisional investigation configurations:

• Uniting the roles of coroner's jury and scientific investigation to produce a single report;

- Splitting up of reports issued by the jury, the company, scientists, the public, and the professional press into combative camps issuing sermons and tirades to each other;
- Uniting the role of disinterested and critical scientific investigation with the defensive company report.

ENDNOTES

1. "How We Exhaust Life," *Harper's new monthly magazine,* 19 (109), June 1859, p. 123.
2. "Steam-boat New England," *Liberator,* 3, 1833.
3. *Connecticut Courant,* 69 (3594), December 9, 1833.
4. George W. Smith, "Explosion of the Boiler and Steam Chimney of the Portsmouth," *Journal of the Franklin Institute,* 3rd Series, Vol. 9, January 1845.
5. Frederick Farley, "Address Delivered by Frederick Farley, Esq., at the Close of the Fourteenth Exhibition of American Manufactures Held by the Franklin Institute of the State of Pennsylvania, for the Promotion of the Mechanic Arts, October 1844," *Journal of the Franklin Institute,* 39, January 1845.
6. Minutes of Meetings, January 16, 1845, cited in [20, p. 247].
7. *Citizens Insurance Company of Missouri v. Glasgow, Shaw and Larkin,* 9 Missouri Reports (1845). Cited in [21, p. 290].
8. *Report to Inquire into the Causes of the Explosion of the Moselle, and to Suggest Such Preventive Measures as May Best Be Calculated to Guard Hereafter Against Such Occurrences,* Cincinnati, Ohio: Alexander Flash, 1838.
9. Fred Irving Dayton and John Wolcott Adams (illustrator), *Steamboat Days,* New York: Fredrick A. Stokes Co., 1928.
10. Drawn from Thomas T. Taber, *Railroad Periodicals Index, 1831–1999: Eighty Periodicals Containing Steam, Electric, and Industrial Railroad Material,* Muncy, Penna.: Taber Publications, 2001.
11. "The Calamity on the Camden and Amboy Railroad," *American Railroad Journal,* 1012 (28), September 5, 1855.
12. "Camden and Amboy Railroad," *American Railroad Journal,* Second series, 11 (50), December 15, 1855.
13. "Camden and Amboy Amusements," *Colburn's Railroad Advocate,* October 13, 1855.
14. "Camden and Amboy Annual Accounting," *American Railroad Journal,* 1041 (29), March 29, 1856.
15. *National Observer,* November 29, 1855.
16. "Railroad Bridges—Terrible Accident," *Scientific American,* 11 (10), November 17, 1855.
17. "The Gasconade Bridge Disaster," *Scientific American,* 11 (13), December 8, 1855.
18. *Report of the Board of Examiners Appointed by the Connecticut River Steam Boat Company to Inquire into the Causes of the Explosion of the Steam Boat New England Which Occurred at Essex, October 9th, 1833,* New Haven, Conn.: Connecticut River Steam Boat Company, 1833.

19. D. Lardner, *Investigation of the Cause of the Explosion of the Locomotive Engine "Richmond" Near Reading, PA on the 2nd of September 1844,* New York: Herald Book and Job Printing Office, 1844.
20. Bruce Sinclair, *Philadelphia's Philosopher Mechanics: A History of the Franklin Institute, 1824-1865,* Baltimore, Md.: Johns Hopkins University Press, 1974.
21. Louis C. Hunter, *Steamboats on the Western Rivers: An Economic and Technological History,* Cambridge, Mass.: Harvard University Press, 1949.
22. Cortlandt Van Rensselaer, A. Review of the Camden and Amboy Railroad's Report on the Accident of the 29th of August 1855. Burlington, NJ, 1855.
23. Commodore Robert F. Stockton, "To the Rev. C. Van Rensselaer, D.D." *Public Ledger and Daily Transcript,* October 15, 1855.
24. Report of the Committee Appointed by the Directors of the Pacific Railroad to Investigate the Causes of the Accident at Gasconade Bridge. St. Louis, MO: Republican Book and Job Office, 1855.

CHAPTER 3

Publicity, Politics, and Emotions Enter the Investigation Constellation—The Steamboat Moselle Explosion, Spring 1838

... and in the excited state of the public mind [in reaction to some explosions], these safety barges became great favorites with travelers, especially with parties of pleasure. But our countrymen never hold their fears long: a short interval of exemption from steamboat accidents ended the excitement, while the greater speed attained with the ordinary boats, and the lower fare, gradually drew off passengers from the safety barges until they could be no longer run with profit to the company, and they were abandoned.

Address on the Scientific Life and Labors of William C. Redfield [1, p. 9]

We are not satisfied with getting rich, but we must get rich in a day. We are not satisfied with traveling with a speed of ten miles per hour, but must fly. Such is the effect of competition that every thing must be done cheap; boiler iron must be made cheap, traveling must be done cheap, freight must be cheap and yet every thing must be speedy. A steam boat must establish a reputation of a few minutes "swifter" in a hundred miles than others, before she can make fortunes fast enough to satisfy owners. All this seems to be demanded by the blind tyranny of custom, and the common consent of the community. And while this is so, is it strange that ambitious young men should run the same risk they would run for the post of honor in the battlefield? That they should jeopard [sic] every thing, even life itself, for that which has become a very deity, and should occasionally encounter a fate at which legislation, with all its terrors at its elbows, stand aghast and powerless?

Professor John Locke, Cincinnati 1838 *Moselle* Disaster Investigation Report [3, p. 28]

THE STEAMBOAT *MOSELLE* EXPLOSION ON THE CINCINNATI WATERFRONT

One of the most popular antebellum journals, *The North American Review,* described a steamboat trip in the spring of 1838 between St. Louis and Cincinnati [2, pp. 29-30]:

In the spring of 1838, it was our lot to embark at St. Louis, in a new and very splendid steamboat bound for Pittsburgh. Her captain was a young man of some experience on the river and of a very ambitious and energetic character. The boat was evidently built with a view of embracing all the accommodations and improvements then known; and our party were congratulating themselves upon the comfort and cleanliness of the cabin, and the order and neatness apparent throughout.

Before casting off her fasts from the shore, steam was got up beyond the limits of safety, and the boat shot up the strong current of the Mississippi, and, turning above the town, dashed by the wharves with a velocity frightful to behold, but which seemed peculiarly exhilarating to both crew and passengers. As this, however, was no more than the usual practice for *crack* boats on leaving port, we thought nothing of it; but the haste, with which her necessary landings for wood and other purposes were managed, and the excited condition of her crew, soon made manifest (what was afterwards confirmed by the express declaration of the captain), that it was intended to make a *brag trip.*

Now there were, no doubt, some few among the passengers, whom a knowledge of this really alarming fact rendered uneasy and apprehensive; but upon a large majority it produced no other feeling than those of pleasing excitement; and the watching of her rapid progress, and estimating from time to time her rate of speed seemed to form an agreeable relief from the usual monotony of a steamboat voyage. No boat was for some time encountered whose speed was equal to our own, and one after another was easily passed; till, between Louisville and Cincinnati, a vessel was discovered in our wake, whose two escape pipes and double engine showed her to be one of the mail-boats that ply between the two places, and reputed to be one of the fastest boats on the Western waters.

As each bend of the river occasionally disclosed her to view it was evident, that she was gaining on us. The excitement on board our boat now became tremendous. Captain and passengers vied with each other in stimulating the exertions of the firemen. Rosin was freely thrown into the furnaces, and the thundering of her paddles, and the quivering of the boat, told of the increased action of the steam upon her engine; while no warning voice was heard from the passengers, those who felt alarm contenting themselves with keeping astern, as far as possible from the scene of danger. These efforts, as it proved, were unavailing.

The power and speed of the mail-boat carried her by us; while our captain concealed his mortification as best he could, swearing a deep oath, that the next time he encountered this rival, he would pass her, or blow his own boat out of the water.... We landed in safety, and all tongues were loud in applause of our captain and his fast boat. The newspapers recorded the trip just accomplished as the quickest ever performed; and the challenge was thus in effect thrown out to all other captains, to emulate this dispatch.

The "very ambitious and energetic" captain [4; 5, p. 65]—and part owner—v Isaac Perrin, the "new and very splendid" steamboat, the *Moselle.* The *Moselle* l only made two or three trips on her intended circuit between Cincinnati and St. Louis, having only been launched March 31 in Cincinnati. In 1838, the year of this *Moselle* voyage, Cincinnati was one of the largest, if not the largest, inland water ports in the United States, and many of the steamboats plying the western rivers were built in Cincinnati [6, p. 50]—as many as thirty-three boats a year [10, p. 18; 11, p. 24].

The *Moselle* was 100 tons lighter than the *New England,* since the swells of Long Island Sound would probably not be encountered on the Ohio River, but, like the *New England,* the *Moselle*'s accommodations were unique in her class [13, p. 52]—"embracing all the accommodations and improvements then known"—as the *North American Review* crowed [2, p. 29]. Moreover with four boilers, the *Moselle* could keep up a high pressure of seventy-five pounds per square inch, maintaining a reputation for speed that would bring customers [5, p. 170]. All this cost her owners some $35,000 [5, p. 64].

The *Moselle*'s return voyage to St. Louis wasn't described in the *North American Review,* but by the following extra in the *Cincinnati Whig:*

CINCINNATI WHIG—EXTRA.
Wednesday Night, 8 o'clock,
April 25th, 1838.
MOST AWFUL
STEAM BOAT ACCIDENT.
LOSS OF 125 LIVES.

It becomes again our painful duty to record one of the most awful and destructive occurrences known in the terrible and fatal catalogue of steam-boat Accidents.

This afternoon about six o'clock, the new and elegant steam-boat, *Moselle,* Capt. Perrin, left the wharf of this city, (full of passengers,) for Louisville and St. Louis, and with a view of taking a family on board at Fulton, about a mile and a half above the quay, proceeded up the river, and made fast to a lumber raft for that purpose. Here the family were taken on board, and during the whole time of the detention, the Captain was holding on to all the steam he could create, with an intention of showing off to the best advantage the great speed of the boat as she passed down the whole length of the city. The *Moselle* was a new brag boat, and had recently made several exceedingly quick trips to and from this place.

Soon as the family were taken on board from the raft, the boat shoved off, and at the very moment her wheels made the first evolution, her boilers burst with a most awful and astounding noise, equal to the most violent clap of thunder. The explosion was destructive and heart rending in the extreme, as we are assured by a gentleman, who was sitting on his horse on the shore, waiting to see the boat start. Heads, limbs, bodies and blood, were seen flying through the air in every direction, attended by the most horrible shrieks and groans from the wounded and the dying.—The boat, at the moment of the accident, was about thirty feet from the shore, and was rendered a perfect wreck. She seemed to be torn all to cinders as far back as the gentleman's cabin, and her hurricane deck (the whole length) was entirely swept away. The boat immediately began to sink rapidly, and float (with a strong current) down the river, at the same time getting farther from the shore.

The Captain was thrown by the explosion entirely into the street, and was picked up dead and dreadfully mangled. Another man was thrown entirely through the roof of one of the neighboring houses, and limbs and fragments of bodies scattered about the river and shore in heart-rending profusion. Soon as the boat was discovered to be rapidly sinking, the passengers who remained unhurt in the gentlemen's and ladies cabins, became panic struck, and with a fatuity unaccountable, jumped into the river. Being above the ordinary business parts of the city, there were no boats at hand except a few large and unmanageable wood flats, which were carried to the relief of the sufferers as soon as possible, by the few persons on the shore. Many were drowned, however, before they could be rescued from a watery grave, and many sunk who were not seen afterwards.

We are told that one little boy on shore was seen wringing his hands in agony, imploring those present, to save his father, mother, and three sisters, all of whom were struggling in the water to gain the shore, but whom the poor little fellow had the awful misfortune to see perish, one by one almost within his reach. An infant child, belonging to this family, was picked up alive, floating down the river on one of the fragments of the hurricane deck.

Doctor Wilson Hughey, of the U.S. Army, (and brother-in-law to our estimable fellow citizen, W. P. Hughes, of the Pearl St. House), is doubtless among the slain, as he was known to have been on board, and some pieces of the military coat he had on, were picked up among the fragments.

Mr. Powell, a highly respectable grocery merchant, of Louisville, and brother-in-law of Mr. Wilson McGrew, of this city, is also supposed to be lost, as he was on board, and no tidings has since been heard of him, notwithstanding the active inquiries of his friends.

We are unable, as yet, to particularize any other persons lost, as the boat sunk in about fifteen minutes after the accident, leaving nothing to be seen but her chimneys and a small portion of her upper works, and also as a scene of distress and confusion immediately ensued that altogether baffles description. Most of the sufferers are among the hands of the boat, and the steerage passengers.

It is supposed that there were about TWO HUNDRED PERSONS ON BOARD, of which number, only from fifty to seventy five are believed to have escaped, making the estimated loss of lives about ONE HUNDRED AND TWENTY FIVE!! O, tale of woe!

The accident unquestionably occurred through sheer imprudence and care-lessness. The Captain of the boat was desirous of showing off her great speed as she passed the city, and to overtake and pass another boat which had left the wharf for Louisville a short time before him. Dearly has he paid for his silly ambition. The clerk of the boat, we, understand, escaped unhurt. These are all the particulars we have yet been able to learn. In to-morrow's *Whig*, we shall no doubt be able to give the names of many others who have been lost or killed [2, pp. 19-22; 14, pp. 119-125].

Almost to the day, both the *Moselle* and the *New England* exploded after only a month in service, and both exploded just moments following the pickup or delivery of passengers. Those moments were when the engines were stopped both for propulsion and for pumping replacement water for that already evaporated into steam in the boiler. Two-thirds of all steam boiler explosions occurred after stopping the engines, thus stopping the pumps [13, p. 56; 15, p. 295; 16].

The next evening, Thursday, April 26, the mayor of Cincinnati, Col. Samuel Davies, presided over a public meeting, and several committees were designated to respond to the disaster—one to ascertain the names of the dead and to notify their families, and another to investigate and explain to the public the causes of the explosion and what preventive measures could be taken. A public proclamation was issued from the meeting:

> That as a public token of our respect, and deep regret for the fate of the deceased, and our sympathy with their surviving friends, and to express our sense of the awful responsibilities which may have led to such a disaster, the Mayor of the city be requested to issue his proclamation for a funeral procession, to take place on this day, at 3 o'clock, P.M. to form on Front street, between Broadway and Main streets; that the stores and shops be closed on the occasion, and that the Reverend Clergy, the members of City Council, and the several committees, be requested to attend in their official capacities [17, p. 3].

On Sunday, April 29, when funerals were held for some of the 266 victims, more than 20,000 people participated, and the city shut down [18, p. 342].

Within a week, the news of the disaster had spread across the United States in the pages of national newspapers [19, p. 3]. In Washington, D.C., not only were the causes of the *Moselle* catastrophe debated, but the large loss of life in its explosion was so shocking that it reached into the private thoughts of diaries such as the one kept by the assistant clerk of the House of Representatives, Benjamin B. French:

> The Nation must shake off its apathy about steam navigation and arouse itself; legislation must be had on the subject or nobody's life will be safe who travels. Only last October the *Home* was lost with many valuable lives—recently the *Moselle* was blown up & hundreds of human beings hurried into eternity in a moment—the paper of today contains the account of the burning of the *Washington* on Lake Erie & the loss of more than 50 lives! Something must be done, or steam navigation had better never been discovered—it will prove, to the human race rather a curse than a blessing [20, p. 88].

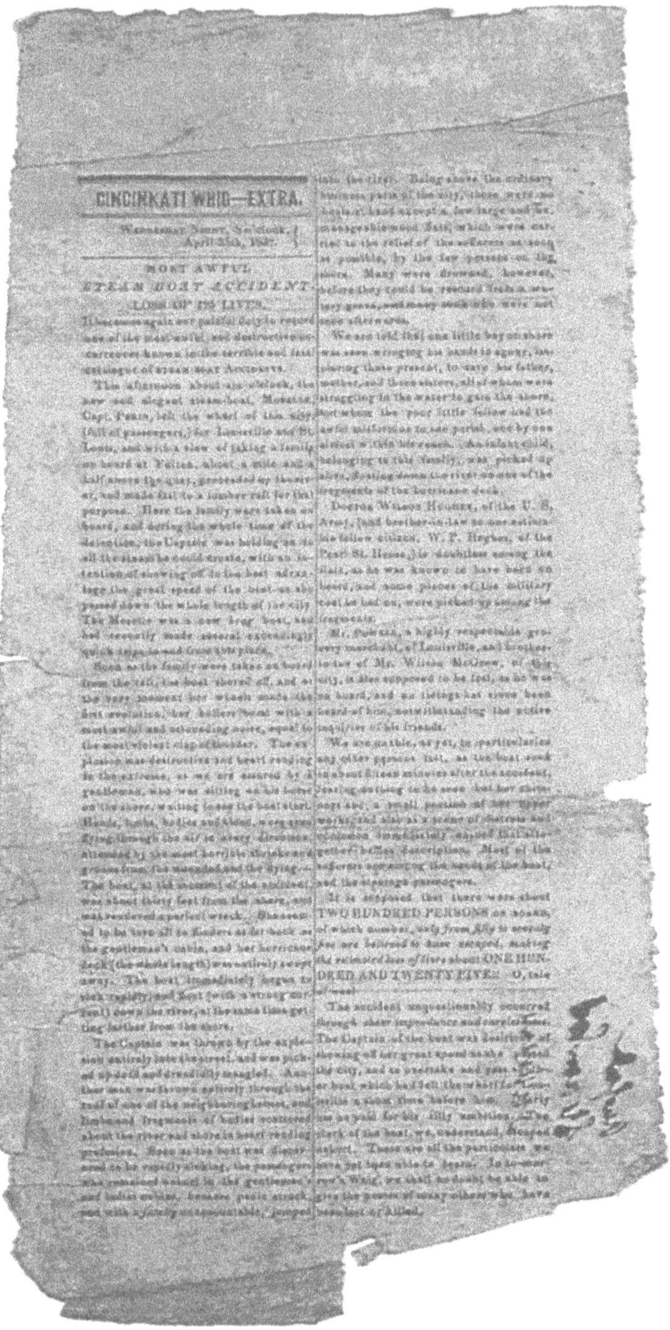

CINCINNATI WHIG—EXTRA.

MOST AWFUL

STEAM BOAT ACCIDENT.

TWO HUNDRED PERSONS

Figure 20. *Cincinnati Whig*—Extra. "Most Awful Steamboat Accident."

Figure 21. The wreck of the *Moselle* in which 266
were killed or injured.

The news reached Washington at an auspicious moment. After four different
Congresses had considered and failed to pass national steamboat safety legislation,
and after both President Jackson and President Van Buren had separately called for
such legislation in their State of the Union addresses, the Senate had finally passed
a national steamboat safety law [21]. While, at the time of the *Moselle* explosion,
the House of Representatives had not yet taken up the bill, the shock of the *Moselle*
reports motivated several Congressmen to request a suspension of the House
procedures so that the bill could be considered [22, p. 342; 23, p. 15]. In this
regard, the investigative committee appointed at the Cincinnati public meeting
hoped that their local investigations could aid the passage of an effective national
bill in Washington:

To devise some means of preventing these deplorable disasters has employed
the attention of Legislative bodies, and of talented individuals for many years.
This Committee, with neither time, money, nor apparatus placed at their
disposal, can add very little to the creditable labors already performed. It may
not be improper, however, to advert to the remote and moral causes which
operate to increase steam boat disasters, especially on the western waters;

causes which it is very possible to obviate, and especially by drawing public opinion to the subject [3, pp. 27-28].

Thus, the *Moselle* investigative committee reacted to a very specific local event in the midst of great publicity locally and nationally, and also participated in both a local and a national political reaction to the problem of steamboat explosions. This would be the moment when, in the typical investigation, the coroner's jury would be called to collect evidence; that did not happen. Nor did the steamboat company produce a report attempting to protect itself from liability. Nor did the Franklin Institute perform its usual investigation. In this investigation, the customary actors and actions were transformed because of public outcry in frontier Cincinnati, with its long lawless history of mob riots.

CINCINNATI IN THE 1830s: FRONTIER LAW AND ORDER

At the time of the *Moselle* explosion, the elected governing body of Cincinnati, the City Council, was led by Peter Neff [24], and primarily included businessmen with independent means. After all, the salary for Council members was only a dollar a week [25, pp. 85, 87; 26, p. 177]. Also at the time of the *Moselle* explosion, the chief executive officer for council was the mayor, Col. Samuel Davies. However, Davies was later remembered less as a faithful executive officer for the Council and more as having been "practically the political dictator of the town" [27, p. 132].

One example of Mayor Davies's approach to governing in Cincinnati can be seen in 1814 when he first was a member of an extra-legislative committee, for he

> served as secretary to a large meeting of citizens protesting the inadequacy of mail service, and was appointed, with Burnet, Ruffin, Jesse Hunt, George P. Torrence, and others, to a committee to make their protest effective [29, p. 100].

In 1835 Davies issued a proclamation, and it was reported in a national paper under the lead, "Judge Lynch arrived here yesterday morning . . ." [30, p. 402]. This 1835 proclamation endeavored to rid Cincinnati of gamblers and read in part as follows:

> Whereas great excitement prevails among the citizens, produced by the presence of a number of persons called gamblers, whose offensive pursuits, it is said, have caused their expulsion from other places:

> And whereas, it is known to me, that strong and violent measures are contemplated and recommended to the citizens, for the purpose of compelling these persons immediately to leave the city:

> Now, therefore, be it known, that to attain the end proposed, the city council have, by a resolution, authorized me to call to the aid of the police, one

hundred effective men, in addition to which I am authorized to say, that FIVE HUNDRED CITIZENS stand ready at any moment to render personal aid to the authorities of the city, in support of such measures, as may be deemed necessary to protect the inhabitants from lawless depredations of all kinds [30, p. 402].

The next instance of Davies's extralegal management of Cincinnati came in April 1836 in response to a mob attack against an abolitionist newspaper, the *Philanthropist*. Mayor Davies was reported to have "stood by approvingly as the mob did its work and addressed them as comrades when he finally asked them to break up":

> Gentlemen—It is late at night, and the time we're all in bed—by continuing longer, you will disturb the citizens, or deprive them of their rest, besides robbing yourselves of rest. No doubt, it is your intention to punish the guilty, and leave the innocent. But if you continue longer, you are in danger of punishing the innocent with the guilty, which I am convinced no one in Cincinnati would want to do. We have done enough for one night. ("three cheers for the Mayor") The abolitionists themselves, must be convinced themselves by this time what public sentiment is, and that it will not do any longer to disregard, or set it at naught. (three cheers again) As you cannot punish the guilty without endangering the innocent; I advise you all to go home (cries of home! Home!) [31, pp. 143, 375].

However, he was not alone in abetting the anti-abolitionist mob actions and circumventing the legally elected council. Contemporary newspapers and later historians have pointed out that "social, political, economic, and even religious leaders sanctioned them" [31, p. 375]. The mayor and a large number of the Cincinnati elite were not necessarily pro-slavery, but did recognize that "trade with the slave-holding South was the lifeblood of the Queen City" [31, p. 390]. Moreover, Southern papers had warned of retribution if the publication of the abolitionist *Philanthropist* was not stopped [31, p. 367]. By abetting the mob, the "Cincinnati elite thus insured the city a long string of future riots. They established the precedent that rioting was an acceptable method of redressing grievances" [31, p. 375]. Indeed, mob riots later occurred in 1841, 1842, 1843, and 1848. Not all were anti-abolitionist riots; yet after the 1836 riots, "no one need ask if rioting were permissible . . . the only question would be whether a particular evil was bad enough to merit a mob" [31, p. 376].

POLITICAL CONTROL OF THE INVESTIGATION

Thursday after the *Moselle* explosion, Mayor Davies presided over a public meeting that designated the investigative committee that was, in effect, going to combine the work of a coroner's jury and the Committee of Science and the Arts from the Franklin Institute. It was to include two academics, John Locke a professor at both the Medical College and at the Ohio Mechanics Institute, and

Figure 22. Mayor Samuel Davies, dictator of Cincinnati in the 1830s.

Thomas J. Matthews, a professor of mathematics and head of a local college. Both were excellent candidates to carry out the investigation. However, the investigative committee was not appointed by the City Council, which should have performed such a task [32; 33, pp. 61, 69], but by the extra-legislative public meeting led by the mayor in much the same fashion that extra-legislative investigative committees had been constituted earlier in the 1836 *Philanthropist* episode [34]. The *Liberty Hall & Cincinnati Gazette* sarcastically observed about that earlier meeting that it was a ". . . rather a new mode of calling a town meeting" [34, p. 2]. Much the same could have been written of this 1838 meeting.

Consider who else was and was not appointed to the *Moselle* investigative committee at that public meeting. A month after the *Moselle* Report was published, a large meeting of steamboat owners and officers was held [35, pp. 180-181] and, in 1843, 128 men were listed as members of the Cincinnati

Figure 23. Professor John Locke, lead investigator and report writer for the *Moselle* Investigation Committee.

Figure 24. Captain Jacob Strader, a member of the 1836 anti-abolitionist
mob and a member of the 1838 *Moselle* Investigation Committee
[38, pp. 328-331; 40; 41, pp. 74-75; 42; 43, p. 3; 44, pp. 77-78].

Practical Steamboat Engineers Association [9]. Of the more than 128 steamboat
captains and engineers listed in these two publications, only Captain Jacob Strader
was both a member of the association and a part of the 1836 mob [36, pp. 173-174;
37]. Davies appointed him to the *Moselle* investigation committee along with
Locke and Matthews [33, pp. 107, 120-121; 38, pp. 328-331; 39, pp. 40-42].

Also appointed were two other anti-abolitionist mob members, Captain Joseph
Pierce (not listed in the 1843 association), and the lawyer Charles Fox. An engine
builder, William Tift, cited as a co-investigator with Locke of the physical
evidence of the explosion, was also a member of the 1836 mob [45, pp. 173-174].
In the report itself, a Mr. Graham [45, pp. 95-100, 173-174; 46], C. Wilder Bailey,
Anthony Harkness, and Abraham Voorhees are cited as steam engine experts far

JACOB STRADER & CO.,
BANKERS,
(Successors to the Commercial Bank of Cincinnati,)
MAIN STREET,

Having taken the Banking House lately occupied by the Commercial Bank of Cincinnati, are prepared to receive Deposits, to collect for Banks, Merchants, and others, Notes and Bills of Exchange, payable at Cincinnati, and at all other places where there are Banks or other facilities for transacting such business; to buy and sell Exchange, and transact business generally as Bankers and Money Agents.

JACOB STRADER,   JOHN R. CORAM,
JOHN M'CORMICK,   JAMES HALL, *Cashier.*

REFERENCES.

Bank of America,
Heran, Lees & Co.,   } *New York.*
Prime, Ward & King,

Bank of Kentucky,
Messrs. Wm. H. Pope & Co.,} *Louisville.*
C. M. Strader & Co.,

Bank of North America,} *Philadelphia.*
Charles Macalester,

Messrs. Robb & Hoge,
"   Shultz, Hadden & Leach, } *New Orleans.*
"   Hewitt, Heran & Co.,
"   J. L. Bogert & Co.,

Union Bank of Maryland, *Baltimore.*
George Collier, Esq., *St. Louis.*

Figure 25. Strader's Cincinnati business interests included more than steamboats [38, pp. 328-331].

more than Captains Strader or Pierce, and yet these experts were not appointed to the Committee. They were also not members of the 1836 mob.

There were other similarities between the anti-abolitionist committee in 1836 and the *Moselle* investigative committee in 1838. Locke and his committee hoped their report might be put to good effect in helping pass the national steamboat legislation then under consideration in the House of Representatives. In this regard, a timely publication of the report was essential. Moreover, if the report could in any way prevent further loss of life, its timely publication was doubly essential. Professor Locke completed the majority of the report within two months in late June (see Table 1. Timeline for *Moselle* Report), and yet, by September 9 it still had not been published by the City Council, which had been delegated that task by Mayor Davies.

To expedite the report's publication, Locke wrote an open letter to the public in a Cincinnati newspaper on September 18. This public letter prefaced the final published report and seemed to refer to business interests opposing the report:

> . . . some opposition has been made, and will continue to be made, by those whose interests it would be likely to affect, and any change in the management of steam must affect private interests more or less [3, p. 2].

Four days later, on the 22nd, in another open letter to the public published in the newspapers, Mayor Davies and 200 others presented a petition to the City Council asking for the report to be published. Of those who signed this petition, some two dozen had been members of the anti-abolitionist mob in 1836 in one form or another [36, pp. 173-174], including Joseph Graham who had, in the 1836 riot, "actually organized and led the mobs" [34, pp. 375-376; 46]. Another who signed the petition, Thomas A. Bakewell, was a local expert on steam engines, as well a member of the 1836 mob.

Both the federal government and the Franklin Institute began their investigations into boiler explosions at the same time, using the same "special observer" in the West for detailed information. This special Western observer was located in Cincinnati and was Thomas A. Bakewell. He described himself in a letter to the secretary of the U.S. Treasury as:

> . . . theoretically and practically acquainted with the steam engine both in the making and using of that agent for nearly 20 years. My experience in its use has consisted chiefly in its application to boats; and I believe no alteration or improvement, either real or pretended, during that period has escaped my notice [47, p. 25].

This same Thomas Bakewell also signed a resolution in 1836 to inform the public that his anti-abolitionist committee, created at a public meeting of a thousand citizens, had informed the *Philanthropist* abolitionist newspaper that "nothing short of the absolute discontinuance could prevent a resort to violence" [38, p. 97], and yet no discontinuance had occurred. The committee, with Bakewell on it, wrote much like Locke's 1838 Committee would: "It only remains, then, in pursuance of their instructions to publish their proceedings and adjourn without delay" [36, p. 173].

A final telling similarity in context between the anti-abolitionist committee of 1836 and the *Moselle* investigative committee of 1838 can be observed in the nearly identical role that The Rev. Oliver Spencer, a local Methodist minister, played in both circumstances. In both 1836 and 1838, Spencer was an elected member of City Council, as well as the individual selected by the extra-legislative bodies to carry communications—such as the September 22 petition with 200 signatures—to and from the City Council.

Was it possible that the City Council heard the implicit threat of riot in all these similarities to the troubles of 1836? Was it possible that when the City Council balked at performing the publishing job delegated to it by Mayor Davies, the council was not objecting to the report content per se but rather to the way the council was being asked to implicitly approve and print a report created by the mayor and the unelected body of the public [33, pp. 61, 69]? Was council alarmed that this particular evil, the *Moselle* explosion, might be bad enough to merit a mob?

If so much of the social context of the *Moselle* investigative committee, its work, and its membership echoed the 1836 mob actions, what effect might such a context have had on Professor John Locke's manner of writing the investigative report? One might also observe, in addition to the highly charged political context of Locke's composition of the report, the highly charged personal involvement of Locke.

LOCKE'S HIGHLY CHARGED PERSONAL EMOTIONAL INVOLVEMENT IN THE INVESTIGATION`

Unlike all the investigators of the disasters in Part One, Locke was in the vicinity when it happened. He could not treat it diffidently. First, the explosion was, according to the records, "equal to the most violent clap of thunder" [14, p. 117], and Locke's residence was within hearing distance of the explosion. Locke was in town the following night at the mayor's meeting, for the funerals involving 20,000 people the following weekend, and said that he undertook the investigation because he was "excited by the melancholy scene occasioned on our shore" [3, p. 17].

Second, Locke personally knew steamboat engineers. Silliman, Redfield, Olmsted, and the *New England* Investigative Board came from a distance, were emotionally detached, and Silliman's work at Yale and his editorship of the *American Journal of Science* did not bring him into contact with mechanics and engineers of the sort who were personally involved in the operation of steamboats. However, as one of the earliest instructors and lecturers in the Mechanic's Institute in Cincinnati [48, p. 23], Locke gave classes to the mechanics in his private apartments at 9th and Plum Street—the mechanics or engineers who would be running engines on such boats as the *Moselle*. Is it any wonder then that Locke burst out in one of the prefatory letters to the report:

> I would ask what has the leisurely enlightened part of the community done for the Engineer? Have you furnished him with a teacher? Have you published for him a Manual to guide him in his important and responsible duties? Have you

Table 1. Timeline for *Moselle* Report[a]

Date	Event
April 25, 1838	*Moselle* explodes. The steamboat bill in Washington, D.C., has passed the Senate and has yet to be considered by the House of Representatives—this explosion and three others occurring around this time push the House's considerations [3, p. 37].
April 26	A public meeting of the citizens appoints the *Moselle* Investigation Committee that includes Locke.
From April 27 to May 7[b]	Professor Locke in consultation with Mr. Tift, an experienced engine builder, examines the physical evidence of the explosion and writes a five-page letter summarizing his findings (3, pp. 23-28).
From June 10 to June 23[b]	Professor Locke writes a second 40-page letter developing a theoretical explanation for the physical evidence, and he uses the published boiler explosion investigations of the Franklin Institute that had appeared in 1836 and 1837 in the *Journal of the Franklin Institute* (3, pp. 28-68).
July 5	The steamboat bill is signed into law in Washington, D.C., by President Van Buren.
Sometime between July 5 and August 15	Seven pages are added by *Moselle* committee at large critiquing the steamboat bill just signed into law (3, pp. 69-76).
August 15	The 76-page report is handed to Mayor Davies who passes it to City Council for printing (3, p. 8).
September 8	When City Council does not move to print the report, the *Moselle* Investigation Committee asks City Council member The Rev. William Spencer [79] to recommend to City Council that the report be withdrawn from consideration so it may be printed through other means. He makes the recommendation on Sept. 8, but City Council does not comply (3, p. 8).
September 18	Professor Locke writes a two-page open letter to the public via the *Cincinnati Gazette* about the slow speed of getting the report published and hints at interference from business interests (3, pp. 9-10).
September 22	Mayor and others with many who were earlier involved in the 1836 anti-abolitionist action publish a petition to City Council to release the report so they may publish it (3, pp. 10-15).

Table 1. (Cont'd.)

Date	Event
September 22	Locke gives a copy of the 76-page report to the mayor and the extra-legislative petitioning group for publication (3, pp. 15-17).

[a]This is based on dates in the report itself and in Locke's portion of the *Second Annual Report on the Geological Survey of the State of Ohio* [51, pp. 277-286]. In it, Locke records his day-by-day schedule of "barometical" observations during the months of May to September 1838, made as he traveled the southwestern counties of Ohio doing his survey.

[b]Locke himself says at the end of his second report letter that, "I hope the citizens, on examining the report, will be satisfied, from the labor it necessarily involved, that, engaged as I have been in my geological duties, and having only the time afforded by occasional visits to the city at my disposal, it could scarcely have been accomplished at an earlier period" [51, p. 68].

appointed and paid a qualified person to hear his ingenuous suggestions and to assist him in the perfecting of his inventions? Has our government made the necessary experiments on steam as used in the West, and then put the result into his hands for his benefit and instruction? None of these things have been; and how soon will they be done, may be inferred from the "struggling to light" of this first attempt at a contribution. We are urging the rod of legislative punishment to be held over the Engineer; and is this all which our City Council, our State Legislature, our National Government, and our enlightened citizens propose to do for him [3, pp. 16-17; 49, p. 45]?

Finally, there is the effect of Locke's personality on his rhetoric. Texts are available that Locke wrote in 1838 both before and after his creation of the *Moselle* report. In these contemporaneous texts, one of Locke's rhetorical characteristics was that he repeatedly moved from a specific topic to a much more elevated or generalized topic discussed in emotionally charged terms. For example, in his portion of the *Second Annual Report of the Geological Survey of the State of Ohio* [51, pp. 201-286], which he was composing before, during, and after his *Moselle* investigation, Locke expostulated:

Many persons suppose that it is the business of the geologist to find gold and silver mines, and that he renders no service to the State unless he does that. While on my excursions, I got out of all patience with being asked if I was hunting for "gold." The State of Ohio has the richest gold mines in the world in the great fertility of her soil, and any geologist who should suggest the means of perpetuating or improving so invaluable a blessing, would confer a greater benefit on the State than by discovering a gold mine to turn the brains and corrupt the morals of the community [51, p. 208].

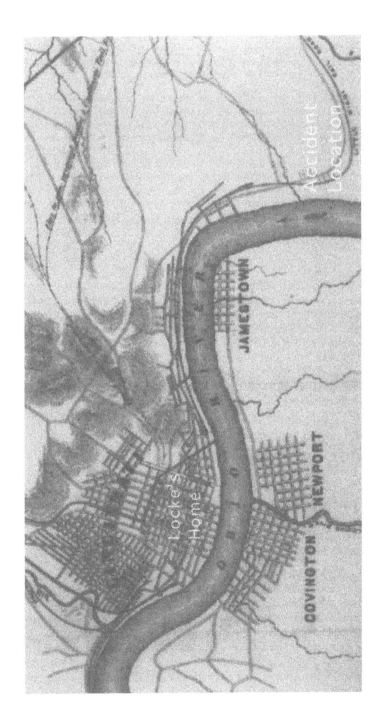

Figure 26. Portion of a Marietta and Cincinnati railroad map—Locke's house (O), and the *Moselle* explosion (X) [50].

Locke is ostensibly discussing the mineral "gold," but he raises it to a figurative level describing the soil of Ohio, and ends by seeing the corrupting influence of gold on the morals of the community. Or consider this passage in the *Geological Survey* when Locke is ostensibly discussing a night horse ride, but ends by quoting the *Bible*'s book of Ezekiel:

On a third occasion my horse took fright in the night at a white boulder in the road, sprang suddenly forward, broke his harness, but had started the carriage into such a speed that as I reined him the shaft pierced his body with a dangerous wound; in his agony he gyrated round and round, stripped the harness entirely from his body, trampled it into the mud and upset the carriage. The temporary pain from the fall and shock was severe, but I had sustained no serious injury—my barometer, strapped to my back, escaped unbroken. There were lights in a house and grocery near, I applied for assistance, and heard the voices of men in the grocery as I approached, but when I knocked, the lights were instantly extinguished, and I was told by some females in the house that there was nobody there to help me, and I must "go to the brick house." But I could get no directions to the "brick house," only it was in a field the other side of the way. My disgust at the treatment prevented me from urging very particular inquiries; and I presently found myself wadding in the mud of the road scarcely darker than the atmosphere above it. A light at a distance gleamed the hope that it proceeded from the "brick house." I directed my course recklessly towards it, left the road, entered the field, waded a muddy brook, but had the mortification to perceive that the light proceeded from a brush-heap in the field. On scanning the visible darkness I discovered the faint outline of the "brick house," but all in darkness and silence. I approached, knocked, made known my case, and heard the call, "My son, you must get up, there is a stranger in trouble." The son came with a lantern; and after sheltering the wounded horse, we found the mother and daughter, an interesting young lady, preparing a hot meal for me. The intelligent reader will feel that I need pay this family no higher compliment. To a geologist suffering as I was, it must always be interesting to discover specimens of hearts made of *flesh*, not of *stone* [51, p. 273].

And in a final example from the *Survey*, Locke describes how experiments in the chemistry lab are important not only for engineers, manufacturers, and agriculturists, but rise to national importance even for poets and philosophers:

The sublime science of geology, the element of which is learned in the chemical laboratory, has attractions for every one. It is now a part of the business of our state, and is attractive to poets, to philosophers, engineers, manufacturers, and agriculturalists. Even sordid avarice is roused by it, and when mines of lead, iron, silver, gold, are mentioned, early enquires where! Where! Domestic economy, searching for coal, gypsum and salt, honestly asks where? Their spirit of internal improvement, enquiring for compact limestone, and hydraulic cement, deserves to be informed where. The wheat and grass grower, whose soil, from ungrateful treatment, is beginning to become pale, sickly, and feeble, asks for a remedy, and must be informed WHERE! [54, p. 13].

We can also see something of this movement from the specific topic at hand to a much more elevated or generalized level discussed in emotionally charged terms in Locke's fall 1838 introductory lecture on chemistry and geology delivered at the Medical College in Cincinnati:

> Are these strata, these fused rocks, and the encompassed animal remains, these medallions of nature, proceeding from the simple polyp by regular progression to the last most perfect terrestrial being, man—are those an unmeaning, unintelligible record? Or are they news of ancient chaos, telling us that the earth was once as it is not now; a physical parallel of the moral Decalogue [52], tablets of ancient history, engraved on stone, and handed down to us by their Divine Author; needing no Champolion [53] to decipher and translate them, being written in a language intelligible to every nation, and in every age, speaking with the deep-toned eloquence of the most inconceivable antiquity, almost realizing, to our finite capacities, the vast idea of eternal duration [54, p. 17].

Is it any wonder then that when Locke ends his description of the causes of the *Moselle* explosion, his language ascends from mechanics to morality:

> These causes are only an excess of those things which are in themselves laudable. They have their foundation in the present mammoth evil of our country, the inordinate love of gain. We are not satisfied with getting rich, but we must get rich in a day. We are not satisfied with traveling with a speed of ten miles per hour, but must fly. Such is the effect of competition that every thing must be done cheap; boiler iron must be made cheap, traveling must be done cheap, freight must be cheap and yet every thing must be speedy. A steam boat must establish a reputation of a few minutes "swifter" in a hundred miles than others, before she can make fortunes fast enough to satisfy owners. All this seems to be demanded by the blind tyranny of custom, and the common consent of the community. And while this is so, is it strange that ambitious young men should run the same risk they would run for the post of honor in the battlefield? That they should jeopard [sic] every thing, even life itself, for that which has become a very deity, and should occasionally encounter a fate at which legislation, with all its terrors at its elbows, stand aghast and powerless? [3, pp. 27-28].

To begin to assess the effects of the unique Cincinnati social context on Locke, one must consider available models of steamboat explosion investigative reports that Locke may have used to create his own. After all, Locke could not have done all the investigating that he performed, as well as invent the form of a technical investigative report, in the short amount of time that he spent on the project—the months of May and June 1838 grudgingly sacrificed from his work on the geological survey of Ohio [55; 56, pp. 14-15]. In regard to models, Locke fortunately had a steamboat explosion investigative report that had been serially published in the pages of the *Journal of the Franklin Institute* in the 1830s—a journal for mechanics [57] that Locke was likely to read since he himself was "one of the earliest instructors and lecturers in the [Ohio] Mechanic's Institute" [56, p. 23; 58, pp. 343-345]. Moreover, someone with whom Locke was in active correspondence with in 1838 wrote such a model report [59, pp. 125-132; 60]. It was, in short, the report written five years earlier by Locke's mentor and professor while Locke was a student at Yale, Benjamin Silliman [48, 60, 61, 62] and his *New England* report [63-66].

HOW LOCKE USED SILLIMAN'S REPORT

Nowhere in the *Moselle* report does Locke specifically quote or cite Silliman's report on the *New England,* as he explicitly does with some Franklin Institute reports [21, pp. 79-80]. Yet Silliman and his investigation provided a general model of scientific investigation applied to very practical technological problem—a genre—as suggested in the following ways:

• Silliman's board of examiners was composed of two professors and three experienced steamboat engineers or designers. The *Moselle* committee also included two professors and two experienced steamboat captains or designers of steamboats.
• Both began their reports by using reprinted letters to define the purposes and constraints of the investigation.
• Both proceeded with a survey of the material evidence of the explosion early on in the reports—in the *Moselle's* case: the grummets, the boiler iron, the boiler workmanship, and the quantitative force of the explosion.
• Both then proceeded from general theoretical information to review the evidence of the catastrophe.

Yet, where his team membership and form may have come from Silliman, Locke's style was all his own. Unlike Silliman's objective-impersonal style [67, Chapter 4], such as avoiding references to himself, Locke included a number of them; rather than employ the passive voice, Locke used mostly transitive verbs; and where Silliman would studiously avoid metaphors or similes, Locke used them. Locke repeatedly addresses his audience in the report, basing his rhetoric on his pedagogical style in the Mechanics Institute, rather than on Silliman's objective-impersonal style:

> Having now disposed of this most important law of the correspondence of the temperature and the expansive force of steam in a manner, so far as I am able, suited to the understanding and education of engineers, I proceed to the consideration of several subjects, essential in a practical point of view, which we have reason to believe are not known to all engineers, or imperfectly understood by them [3, p. 33].

...

As the report which I now offer is intended, in part at least, as a piece of brief instruction to plain, practical men, I feel myself called upon to lay down in the beginning the most important mechanical principle in relation to the force of steam, a knowledge of which is necessary for·understanding all that follows [3, p. 29].

...

Having discussed, as briefly as possible, some of the most important points connected with high pressure steam engines, I proceed to suggest a few rules for the consideration of Captains and Engineers [3, p. 44].

...

Here engineers will please to observe, that when they stop the engine, and keep all of the valves closed, having a full fire, the pressure will be doubled, that is, from one hundred pounds on the square inch to two hundred pound in four minutes and fifty second [3, p. 61].

Also Locke offered a background to explosions of high pressure steam boilers on pages 29 to 44, and it was in these pages that Locke specifically referred to the "very able" Franklin Institute's reports thirteen different times and used them as his experimental foundation [21]. However, since Locke saw as his goal "a piece of brief instruction to plain, practical men," he excerpted and used a simpler approach, yielding such aphorisms as:

The expansive force of steam produced in a closed boiler contains a sufficient supply in water increases as the heat increases, but not at the same rate, the force increasing faster than the heat [54, p. 29].

At other times Locke would directly quote from the Franklin Institute's report *Part 1* for other aphorisms that would be understood by "plain, practical men":

All the circumstances attending the most violent explosions may occur without a sudden increase of pressure within the boiler [3, pp. 39, 69].

When Locke reviewed his work a month after its completion in one of the open letters to the mayor and newspapers, he highlighted the work he did in making the experiments of the Franklin Institute Reports plain:

I hope that it will be anticipated by our citizens, that had their Committee merely collected the principal facts in relation to the disaster which led to their appointment; or had they reduced a few elementary principles of science to a popular form; or had they collected a few of the results of well directed experiments on the subject of high pressure steam, and made them accessible to our practical men; or had they, by experiments, or by calculation discovered one new fact, or opened one new view of the management of steam, and the prevention of steam accidents; their labors would not deserve to be slighted. We hope something of all these things, briefly, and no doubt imperfectly, sketched, will be found in the Report [3, pp. 15-16].

In contrast to the inexorable nature of Silliman's report with its unanimous opinions instantly reached, Locke's report embodied much more of the serendipity of the investigation. For example, rather than presenting his findings as a single piece, Locke presents them in the form of two letters [3, pp. 23-28; 28-68] separated in time by a month (see Table 1). And, even in the second letter, there seems to be a break in the action when he notes: "Since I wrote the foregoing, one boiler of the *Moselle,* which was seen, at the time of the explosion, to go over-board entire, has been removed from the river" [3, p. 58].

This explicit rendering of the scientific process as time-bound also allowed Locke to reveal the provisional nature of his findings:

> These effects are so gunpowder-like, that they excite a common impression of some sudden and violent expansion, beyond that produced by a gradually increasing temperature; and it was not until I had applied the principles of calculation, revolved the subject in my mind, and conversed with intelligent, practical men, that I came to an opposite conclusion myself [3, p. 36].

Locke even included opinions and ideas at odds with his, via footnotes:

> Capt. Pierce's opinion, which coincides with that of many others, is entitled to every degree of respect and consideration, yet I am compelled, from the evidence before me, to differ from his views [3, p. 36].

Or by sarcastic asides:

> A very common opinion prevailed immediately on the occasion [of the explosion] that the water was too low, or was entirely dissipated, and that the boilers had been heated red-hot. While I was at the place of the accident, most of those who came to see the fragments of the boilers seemed inspired with peculiar sagacity, and each discovered unquestionable signs of a red heat. I ventured in one instance to dissent, and informed the person, that lead in the inside of the boilers had not been melted. On his disputing it, I took a piece from my pocket, a collet in perfect shape, which I had just removed from the boiler. He took it, and, with an oath, declared it had been melted. I, of course, urged no further argument [3, pp. 47-48].

And:

> I am well aware that, in the above opinion, in relation to the explosion of the *Moselle,* I encounter a very respectable opposition, in a part of our practical men [3, p. 51].

Locke also continued his characteristic technique of moving from the immediate and specific to the general, abstract, and highly emotionally charged. For example, he moves in one paragraph from considering the specific force of the *Moselle* explosion by perpendicular velocity of objects and individuals

> To devise some means of preventing these deplorable disasters has employed the attention of Legislative bodies, and of talented individuals for many years. This Committee, with neither time, money, nor apparatus placed at their disposal, can add very little to the creditable labors already performed. It may

not be improper, however, to advert to the remote and moral causes which operate to increase steam boat disasters, especially on the western waters; causes which it is very possible to obviate, and especially by drawing public opinion to the subject.

These causes are only an excess of those things which are in themselves laudable. They have their foundation in the present mammoth evil of our country, the inordinate love of gain. We are not satisfied with getting rich, but we must get rich in a day. We are not satisfied with traveling with a speed of ten miles per hour, but must fly. Such is the effect of competition that every thing must be done cheap; boiler iron must be made cheap, traveling must be done cheap, freight must be cheap and yet every thing must be speedy. A steam boat must establish a reputation of a few minutes "swifter" in a hundred miles than others, before she can make fortunes fast enough to satisfy owners. All this seems to be demanded by the blind tyranny of custom, and the common consent of the community. And while this is so, is it strange that ambitious young men should run the same risk they would run for the post of honor in the battlefield? That they should jeopard [sic] every thing, even life itself, for that which has become a very deity, and should occasionally encounter a fate at which legislation, with all its terrors at its elbows, stand aghast and powerless [3, pp. 27-28]?

Unlike Silliman and the other investigations yielding blamelessness as a result, Locke was unafraid to point to a number of culprits [18, p. 342; 68; 69, p. 424; 70, pp. 23-25; 71; 72, pp. 2, 664-673]. Besides placing blame with society in general, he also had room to assign blame to the engineers of the *Moselle:*

It is with pain, that I feel myself obliged to recorded the evidence, which I obtained from the above gentleman, that the elder or first engineer, although usually temperate, had that day been several times to a drinking shop, leaving the engine in the care of the second engineer, who was a temperate young man. On starting the boat, the first engineer resumed command of the engine, but was in a passion of anger, which he expressed by oaths, because he was compelled to go up river to the raft, instead of proceeding directly towards Louisville. Under these circumstances, it is not likely that he exercised his usual prudence. Very unwarrantable liberties have been occasionally taken by engineers with the safety valve [3, p. 53].

He blamed also the designers of engines that were without gauges or any means of accurately understanding their status:

It is probable the Engineers have not a proper knowledge of the fearful force which is accumulating under their hands, and of its rapid and sudden increase by heat, only 123 degrees from security to the most violent and general destruction. Could they see a twenty thousand pound weight suspended over their heads by a ribbon of boiler iron, one inch wide and one-sixth of an inch thick, they would recoil from the danger with horror. Yet they carelessly suffer a more frightful force to impend, because there is no way in which it is made to stare them in the face. Our community are called upon, for their own safety, to furnish the engineer with better means, than he now has, of knowing, at all times, both the quantity of water, and the strength of the steam [3, p. 40].

He blamed captains who overlooked dangerous engine situations:

It is in the department of exact discipline and order, that great improvement might undoubtedly be made in our internal navigation. . . . He is a bad general who suffers himself, even in time of peace, to be surprised, and nothing would be more absurd than for a commander, after having stationed his watch one night, to omit that duty the next, because no enemy has appeared. And is this very absurdity practiced too frequently in the responsible station of steam boat commanders? The force pump has done its duty for a long time, and it is trusted, that without any particular attention, it will continue to do so. The safety valve has been over-loaded again, and even further than before, until the bad general is surprised by an artillery, which overwhelms him in a moment [3, pp. 45-46].

And, he blamed the technology that made its misuse easy:

In the present more complicated, and more objectionable plan, a long rod, or axis, running from the engineer's station, at right angles, to the steel-yard, engages it by a short arm for that purpose, in such a manner, that, when the rod is twisted auger-like, it shall lift the valve in one direction, and hold it down in the other. This rod terminates at the other end, near the engineer's station, in a cross of T, like the handle of an auger; but the two ends of this cross piece are not alike, one is a handle by which to raise the valve, and the other is a HOOK intended expressly for the application of EXTRA WEIGHTS. The area of the *Moselle*'s safety valve, was about twelve inches, the lever's power was about twelve, make every pound of weight, at the extreme notch of the beam, cause one pound of pressure on the square inch of the valve and boiler. The lever, or "arm," of the cross rod, had a power of two, which would make every pound added to the *death-hook,* increase the pressure two pounds on the square inch. One of the under officers of the *Moselle,* says that, at the time of the explosion, three large iron wrenches and a piece of lead, were hung on the "hook." A similar wrench made at the same shop, weighed 12 lbs., and the lead, which was part of a common "pig" of metal, was estimated at twenty pounds, making, in all fifty-six pounds, or one hundred and twelve pounds to the square inch, more than the proper weight, which was more than one hundred pounds, probably one hundred and twenty-five, making, in all two hundred and thirty-seven pounds to the square inch. . . . It appears from the above, that *safety valve* is a nick-name. There is a *valve,* which can be raised to let off steam; but, when thus indefinitely loaded, it scarcely affords *safety* [3, pp. 52-53].

The *Moselle* investigation was unique because Professor John Locke was the ideal scientist-investigator, a Cincinnatus of the laboratory. He did not covet any new position, for he spoke in the Report of his desire to get back to his first love, the Geological Survey of Ohio. Thus, he had a quality of disinterestedness shared with the volunteer members of the Franklin Institute's Committee on Science and the Arts. Locke also knew he was working for the public and the government . . . even if it was constituted in an unusual manner. Silliman worked to defend the Connecticut River Steam Boat Company, and thus the company had a preponderance of scientific expertise. Lardner worked for Norris Brothers in the same way. For the first time, in the case of the *Moselle,* the public had a preponderance of scientific expertise.

THE BEGINNING OF A NEW APPROACH TO ACCIDENT INVESTIGATION

The happy accident of Cincinnati's ability to circumvent traditional legal approaches to accident investigation bore good fruit. Rather than a coroner's jury with no expertise collecting evidence, the leading scientist of the town collected the evidence and interviewed witnesses. Rather than looking to blame the immediate causes of the accident, Locke was able to examine the root causes of the accident and the systemic problems. Locke was able to assign the complexity of blame where it belonged: to society in general, to the engineers, to the designers of engines, to captains, and to the technology itself that made its misuse easy.

This time, the "disinterested" investigation and its findings were the sole report produced, and it has never been questioned. Moreover, the report came out in such a timely fashion that it truly had an effect. Unlike Silliman's report, which received excellent and rapid diffusion in the key scientific journals and societies and was reprinted by government publications, Locke's report was never reprinted nor included in any larger government publications [73, p. 529]. However, the report was well-respected in Cincinnati. When Charles Cist, editor of a Cincinnati daily paper and five business directories, wrote to the Secretary of the Treasury about the *Moselle* a decade after Locke had made his investigation, Cist reported that a "systematic investigation" was done and, he found, unlike the *New England* report critics, there was, after ten years, "little doubt" of Locke's conclusions [5, pp. 63-64, 170; 74, pp. 40-42].

Locke's report also established a regional reputation for a year later when Cadwallader Evans, a Pittsburgh inventor, son of the man who invented high-pressure steam engines [69, Chapter 1; 75, pp. 63–89], and a major manufacturer of engines in Pittsburgh, wanted to have his fusible alloy steamboat safety device tested outside his own city, he sent instruments and samples to Locke, who confirmed his earlier findings [39, pp. 40-42; 76, pp. 182-183]. In *A Treatise on the Causes of Explosions of Steam Boilers,* Evans not only lists Locke as first among the scientific professors who offer testimonials regarding his invention, and includes two pages of Locke's description of his tests, but also lists Locke before he lists Silliman [76, p. 30], and quotes from Locke at length four times, while quoting Silliman only once [76, pp. 36, 40-42, 43, 52-53].

IN THE END

In the end, Captain Perrin was found negligent in the courts [77], but frontier society's desire for speed continued. Jacob Strader, a member of the committee itself, built the steamboats *Pike* and *Franklin* the following year, 1839. Descriptions of these two steamboats have recently been found in a report by Franz Gerstner to the German government, where he noted that the *Pike* and the *Franklin* "carried the mails and were particularly outstanding because of their accoutrements and speed of travel" [44, p. 778].

Locke's call for instruction and improvement of the engineers was answered positively by the unique creation of the Cincinnati Association of Steamboat Engineers, which described the goals of its association in the following fashion: ". . . for the purpose of improving ourselves in a knowledge of their business, by discussions and experiments on steam" [9, p. 8; 78]. Locke's report had tangible results and was a sign that American society was moving beyond helplessness in the face of the awesome power of technology.

ENDNOTES

1. Denison Olmsted, *Address on the Scientific Life and Labors of William C. Redfield*, New Haven, Conn.: E. Hayes, 1857.
2. A Review of "Inquire into the Causes of the Explosion of the *Moselle*, and to Suggest such Preventive Measures as May Best Be Calculated to Guard Hereafter Against Such Occurrences, Cincinnati, 1838," *North American Review*, 50, January 1840.
3. "Report of the Committee Appointed by the Citizens of Cincinnati, April 26, 1838, to Enquire Into the Causes of the Explosion of the *Moselle*." Cincinnati: Alexander Flash, 1838.
4. *Niles Register*, 54 (1389), May 19, 1838: "The *Louisville Journal* contains the following paragraph respecting the mad ambition of Capt. Perrin, to which is justly attributable the late melancholy accident, and the loss of life attendant to it. There is no doubt, that the deplorable occurrence is to be attributed to the overweening anxiety of Capt. Perin to gain for his boat the reputation of unrivaled speed. We have always had the kindest feelings for Capt. P. and when, a few weeks ago, he made a swift trip to this city from above, we cheerfully, in compliance with his request, took notice of the fact. From Louisville he made an extraordinary passage to St. Louis, whence he wrote as by express mail, requesting that we would again proclaim his matchless speed, and say that his boat was and would be 'the eagle of the waters.' We declined to comply with this second request for we saw that his ambition was already roused to a most dangerous pitch" [p. 176].
5. *Report of the Commissioner of Patents on the Subject of Steam Boiler Explosions*, 30th Congress, 2nd Session, Serial Set 529, Executive Report No. 18. The first engineer was Madden who Charles Cist described in the following manner: "The first engineer, Madden, was well known to be one of the most reckless men in that capacity on the river, and had been drinking freely before coming aboard, just as the boat started from the dock. He, too, shared the feeling of the captain, that no boat should be suffered to pass the *Moselle* . . ."

6. "Report No. 478, Steamboats, May 18, 1832," in *Reports of Committees of the House of Representatives at the First Session of the Twenty-Second Congress, Begun and Held at the City of Washington, December 7, 1831,* Washington, D.C.: Duff Green, 1831. Not only was Cincinnati a center for the creation of steamboats, and its economy very much tied to its manufacturer, but it also appears that Cincinnati was one of the very few cities where there was a society of steamboat builders, masters, and owners. Such groups evidently met as early as 1831, only fifteen years after the first steamboat traveled on western waters.

7. Locke noted at the time of his report that "I am happy to see a large number of their highly respected names attached to this letter [the petition]" [2, p. 16].

8. *Niles Register,* 55 (1416), November 17, 1838. Two weeks after Locke sent his report to the mayor for publication in 1838 there was a large meeting of "steamboat owner's officers, etc. held in Cincinnati."

9. Cincinnati Practical Steamboat Engineers, *Relative to Steamboat Explosions*—27th Congress, 3rd Session, House Report No. 145, Serial Set #429, 2/13/1843, Association Response. By 1843, this group was sufficiently organized as to adopt a name, the Cincinnati Practical Steamboat Engineers Association.

10. Rosalie C. Jendrek, "The Contribution of the Steamboat to the Growth of Cincinnati: 1815-1860," Masters Thesis, University of Miami, Oxford, Ohio, 1953.

11. Daniel Drake and Edward D. Mansfield, *Cincinnati in 1826,* Cincinnati, Ohio: Morgan, Lodge and Fisher, 1827. "The commerce of Cincinnati is co-extensive with steamboat navigation on the western rivers."

12. James Hall, *Statistics of the West, at the Close of the Year 1836,* Cincinnati, 1836: p. 217. "It was all that the western country needed, and the name of Fulton should be cherished here with that of Washington: If one conducted us to liberty, the other had given us prosperity—the one broke the chains that bound us to a foreign country, the other had extended the channel of intercourse, and multiplied the ties which bind us to each other."

13. Melanchthon W. Jacobus, *The Connecticut River Steamboat Story,* Hartford, Conn.: The Connecticut Historical Society, 1956.

14. S. A. Howland, *Steamboat Disasters, and Railroad Accidents in the United States,* Worcester, Mass.: Dorr, Howland & Co., 1846.

15. Louis C. Hunter, *Steamboats on the Western Rivers: An Economic and Technological History,* Cambridge, Mass.: Harvard University Press, 1949.

16. Even with their similarities in how they both exploded, the casualties from the explosions differed because of the varied designs of the boats. Professor Silliman's 1830 idea for design safety—the placement of the boilers to the outside of the boat—did work in the case of the *New England,* when 30 percent of those aboard were killed or injured. On the *Moselle,* however, where this safety feature was not followed and where the boilers were placed amidships and below the deck in the center of the craft, 56 percent were killed or injured. The *New England* also suffered less physical damage ($17,500) and returned to her circuit in the following spring. The *Moselle* was a total loss.

17. *Philanthropist,* 1 (17), May 1, 1838.

18. Fred Irving Dayton and John Wolcott Adams (illustrator), *Steamboat Days,* New York: Fredrick A. Stokes Co., 1928.

19. *National Intelligencer* 26 (7866), April 30, 1838, p. 2; 26 (7869), May 2, 4, 7, 8, 1838.

20. Benjamin B. French, *Witness to the Young Republic: A Yankee's Journal, 1828–1870,* Hanover, N.H.: University Press of New England, 1989. June 21, 1838 journal entry.
21. R. John Brockmann, *Exploding Steamboats, Senate Debates, and Technical Reports: The Convergence of Technology, Politics and Rhetoric in the Steamboat Bill of 1838,* Amityville, N.Y.: Baywood, 2001.
22. *Congressional Globe,* 6 (22), May 7, 1838, 25th Congress, 3rd Session, Discussion of Bill Now in House.
23. John C. Burke, "Bursting Boilers and the Federal Power," *Technology and Culture,* 7 (1), 1966.
24. Other members of the City Council at the time included: Oliver Spencer, Archibald Irwin, John Hare, Ebenezer Hinman, S. Hubbell, Septimus Hazen, Oliver Fairchild, E. S. Haines, David Griffin, David Loring, Aaron Valentine, Edward Woodruff, Ebenezer Hulse, and W. J. Vanhorne.
25. Daniel Aaron, *Cincinnati, Queen City of the West: 1819-1838,* Columbus, Ohio: Ohio State University Press, 1992. "The men who managed local affairs, although honest and conscientious, entertained few unconventional notions about the function of city government. Passing ordinances and issuing licenses, regulating and prohibiting, maintaining public safety and order were the accepted duties of municipal officials" [9, p. 850].
26. Richard T. Farrell, *Cincinnati in the Early Jackson Era, 1816-1834,* Ph.D. Dissertation, Indiana University, 1967.
27. Otto Juettner, *Daniel Drake and His Followers, 1785–1909,* Cincinnati, Ohio: Harvey Publishing Company, 1909.
28. Burnet later played a key role with Davies in anti-abolitionist riots and was the second signature after Davies's on the *Moselle* petition to City Council.
29. Harry R. Stevens, "Samuel Watts Davies and the Industrial Revolution in Cincinnati," *The Ohio Historical Quarterly,* 70 (2), April 1961.
30. *Niles Register,* 48 (1246), August 8, 1835.
31. Patrick A. Folk, *"The Queen City of Mobs: Riots and Community Reactions in Cincinnati, 1788-1848,"* Ph.D. Dissertation, University of Toledo, 1979.
32. Edwin Henderson, City Clerk, *An Address on the History of Council: 1802-1902,* Cincinnati, Ohio: Board of Legislation, 1902.
33. Alan I. Marcus, *Plague of Strangers: Social Groups and the origins of City Services in Cincinnati, 1819-1870,* Columbus, Ohio: Ohio State University Press, 1991: Council had the power to designate special committees in time of catastrophe.
34. *Liberty Hall & Cincinnati Gazette,* 31 (1672), July 28, 1836. "It was then resolved that the committee publish the results of their interview [with the abolitionists], and that these proceedings be published in all the papers of the city," p. 2.
35. *Niles Register,* 55 (1416), November 17, 1838. However, only six specific names are cited.
36. Leonard L. Richards, *"Gentlemen of Property and Standing:" Anti-Abolition Mobs in Jacksonian America,* New York: Oxford University Press, 1970. In the published report, Piece and Strader are never cited as technical informants.
37. Other suggestive links between Strader and Davies are that both were involved in a complex financial interweaving of banking, boat building, and cotton manufacturing. In 1818, Davies was the cashier for the Farmer and Mechanic's bank, and loaned money for the building of five steamboats to a family of boat builders whose uncle was

a director of the bank. Davies also was a major shareholder and incorporator of a cotton manufacturing company.

38. M. Joblin & Co., *Cincinnati Past and Present: Or, Its Industrial History, As Exhibited in the Life-labors of Its Leading Men*, Cincinnati, Ohio: Elm Street Publishing, 1872. Strader was president of the Commercial Bank for many years, during which he built twenty-three steamboats, and in 1844 he founded a large cotton manufacturing company with Anthony Harkness, who built boat engines, was the third signature on Davies 1838 petition to Council, and was a major information source for John Locke in his report.

39. Cadwallader Evans, *A Treatise on the Causes of Explosions of Steam Boilers*, Pittsburgh, Penna.: Whitney, 1850. Finally, there are later links between Locke and Strader that suggest that Locke simply saw Strader as "a judicious and reliable" man, and Locke later chose him himself for a committee to review steam boiler safety devices made by a Pittsburgh inventor.

40. Strader built twenty-three steamboats between 1824 and 1847—he built six different boats with the appellation, *Ben Franklin*.

41. James T. Lloyd, *Lloyd's Directory and Disasters on the Western Waters*, Cincinnati, Ohio, 1856. After owning and running one of the *Franklins* for fifteen months, it was sold to owners in Mobile in 1836 and was destroyed like the *Moselle* by having its boilers explode in March 1836.

42. Moreover, despite the fact that the editor of the *Gazette* wrote the following in sharing the blame for the explosion of the *Moselle* in 1838: "For this sad result we in part, take blame. We plead guilty, in common with other presses, to having praised the speed and power of the boat—a circumstance that doubtless contributed to inflate the ambition of its captain and owners, to excel in rapidity. We feel confident, that if the public are to have any security against steamboat accidents—the press must change its tone. Boats must be praised for their comfort, convenience, and the care and discretion of their managers—but not for their speed" [18, p. 276].

43. *Philanthropist*, 1 (17) May 1, 1838, "They will always have as much speed as their machinery will bear, without the aid of foreign excitement. Safety is better than speed" [p. 2].

44. Franz Gerstner, *Early American Railroad (Die innern Communicationen 1842-1843)*, Stanford, Calif.: Stanford University Press, 1997). We find the following applied to Strader's boats: "They [the *Pike* and a second *Franklin*, two of Strader's boats in 1839] carried the mails and were particularly outstanding because of their accoutrements [like the *Moselle*] and speed of travel" [pp. 77-78].

45. It is unclear, however, in the case of Mr. Graham, who is a technical informant of Locke's. It is unclear whether this is Joseph Graham (although a Jos. Graham does sign the mayor's petition, suggesting it might be he). If it is Joseph Graham, then one of the ringleaders is himself one of Locke's informants.

46. Folk goes on to note that when Graham later became an editor of a Cincinnati newspaper along with two others heavily involved in the 1836 riot who also became editors, John C. Wright and John C. Vaughan, who could all little criticize later mob actions in 1841, 1842, and 1843 without repudiating their own positions in 1836. Wright and Vaughan both signed the petition.

47. "Report No. 478, Steamboats, May 18, 1832," in *Reports of Committees of the House of Representatives at the First Session of the Twenty-Second Congress, Begun*

and Held at the City of Washington, December 7, 1831, Washington, D.C.: Duff Green, 1831.

48. M .B. Wright, *An Address on the Life and Character of the late Professor John Locke Delivered at the Request of the Cincinnati Medical Society,* Cincinnati, Ohio: Moore, Wilstach, Keys & Co., n.d.

49. Christian H. Hewison, *Locomotive Boiler Explosions,* North Pomfret, Vt.: David & Charles, 1983. One needs to keep in mind that this was not only a Cincinnati problem or an American problem, or even just an international problem in regard to steamboats, but rather was equally a problem on early railroads. Hewison, commenting on British locomotives, observed, "in 1856 locomotive superintendents were not as yet very experienced; there were virtually no textbooks on boilers that were of any real use, and in drawing offices and workshops there was still much to be learned about boiler design" [p. 45].

50. Library of Congress Map 455.

51. W. W. Mather, *Second Annual Report on the Geological Survey of the State of Ohio,* Columbus, Ohio: Samuel Medary, Printer to the State, 1838.

52. Ten Commandments.

53. Frenchman Jean-François Champollion (1790-1832) deciphered the Rosetta Stone.

54. John Locke, "An Introductory Lecture on Chemistry and Geology: Delivered November 6, 1838," Cincinnati, Ohio: Republican Printers, 1839.

55. House Executive Document 239, 26 Cong., 1 Sess., and republished in enlarged form in 1844 (Senate Document 407, 28 Cong., 1 Sess.), Locke did geological survey work for both the state of Ohio and the federal government. One of his subsequent reports on the mineral lands of Iowa, Illinois, and Wisconsin was published by Congress in 1840.

56. Adolph F. Waller, "Dr. John Locke, Early Ohio Scientist (1792-1856)," *Ohio State Archaeological and Historical Society Quarterly,* 1946.

57. David Freeman Hawke, *Nuts and Bolts of the Past: A History of American Technology, 1776–1860,* New York: Harper & Row, 1988, p. 31. Persons "skilled in the operation, repair, and creation of machinery."

58. *Journal of the Franklin Institute* 29 (5), pp. 343-345. Another clue that Locke was probably a reader of the *Journal* is that the year before Locke participated in the *Moselle* investigation, in 1837, he had created a piece of equipment to aid in his Ohio Mechanic's Institute lectures called a thermoscope galvanometer, a description of which was published in the May 1838 edition of the *Journal of the Franklin Institute.*

59. *American Journal of Science,* 34 (1838). Locke wrote to Silliman in 1838 as recorded in his own letters to Silliman regarding "Magneto-electricity."

60. Silliman and Locke had remained in contact, as can be seen in Locke's January 1838 letter to Silliman on magneto-electricity.

61. And, since there is ample evidence of Locke's use of the Franklin Institute Bache Committee report on steam boiler explosions, it can be inferred that as a professor at the Ohio Mechanic's Institute, he read the *Journal of the Franklin Institute* (the premier mechanic's institute at the time) in which Silliman's 1835 report was published in its entirety. Also, on November 24, 1843, both Benjamin Silliman and Denison Olmsted wrote to the committee in Washington, D.C. then considering whom to appoint as the new leader of the prestigious Coast Survey, and they recommended Alexander Dallas Bache, the leader of the Franklin investigation team.

62. Alexander Dallas Bache Papers, 1821-1869, Smithsonian Institution Archives, Record Unit 7053, Box 6.

63. There was also, of course, the three-part steamboat boiler explosion investigation done by Bache and his committee at the Franklin Institute; see the three reports coming out of the Committee, which included: *Communications Received by the Committee of the Franklin Institute* (1832)—*Franklin Institute and the Making of Industrial America*, Microfiche Collection (1987): Committee on Boiler Explosions #148-9; *Part 1—Explosions of Steam Boilers* (1836).

64. Stephanie Morris, *Franklin Institute and the Making of Industrial America*, Microfiche Collection (1987): Committee on Boiler Explosions #149-51; *Part 2–Strength of Materials* (1837).

65. Stephanie Morris, *Franklin Institute and the Making of Industrial America*, Microfiche Collection (1987): Committee on Boiler Explosions #151-3; and the General Report.

66. Bruce Sinclair, *Early Research at the Franklin Institute: The Investigation into the Causes of Steam Boiler Explosions, 1830–1837*, Philadelphia, Penna.: The Franklin Institute, 1966. However, these reports and this Franklin Committee, although referred to often by Locke, were not alike in how they focused on a single explosion with actual casualties and individuals like Silliman's *New England* report. The Franklin Institute approached the problem of explosions from a "basic science" standpoint, and, in doing so, wound up inventing the science of materials testing. The Franklin Institute hoped to see the practical application of this "basic science" in national legislation, but not in an immediate application as both the Silliman and Locke reports sought.

67. R. John Brockmann, *From Millwrights to Shipwrights to the Twenty-first Century: Explorations in a History of Technical Communication in the United States*, Norwood, N.J.: Hampton Press, 1998.

68. An editorial in one of Cincinnati's papers (*Advertiser and Ohio Phoenix*, April 28, 1838) made a similar observation about the public fascination with speed: "For this result we are in part to blame; we plead guilty, in common with other presses, of having praised the speed and power of the boat—a circumstance which doubtless contributed to inflate the ambition of the captain and owners to excel others in rapidity. If the public are to have any security against steamboat accidents, the press must change its tone. Boats must be praised for their comfort, convenience and the care and discretion of their commanders—but not for their speed" [p. 2].

69. Robert B. Shaw, *A History of Railroad Accidents, Safety Precautions and Operating Practices*, Binghamton, NY: Vail-Ballou Press, Inc., 1978. In September 1958, ICC examiner Howard Mosmer wrote "Almost the only advantage which railroad passenger service now has to offer in competition with motor and air travel is an incomparably better safety record. This facto is of negligible value . . ."

70. Michel Chevalier, *Society, Manners and Politics in the United States: Being A Series of Letters on North America*, Boston, Mass.: Weeks, Jordan and Company, 1839. Frenchman Michel Chevalier wrote about the America of the 1830s in his book, and described how Americans both felt about speed and the possible loss of life in military metaphors quite similar to Locke's: "In the West, the flood of emigrants, descending from the Alleghenies, rolls swelling and eddying over the plains, sweeping before it the Indian, the buffalo, and the bear. At its approach the gigantic forests bow themselves before it, as the dry grass of the prairies disappears before the flames. It is for civilization, what the hosts of Genghis Khan and Attila were for barbarism; it is an

invading army, and its law is the law of armies. The mass is everything, the individual nothing. Woe to him who trips and falls! He is trampled down and crushed under foot. Woe to him who finds himself on the edge of a precipice! The impatient crowd, eager to push forward, throngs him, forces him over, and he is at once forgotten, without even a half-suppressed sigh for his funeral oration. *Help yourself!* is the watchword. The life of the genuine American is the soldier's life; like the soldier he is encamped, and that, in a flying camp, here to-day, fifteen hundred miles off in a month...Like the soldier, the American of the West take for his motto, *Victory or death!* But to him, victory is to make money, to get the dollars, to make a fortune out of nothing, to buy lots at Chicago, Cleveland, or St. Louis, and sell them a year afterward at an advance of 1000 per cent; to carry cotton to New Orleans when it is worth 20 cents a pound. So much the worse for the conquered; so much the worse for those who perish in the steamboats! The essential point is not to save some individuals or even some hundreds; but, in respect to steamers, that they should be numerous; staunch or not, well commanded or not, it matters little, if they move at a rapid rate, and are navigated at little expense. The circulation of steamboats is as necessary to the West, as that of the blood is to the human system. The West will beware of checking and fettering it by regulations and restrictions of any sort. The time is not yet come, but it will come hereafter" [pp. 23-25].

71. Mrs. Houston, *Hesperus, or Travels in the West* (1850), London: J. W. Parker, 1850. A similar observation appeared in which she commented about railroads: "I really think there must be some natural affinity between Yankee 'keep-moving' nature and a locomotive engine" [p. 238].

72. "The Wonders of Modern Locomotion," *The Dublin University Magazine*, 210 (35), June 1850. This article excerpts from Dionysus Lardner's *Railroad Economy* and notes: "[Engine-drivers and captains] are too intent on obtaining speed—and to use their own phrase, "going a-head"—and they have little hesitation in risking their own lives and those of the passengers, rather than allow themselves to be outrun by a rival boat" [p. 669].

73. In fact, when W. B. Hale sought to use the *Moselle* explosion in a discussion of steam boiler explosions in the *Journal of the American Institute*, 3 (10), July 1838, he referenced the *Niles Register* article about the report and not Locke's report itself. He does in the same correspondence refer to the Bache report and in the reply they refer to the Silliman report.

74. *Report of the Commissioner of Patents on the Subject of Steam Boiler Explosions*, 30th Congress, 2nd Session, Serial Set 529, Executive Report No. 18. Thomas Halderman concurs with this confirmation of Locke's findings.

75. R. John Brockmann, "Oliver Evans and His Antebellum Wrestling with Rhetorical Arrangement," in *Three Keys to the Past: The History of Technical Communication*, Teresa Kynell and Michael Moran (eds.), Stamford, Conn.: Ablex Publishing Corp., 1999.

76. Cadwallader Evans, *A Statement upon the Temperature of Steam*, Pittsburgh, Penna.: Keenan & Hopkins, 1854.

77. *The Case of Administrators of Isaac Perrin vs. the Protection Insurance Company*, Supreme Court of Ohio, 11 Ohio 147; 1842 Ohio (December 1842).

78. "Witnessing these facts, we have thought it necessary to make an attempt to vindicate the character of Western engineers against such aspersions as they have heretofore

been subjected. This can only be effectually done by unity of action and sentiment among the engineers of the West, (which we are happy to say, seems to have taken place,) which will enable them to present to Congress for the consideration, a synopsis of the art of practical steam engineering, and at the same time show to the public the true nature of Western engineers. With this object in view, and for the purpose of improving ourselves in a knowledge of their business, by discussions and experiments on steam, we have associated ourselves under the name and title of the "Cincinnati Association of Steamboat boat Engineers." One hundred forty three signatures are appended. Cited from [9].

79. Spencer evidently suffers no ill effects from his holding up of the report since in the next City Council election in 1839 he is re-elected.

CHAPTER 4

What Happens When the Scientific Ethos is Missing in Investigation Reports: The Camden and Amboy Railroad Disaster, 29 of August 1855

Rock away, passenger, in the third class,
When your train shunts a faster will pass;
When your train's late your chances are small
Crushed will be carriages, engine and all.
To the tune of Hush-a-by-baby,
"The Railway Nursery Rhymer" [1, p. 1]

RAILROAD DANGERS

A cartoon in the January 1856 edition of *Harper's Weekly* depicted the dangers haunting antebellum America. As expected, the cartoon featured explosions on steamboats and accidents aboard trains. However, the train accident in the third box specified a very specific road in the accident, the Camden and Amboy Railroad (Figure 27).

Moreover, the *Harper's Weekly* cartoon wasn't the only cartoon directed specifically at Camden and Amboy Railroad accidents. Another had the following conversation between an attractive young housewife and a railroad employee toting a large bag over his shoulder. Knocking at her door, he asked:

Benevolent Employee: Does Mr. Jones live here?
Mrs. Jones: Yes, but he's not in.
Employee: Well, I guess not, seein' as I've got him here, a little mixed up with a few other fellows [3, p. 93].

On the large bag over his shoulder was the name of his employer, and the name, little disguised, was: "C_____n and A_____y Railroad."

Americans had a right to fear the dangers of this particular railroad, for it had had more than its share of accidents, many of them making the record books of American railroad history:

Figure 27. *Harper's Weekly* cartoon on antebellum technology's dangers to life and limb [2, pp. 284-285].

- On November 8, 1833, it made the record books by suffering the first passenger fatalities on an American railroad. Both the former president, John Quincy Adams, and the soon-to-be-famous entrepreneur of steamboats and railroads, Commodore Cornelius Vanderbilt, were jostled and slightly injured in the accident.
- On March 2, 1836, it again made the record books by having the first head-on collision on an American railroad; one person was killed [3, p. 18; 4, pp. 301-302].
- On September 12, 1839, the brakes failed on eight passenger cars coasting down the tracks onto the pier for the ferry across the Hudson. The cars hit a baggage car, and that baggage car and the two forward most passenger cars crashed into the steamboat *Commerce*. Thus, the company made it into the record books again for the first collision between a train and a boat. One person died, and one was injured.

Five more accidents occurred on the line between October 1845 and September 1853 killing twelve and injuring twenty-four [5; 6, p. 154; 7]. In each of these cases, coroner's juries had found either no liability for these injuries on the part of the Camden and Amboy, or had indicted low-level personnel operating the particular train in question. Not once did the Camden and Amboy investigate the causes of these accidents or issue a report to the public.

However, in August 1855, that all changed. Again the Camden and Amboy made the records books, this time for the worst railroad disaster ever to occur in New Jersey up to that date:

ACCOUNT OF A TERRIBLE ACCIDENT ON THE CAMDEN AND AMBOY RAILROAD.

It appears, that the 10 o'clock, a.m., train from Philadelphia, proceeded as usual on the way, until they got about two or three miles above Burlington, N.J., when they discovered the train from New York coming down at full speed. The eastward bound train then attempted to back up to a turnout to let the New York train pass, when the track was crossed by a carriage and two horses, driven by Dr. Heineken, of Columbus, N.J. The horses were caught by the hindermost car, knocked down, and crushed to death. The Doctor was thrown out and made a very narrow escape, the carriage being shivered to pieces. This contact with the horses threw the rear car, now the first advancing one of the train, off the rails. Here it ran for some distance without injury, until the embankment, about five feet high, commenced shelving off. The wheels outside the rail, of course, followed this downward direction, until the car was entirely off the track. The second car was thrown directly across the first, and the third went completely through that, and stopped diagonally across the road. The fourth car followed, and plunged headlong into the third. The way-car was also very much injured, but none of the passengers in it were killed. It is to this remarkable jumbling up of the cars that the enormous loss of life is to be attributed. The major part of the passengers in the rear cars were instantly killed or seriously injured.

The scene that ensued baffles all description. The consternation was so great, that a panic of horror seized on all who survived the awful calamity. About twenty persons were killed, and about twenty wounded most shockingly—some so badly that recovery is almost impossible. That night the remains of the dead were carefully deposited in coffins, furnished by the authorities of Burlington. The spectacle at the Town Hall was of the most painful character, fifteen coffins being arranged around the center of the room. Almost every house in Burlington contained one or more of the sufferers by this terrible catastrophe. During the entire day that usually quiet town was the scene of the wildest excitement.

Four of the cars were smashed to pieces. In some cases the mutilation was horrible. One man had his arm torn off in a fearful manner. Another had an arm also torn off and thrown some distance up the embankment, and his legs separated from his body, his heart and viscera strewn along the track for a great distance. One or two others were buried in the sand, and others were crushed to death between the sleepers. One man had his scalp taken off; another had his thighs broken. Several others had arms broken and were lacerated and bruised in the most dreadful manner. The women and children on board of the train appear nearly all to have escaped. We have but four or five females reported among the dead.

The killed and wounded are as follows: Died on the spot, 19; at Burlington, 1; at Bordentown, 1; at Philadelphia, 1; —Total, 22. Not likely to live, 1; critical, 3; left for home, 4; doing well at Burlington, 20; injured, but returned to their respective homes, 51. Total, killed and wounded, 101.

The total number of passengers on the train is said to be 193; so that more than half were either killed or wounded.

Yesterday we visited the scene of carnage. Crowds of workmen were engaged in clearing away the broken fragments of the ruined cars, and searching among the ruins for the numerous valuables of which the concussion had despoiled the ill-fated passengers. Of the four cars thrown off the track, not one is worth repairing—the wreck has been total. We have never witnessed many railroad accidents, but we can hardly conceive of any so overwhelmingly destructive of car-work as this.

The accident occurred a short quarter of a mile above Burlington, at the first road which crosses the track—the same crossing where a man was killed in his wagon, a year or two ago, while attempting to pass the track [8, p. 49; 9].

After this accident, the Camden and Amboy refused not only to pay compensation to the victims or their families for injury or death, but also even for the destruction of baggage. The railroad did this, they said, because they feared such payments would establish precedents for the assumption of liability [6, p. 166; 10, pp. 206-207].

In response to this accident, the usual participants in the investigation triangle, a coroner's jury, the company, and the scientists at the Franklin Institute, convened and offered three separate investigations. The unique feature, however, of all

ACCIDENT ON THE CAMDEN AND AMBOY RAIL ROAD,
NEAR BURLINGTON, N. J.
APE. 29TH 1855.
21 PERSONS KILLED_75 WOUNDED

Figure 28. Picture of the Camden and Amboy accident scene in Burlington, 1855.

these reports is that they eschewed a disinterested scientific ethos, with the result that the rhetoric of investigation fell into a series of combative accusations and rejoinders.

The coroner's jury issued a report that for once spoke of more than proximate causes and the mistakes of low-level train operating personnel. This time the jury saw that part of the cause of the death of twenty-two people was the company itself:

> And the Jurors aforesaid, upon their oaths and affirmations aforesaid, do further say, that, by the "Running Regulations" issued by the said Camden and Amboy Railroad and Transportation Company, the possibility and probability of collision between opposing trains on a single track, is so great, as to prove that some efficient means should he adopted to prevent the recurrence of the cause which has called this Inquest together, and that the safety of the passengers in life and limb, is of more importance than the saving of a few minutes of time [9, pp. 4-5].

The Board of Directors of the Camden and Amboy then issued its investigation report, and it did not use any scientific approach to analysis, nor did it accept the veracity of thecoroners jury's witnesses. However, the Board of Directors of the Camden and Amboy did use dozens of rhetorical questions.

Later still, the Franklin Institute published its scientific investigation into the accident in the *Journal of the Franklin Institute.* However, just like the coroners jury's and company's reports, this report used a combative tone that did not partake of scientific objectivity. Consider the following:

- But we differ from them in this . . .
- . . . we know of no road which has been so complained of, as this very road has been . . .
- . . . but surely they have overlooked . . .
- Another assertion of the report that strikes us as inaccurate . . .
- . . . we must reply, no, gentlemen . . .
- How can this be the case . . .
- Is it true, moreover, as the report asserts, that a double track is not compatible with economy? Is it not, on the contrary the result of both reasoning and experience . . .
- It appears to us, that the moral of the late fearful and deplorable accident which has furnished the text of these remarks is . . . [11; 12, p. 21; 13].

The last turn of phrase appearing in the last paragraph of the report is most interesting. In the mid-nineteenth century, "furnishing the text" was most often used in regard to scripture and sermons [14, p. 705; 15, p. 71; 16; 17]. Moreover, if the Camden and Amboy report did not use science to support its observations, but rather its reasoning and experience, that was exactly what the Franklin Institute used, too. In doing this, the disagreement between the two groups did not have the emotional buffer of "disinterested science," to keep the two parties from becoming polemical. In fact, the arguments seemed very pointed, personal, and combative.

These three customary investigators (the coroner's jury, the company, and the Franklin Institute) were joined by a barrage of other voices, all critical of the company report, and none employed the emotional buffer of "disinterested science":

- Sermons such as this one by H. A. Boardman, *God's Providence in Accidents:*

  The animus which pervades the entire administration of this opulent and powerful monopoly may be seen with noonday clearness in the official "REPORT" of the Directors of the Company, on the recent accident. The gentlemen whose names are appended to this paper, are, several of them, my personal acquaintances—I hope I may say, my personal friends; and they are, as a body, known in society as high minded and honorable men—exemplary, not only as citizens, but as husbands and fathers. And yet these gentlemen have affixed their signatures to as heartless a document as ever emanated even from a railroad corporation. One of their trains has killed twenty-four persons, and wounded some sixty or seventy others. And while hundreds, perhaps thousands of hearts are still bleeding under the anguish of this terrible slaughter, they put forth a paper; in which they not only undertake to vindicate the every act of every one of their officials concerned in this tragedy, but scrupulously abstain from the use of any phrase or syllable which might be interpreted into an expression of sorrow for the dead, or of sympathy for the mourners! Even allowing, what few have denied, that a culpable degree of carelessness attached to the driver of the *carriage,* this is no justification of what one of the Philadelphia papers properly described as the "haughty, and defiant," and unfeeling tone of this report. It supplies another illustration of the sinister effect produced upon men by consolidating them in a society or corporation. Many a corporation has done things which its members would no more have done as individuals, than they would have turned highwaymen. It might be well for such persons to consider, in some leisure moment, how the moral responsibility of these transactions is to be apportioned *hereafter,* as between the individual and the corporator [18, p. 39].

- Local newspapers:

  I think the employees of the Company are far less to blame than the Executive Committee and Stockholders, who attempt to excuse their conduct. Better for the reputation of the latter, if their Report had never emerged from the secret council-chamber at Bordentown. The statements and language of the Report are highly censurable; and this, so far as I have heard, is the general sentiment of the public. One of the severest sufferers among the bereaved declared, after reading the Report, that, afflicted as he was, he considered himself in a better condition than the signers of that document [19, p. 2].

- Newly founded railroad professional journals such as the following from the front page of the *American Railroad Journal:*

The Camden and Amboy Company have published a report prepared by their Executive Committee regarding the late disaster on their road, at Burlington. The report takes issue with the verdict of the Coroner's Jury, extols the Company's regulations, exculpates its servants in charge of the ill-fated train, throws the entire blame upon Dr. Heineken, and winds up with various reflections and suggestions. It is quite natural that the Company or its Executive Committee, should put the best face on the matter, on their own side; and they are entitled to be heard in their own defense. But there is little probability that the public will accept their conclusion or consider their defense complete [20, p. 785].

• Or the front page of the *Colburn's Railroad Advocate:*

But seriously,—here is a road, denying all responsibility to public opinion,— and which openly and daringly violates the very first and essential rules of safety,—killing two dozen or more human beings one day, and the next, recklessly and defiantly *backing* its trains at full speed,—without signal, without flagmen, without thought, without care. In fact, not two weeks after the first accident, there was another, and another death, and for the year, in addition to the Burlington deaths and injuries, there were another three deaths and four injuries [21, p. 3; 22, p. 196].

Why would this corporate report generate such negative responses? The cause of this unique response had to do with the company, its monopoly, and the company spokesman, Commodore Robert F. Stockton.

THE JOINT COMPANIES (THE CAMDEN AND AMBOY RAILROAD AND THE DELAWARE AND RARITAN CANAL) AND COMMODORE ROBERT F. STOCKTON

In the 1830s, when New Jersey was soliciting entrepreneurs to build railroads and canals across the state, the legislature authorized thirty years of monopoly rights for such entrepreneurs in exchange for shares in any railroads and canals built. Twenty years later, the exchange seemed much less favorable to the public, with the cost per mile on one of these roads with monopoly rights, the Camden and Amboy, averaging 63 percent more per mile than the average of all Northeast railroads [4, p. 343]. The profits of the Joint Companies (the Camden and Amboy Railroad and the Delaware and Raritan Canal) reaped by this higher average were so large that

... by 1840 the Combined Company was paying annual revenues to the state [of New Jersey] sufficient to take care of all the expenses of state government, and yet its profits were such that by that date $1,595,000 had been paid to the stockholders in dividends [23, p. 52; 24; 25, pp. 428-476].

By August 1855, the date of the accident, Commodore Robert F. Stockton, the President of the Delaware and Raritan Canal, a member of the Board of Directors

Figure 29. Commodore Robert F. Stockton—business entrepreneur
and political powerbroker.

of the Joint Companies, and its usual spokesman, had served with great distinction
in the War of 1812, the War with the Barbary Pirates, and the Mexican War.
In the latter, he was commander-in-chief of both civil and military operations
in California liberating it from Mexican forces in 1846–1847. In 1849, he
resigned his commission in the Navy and was elected senator from New Jersey
in 1852—the first career naval officer to sit in the Senate. His nomination for
president was repeatedly discussed by members of the Democratic Party and
was decided upon by the American Party in 1856 [4, p. 361; 26, Chapters 8–15;
27, pp. 38-39; 28, pp. 1-2].

Also with the resignation of his naval commission, Stockton took over more
day-to-day operations of the Joint Companies [26, p. 183]. Stockton probably

Figure 30. Camden and Amboy Railroad as pictured on
1834 stock certificate.

would have preferred to be shot at by enemy cannon than to endure the political
and economic controversies surrounding the Joint Companies. For, beginning
in 1848, a number of withering anti-monopoly pamphlets and newspaper articles
began to put pressure on the Joint Companies to break up their monopoly.

One author, the noted economist Henry C. Carey, who signed his pamphlets
with the nom de plume, "A Citizen of Burlington," wrote most of the newspapers
articles and letters that were later collected into pamphlets:

- *The Beauties of the Monopoly System of New Jersey* (1848)
- *Letters to the People of New Jersey, on the Frauds, Extortions, and Oppressions of the Railroad Monopoly* (1848) [29]
- *A Review of an Address of the Joint Board of the Delaware and Raritan Canal and Camden and Amboy Railroad Companies to the People of New Jersey* (1848)
- *Correspondence Between the Commissioners for Investigating the Affairs of the Joint Companies and a Citizen of Burlington* (1849)
- *Review of the Report of the Late Commissioners for Investigating the Affairs of the Joint Companies and a Citizen of Burlington* (1850)

Carey's work was the epitome of accountancy detail, using data from the financial reports provided by the Joint Companies to the state. His financial attacks on the monopoly of the Joint Companies, however, were not the only way he illustrated the problems of monopoly.

Customarily, a railroad would begin a line by building a single track, and then use the profits to build a double track allowing trains to freely go at their own rate and on their varied schedules in opposite directions. However, despite the large profits of the Joint Companies, as of 1853 no double track had been built. Not building such a double track was a very concrete, nonfinancial illustration that Carey used to show how the Camden and Amboy Railroad with its monopoly status was insulated from public demands and even from the normal developments of a railroad's infrastructure. The single track made delays inevitable when trains of different direction met, necessitating what Carey called a "railroad quadrille":

> First among them, we find a piece of very bad railroad from Camden to Amboy, sixty-two miles long, and but half made. It has one track only, but to make amends for this there are various turn-outs, also half made. The consequence of this, that when one train meets another there ensures a series of movements not unlike that of a quadrille. First we have that of "one lady forward and back." Next comes that of "one gentleman forward and back." After that comes "lady and gentleman back to back," and at last, after much delay, we read the final movement of "cross over and chassez." All this would be as amusing as it is ridiculous, occurring as it does on the most important part of the main line of communication throughout the Union, were it not that it is so often witnessed, unwillingly, by hundreds of people whose time might be elsewhere so much more profitable employed. The proverb says that time is money. Of the truth of this the Company is fully convinced. They consider their customers' time to be their money, and they act on the principle of giving the poorest machinery, that they make take the most time, and get the most money . . . [29, p. 8].

A single line was not only inconvenient, but it invited dangerous collisions; a fact Carey discovered when he himself was in a head-on collision on the road in August 1853 [30, p. 1].

By 1854, Carey and his pamphlets had proved so persuasive that the New Jersey Senate passed a resolution to inquire of the Camden and Amboy on what terms they would surrender their monopoly grant. Stockton himself answered them in his own signed pamphlet, *Answer of Robert F. Stockton in Behalf of the Joint Board of the D. & R. Canal and C. & A. R. R., Companies, to a Committee of the Senate of New Jersey, in Relation to Surrendering the Works of the Companies to the State* (1854).

In this pamphlet, the commodore, the senator, the hero of the Mexican War and, quite possibly, the richest and most powerful man in the state:

- First pointed out that the Camden and Amboy Railroad was not the only means of transportation in New Jersey; there were nine other railroads and canals. Thus, the Camden and Amboy did not have a monopoly of all New Jersey transportation, as critics charged.

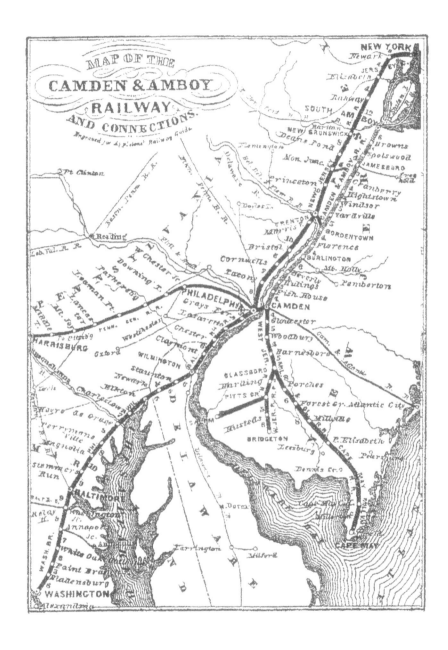

Figure 31. Map of Camden and Amboy Railway and connections [31].

- Moreover, the Camden and Amboy Railroad as part of this group of railroads and canals helped increase New Jersey's population, gave New Jersey revenues from transit duties, and increased the value of her land "to the highest in the Union" without the state incurring any debt in its creation; it was all created by entrepreneurs. Thus, the Joint Companies, be they monopoly or not, have aided rather than hindered the development of New Jersey.
- Stockton then conceded that there were safety problems on the Camden and Amboy Railroad, but these were due to the fact that the roads were originally designed for lighter and slower trains. The public, however, not the company, demanded increased speed, thus increasing the weight of engines with the resulting accidents. Stockton assured the public that the Joint Companies had heard their demands for some safety solutions. However, to improve the lines to handle these increased speeds and loads more safely required large expenditures, and these large funds were only available abroad at high interest rates. And although "ambitious demagogues" (like Carey) who attacked the company were exercising their free rights, such attacks did cause foreign investors to think twice about the stability of the company, and charge even higher rates of interest, thus hindering the company's ability to rectify the safety problems.
- However, if these points do not prove persuasive, and the state still requires that the Joint Companies surrender their monopoly status, then the Joint Companies are willing to comply and will sell out to the state at a fair market price. To aid the state in eventually purchasing the Joint Companies, the amount of money provided to the state by the Joint Companies appeared to be $75,000 more than is needed for the annual state budget, and, if these surplus funds were put aside and invested each year at 6 percent, after fifteen years they would yield the sum necessary to purchase the Joint Companies.
- In conclusion, Stockton suggested that to give the state more time to consider the purchase of the Joint Companies, to save up the necessary funds, and for the Joint Companies to add more miles of rails to reach western New Jersey, an extension, not surrender, of the monopoly was required.

A decade earlier, Stockton, using political leverage, had inserted into the New Jersey Constitution a debt ceiling of $100,000 for any single work or object [25, p. 449]. Thus, the offer by Stockton to sell the Joint Companies to the state that appeared so conciliatory was, in reality, an empty gesture once the debt ceiling was taken into account. His concluding request for the monopoly extension, clearly the opposite of what was desired by the popular uproar, Carey's pamphlets, and the Senate vote, was signed into law on March 16, 1854 [25, p. 470].

Some years before, Stockton reportedly had said that he "carried the State in his breeches's pocket, and meant to keep it there" [25, p. 468]. This tussle on the state level and with Carey had certainly shown that it remained in his breeches' pocket . . . but that did not mean that the New Jersey electorate would enjoy being kept there, and it probably meant that they would leap at any weakness displayed by the Joint Companies or Stockton. This August 1855 accident seemed to be the rallying point for just such retaliation. Thus, much more than the mere investigation of an accident would be communicated in the reports of the jury and company, for as the *American Railroad Journal* wrote:

> If public opinion and the dissatisfaction of the millions of travelers who have been obliged to resort to that miserable route, can have no effect,—it is hoped that a just and vigorous retaliation on their recklessness can at least move them to some caution in their future operations [32, p. 3].

THE CORONER'S JURY VERDICT

Five days after the accident, on September 4, the coroner's jury met in Burlington and began taking evidence. It met for over a week [8, p. 49], and then on September 5 offered the following verdict. First as to the proximate causes, the usual focus of attention of such juries, it noted:

> And the Jurors aforesaid, upon their oaths and affirmations aforesaid, do further say, that due diligence was not exercised by the driver of said horses.
> And the Jurors aforesaid, upon their oaths and affirmations aforesaid, do further say, that the Engineer of the said backing train did not observe the rules of said Camden and Amboy Railroad and Transportation Company, and the laws of the State of New Jersey, in reference to the blowing of the steam-whistle on the engine in approaching and crossing the said River Road.
> And the Jurors aforesaid, upon their oaths and affirmations aforesaid, do further say, that the Conductor of the backing train should be, and is exonerated from blame, inasmuch as he is found to have been acting in accordance with the instructions laid down in the "Running Regulations" of the Camden and Amboy and Branch Railroads, No. 3, the same having been issued to take effect on the twentieth day of August, A. D. one thousand eight hundred and fifty-five, and which regulations governed the running of trains of cars upon said Railroad, on the twenty-ninth day of August, eighteen hundred and fifty-five.
> And the Jurors aforesaid, upon their oaths and affirmations aforesaid, do further say, that the forward Brakeman on the said backing train is censurable.
> And the Jurors aforesaid, upon their oaths and affirmations aforesaid, do further say, that one of the immediate causes of the said collision, was the carelessness and recklessness of Dr. John Heineken driving his horses on the Railroad track, and attempting to cross the same in close proximity to a backing train of cars.
> And the Jurors aforesaid, upon their oaths and affirmations aforesaid, do further say, that another immediate cause of the said collision, was the carelessness and recklessness in which the said train of cars was proceeding backwards at a rate of speed unsafe and imprudent [9, pp. 4-5].

However, this jury then also moved to indict more remote causes of the accident:

And the Jurors aforesaid, upon their oaths and affirmations aforesaid, do further say, that, by the "Running Regulations" issued by the said Camden and Amboy Railroad and Transportation Company, the possibility and probability of collision between opposing trains on a single track, is so great, as to prove that some efficient means should be adopted to prevent the recurrence of the cause which has called this Inquest together, and that the safety of the passengers in life and limb, is of more importance than the saving of a few minutes of time.

And the Jurors aforesaid, upon their oaths and affirmations aforesaid, do further say, that as by the "Running Regulations" of the said Company, an Express train is permitted to leave one station when it is known by the Conductor thereof that an opposing Express train is on the road from the next station, such a regulation has been proved by the event of the twenty-ninth of August last, to be inconsistent with the safety of each of said trains, and the passengers and employees thereon [9, pp. 4-5].

The next day, the *American Railroad Journal* noted the unique features of the jury's report and saw the accident as "the commencement of a new sentiment on the part of the State":

We think the Jury should have found what is palpable to every one, that upon a road which is the main thoroughfare between two such cities as New York and Philadelphia, a road too which pays its stockholders from 12 to 16 per cent, annually, should have a *double* track. This would have rendered the accident impossible. It should have guards stationed at every crossing to shut out travelers on the approach of trains. It should cross no public highway upon a surface grade. But all these precautions were omitted, and by the awkward arrangements of the company to get along without a double track, the most reckless running was resorted to, and 22 persons killed outright, and 70 wounded, for which no more valid apology can be offered, than by a man firing into a crowd and claiming to be excused of murder, because he aimed at no one.

We hope this accident may mark the commencement of a new sentiment on the part of the State—that it will be the signal for a successful outbreak against a despotism which has so long held it enslaved. Some flagrant illustration of its evils was needed as a rallying point. If the spirit and temper of the people are not utterly broken, we shall date this accident as the commencement of a new era in their history; one In which a generous competition may be allowed to correct the abuses of railway management in which the burdens imposed upon the traveling public shall be only a fair equivalent for services rendered, and one in which the territory of the State shall be thrown open, a free, field for the development of what is the great characteristic and improvement of modern times, instead of selling this, with the right and capacity for future progress for a mess of pottage [33, pp. 570-571].

Thus, the findings of the jury were not only a legal judgment, but they also signified a "rallying point" "for a successful outbreak against a despotism which has so long held" New Jersey "enslaved." Kind in mind that the word "enslaved" in 1855 was not used lightly, given the "peculiar institution" that was even then ripping the nation apart. Five days later, September 10, the Executive Committee of the Joint Companies issued its accident investigation report, signed by Commodore Stockton.

THE JOINT COMPANIES TRY TO EXONERATE THEIR ACTIONS BUT MEET WITH DISDAIN

The accident and the public outcry could not have happened at a worse time for Stockton. His national ambitions for the presidency were, at that very moment, precarious. An impromptu speech of his had been twisted and "strangely tortured, or rather caricatured, so as to make it as offensive as possible to his political friends" [26, p. 202]. The reports of these remarks, true or not, cost him the Democratic Party nomination and could cost him the nomination of the breakaway American Party that would meet later that fall. Stockton quickly needed damage control. Thus, the report was published only a week after the coroner's report.

In the report, the Companies first reviewed the facts of the case, pointing out the effectiveness of Companies's regulations and operators to rebut the coroner's jury's findings concerning the proximate causes of the accident. The report also pointed out the impossibility of preventing carriages and horses from entering onto the tracks. Thus, in answer to the jury's criticism of the Companies's rules, the report demonstrated that the rules were effective and followed by personnel.

With this counter-coroner jury version of the accident established, the report proceeded to undermine the creditability of the coroner's jury itself. Stockton and the Executive Board of the Joint Companies suggested the jury ignored evidence that

- exonerated the engineer's actions in his blowing of the whistle;
- the watch of the brakeman, conductor, and engineer was properly fixed on the tracks;
- the speed backing up was the same that had been used for going forward over the same track minutes earlier; and
- the Companies's regulations are proper and safety-conscious.

In fact, the report assigned proximate and remote blame for the accident to the driver of the horses, Dr. Heineken, suggesting: "Had he been at home, there would have been no accident" [9, p. 9]. Thus for the first three and half pages out of a total of five, the Companies's report explicitly sought to protect them against liability for the accident without any pretense of scientific objectivity [34].

In the last page and a half, the Joint Companies' report left the specifics of this accident and responded directly to what the sermons, newspapers, and the professional press had indicted as the root cause of the accident, the single-track aspect of its system. The company defended its single-track system by claiming to be unfairly singled out for such criticism: ". . . we are not aware that there is any railroad in this country which is so exclusively appropriated for the carriage of passengers as this road is, that has a double track" [9, p. 9].

Moreover, the reason why the Joint Company's pledge of the previous year to build a second track had not been carried out was because of the depressed market for selling railroad securities aboard—a problem already stated by Stockton in his 1854 pamphlet. Finally, the Joint Companies's report questioned the need for a double track because such a track might make the "temptation to maintain high speed almost irresistible" [9, p. 10].

In his 1854 pamphlet, Stockton had included a *peroratio* that had turned the tables on his audience, which had been clamoring to break up the monopoly of the Joint Companies; he had asked for an extension of the monopoly and, in time, received it. In this 1855 company investigation report, Stockton used the same tactic. For an audience clearly wanting more restrictions on the Joint Companies, Stockton and the Board concluded by suggesting that the real way to ensure safety on the railroad was to give railroads more support and protection from liability suits:

> We would suggest, however, that the best means to obtain the desired safety, would be to alter the whole system of hostile legislation in regard to railroads; to consider them as useful public conveniences entitled to the liberal support and just consideration of the people, and to that protection from the courts and juries which every American freeman has a right to claim; not as nuisances to be reviled without measure and to be libeled and persecuted on all occasions, right or wrong; to make them exclusive; to fence them in from one end to the other; to take the public roads under or over them; to reduce the speed of the trains to twenty-five miles per hour, and to hold all persons trespassers, who without authority from the Company go on the road or suffer their cattle to go on it [8, p. 54; 9, p. 10].

Stockton's report stirred up a series of responses, many of which we have already seen. The bottom line was that "there is little probability that the public will accept their conclusion, or consider their defense complete" [35, p. 1].

The front page of the *American Railroad Journal* two months after the release of the report had the following harsh reaction:

> We have been in hopes, and we believe it has been general expectation, that the recent dreadful accident on this road would lead to a change in the policy, by which the company has been governed, and to such reforms and improvements in the management of the road, as would secure to this greatest thoroughfare in the United States, and probably in the world, that degree of safety, comfort, and speed, with rates of charges, which, from the vast

patronage it receives, the public have a right to demand. This expectation is, we fear, likely to be disappointed. With the exception of a few churlish utterances, which could not be well suppressed in the universal burst of indignation which overwhelmed them, we see nothing in the action of the company to lead us to suppose that any change for the better is to be hoped. A company, whose policy for the past twenty years has been a subject of general execration, must be callous to any public appeals and have lost that ambition and desire to please which lies at the foundation of efficient management and courteous demeanor. Their policy has degenerated into a mere lust for money [20, p. 785].

Bear in mind that it was not inevitable that the Joint Companies' report would find this kind of reception from this journal. The same journal, two weeks earlier, had accepted an investigation report from the directors of the Pacific Railroad on an accident with a larger loss of life (the subject of Chapter 5) without editorial qualification or criticism [36, p. 760]. The difference in the responses from the journal may have arisen because Stockton defended his road's action, all members of his staff, and asked for further concessions from the state. No apologies were given. In contrast, the Pacific Railroad directors concluded that their engineer had approached the bridge at too high a rate of speed for its temporary nature. Moreover, where the Pacific Railroad report included a critical minority report, and, in this minority report, blame for the accident went beyond the proximate cause involving the individual engineer to those remote causes including the construction process used on the bridge, and the Pacific Railroad's management. In essence, the Pacific Railroad report cast a critical eye on its own actions, and the professional press accepted its report as the Report of Record. Stockton and the Board of the Joint Companies had not, on the other hand, taken a critical eye toward their actions, and thus the jury and the press . . . and the Franklin Institute felt obliged to do it for them.

THE FRANKLIN INSTITUTE SCIENTISTS
OFFER A SERMON, NOT SCIENCE

Scientists from the Franklin Institute joined the fray in November of 1855, just weeks after the Joint Companies's report was published [37, pp. 347-351]. That November issue of the *Journal of the Franklin Institute* first reprinted the Companies's report and then the institute's response. It is interesting that whereas the company report was subsumed by defending the company against liability, criticism of the Joint Companies' operations, and soliciting aid and protection from the state, this "disinterested" external report noted:

> . . . it is not our intention to dwell upon anything which relates merely to the disaster itself; that is past, and if retribution is to be exacted, it must be in due course of law, which we have no desire to forestall by prejudging the case either to condemnation or acquittal of any one concerned. Nor shall

we dwell upon the tone of the report in question, which has been complained of as cold and unfeeling: but we desire to advert to parts of it, in which opinions are expressed as to the possibility of lessening the liability to accidents upon this and other roads, and the means to be used for such a purpose [37, p. 347].

In their report, the scientists at the Franklin Institute take as "given" the facts contained in the Joint Companies' investigation report, appearing immediately before their own, and probe the Joint Companies' conclusions on the basis of logic and the experience of other roads. The Franklin Institute report did not use any independent research, but rather proceeded very much like a rebuttal in following the order of presentation of the Joint Companies's report, and rebutting seven specific points:

- The Joint Companies's rules regarding the need to give way on the single track and for keeping on schedule is theoretically good, but, for a company infamous for its inability to adhere to its own schedule, it's not practical for the Camden and Amboy. In order to best handle trains that may not always be on schedule, the use of the telegraph is strongly urged as a means of maintaining right of way [38].
- Company regulations permitting a speed rate of 15 mph for backing-up on the tracks ignore the problems accompanying such rearward movement that have occasioned other companies to set limits at 6 mph.
- Company regulations should require engineers or brakeman to look left or right and not just directly backward along the track. They should be especially wary of oncoming traffic at road-level crossings.

> But when the Committee go on to exclaim, "how impossible is it to devise means for the protection of railroad trains from so sudden and unforeseen destruction!" we must reply, "No, gentlemen," there is a very simple and effectual way of fully guarding against the possibility of every such disaster—a way, which has been tested by experience in countries where it is considered the duty of government to take human life under its protection, and should be required of you, and of all railroads running through thickly populated sections of country—it consists in passing all roads over the railroad by means of properly elevated bridges. This method would not be very expensive, certainly not too much so in view of the end to be attained; it would be, as it has always been found, effectual, and it ought to be adopted by all railroads: or, if not willingly, then they should be compelled to adopt it by law. Until this is done, we agree with the Committee, "the safety of the trains can best be secured by requiring all persons before crossing a railroad, to stop and ascertain whether the road is clear" [37, p. 348].

- The Joint Companies were critical of being required to install double tracks because they claimed double tracks will not alleviate the problem of backing. The Joint Companies claimed it will continue, but the Institute Committee found that very curious and was sure that such backing on double tracks would be highly unusual.

- The Joint Companies were critical of being required to install double tracks because double tracks would greatly increase the number of switches for the railroad, thus raising construction costs. Again, the Institute Committee found that very curious, and was sure that the number of switches on double tracks would decrease in number.
- The Joint Companies were critical of being required to install double tracks because double tracks were not economical. The Institute Committee conceded that most lines begin with single line tracks and then use the profits from that track to build a double track line, since "reason and experience" suggest that double tracks will last longest for lines having traffic in two directions.
- As to suggesting that the liability laws should be changed to further protect the company, it is true that such legal changes will help prevent some classes of accident:

> The second is the most fertile source of accident, and will remain so, so long as the farmers will allow their cattle to have access to the railroad track, and so long as our people are not reckless in the manner in which they pass on, to, and across it. After obstacles are guarded against as far as possible by fencing the road and passing all other roads across at a different level, we fully agree with the report, that the means of remedying the danger "would be to alter the whole system hostile legislation, &c." So long as a farmer could claim damages for the loss of a cow which must have been on the track by his own fault or negligence, or an individual who has been injured by placing himself in a danger of which he must be aware, could get a verdict against a railroad, whose servants could not, by any possibility, avoid the accident, there can be no hope of any important reduction in this class of accidents; but this state of things we trust is now an end, and we hope soon to see all the courts in the land join to make the individuals in question responsible to the extent of their abilities, for the actual or possible damage in such cases to the train [37, p. 350].
> However, the collision between two trains going in opposite directions would not be resolved by any legal changes and is best solved by a double track system [37, p. 35].

Thus, the Franklin Institute Committee looked at more systemic problems in the Companies's regulations and its use of a single-track system, and used logic and experience. It is interesting to observe the tone of address sometimes used by the Franklin Institute Committee in its rebuttal, e.g., "we must reply, 'No, gentlemen,'" suggests it is much more of a rebuttal sermon than a disinterested scientific one. And, as already noted, such phrases as "the late fearful and deplorable accident which has furnished the text of these remarks" suggest that the Franklin Institute considered itself to be writing something like a sermon with all the attendant polemics and rhetorical flourishes.

The "late fearful and deplorable accident" also "furnished the text" for a series of letters published in the local papers from a minister in the town of the accident, Burlington. This wasn't an ordinary minister, though, but one of the national leaders of the Presbyterian Church in America, as well as a long-time colleague of Stockton in the African Colonization Society. This argument between Stockton and The Rev. Dr. Cortlandt Van Rensselaer was again combative rather than disinterested [39, p. 34].

THE STOCKTON-VAN RENSSELAER CONTROVERSY

Stockton did not reply to the harsh criticism of the Franklin Institute sermon, nor did he reply to the inflammatory editorials of the *New York Herald* printed under headlines such as "The Slaughter on the Camden and Amboy Railroad" (9/1/1855); "The Value of Life in New Jersey as Shown by the Late Railroad Accident" (9/3/1855, p. 4); "The Camden and Amboy Homicide" (9/7/1855, p. 4); and "The Tender Mercies of the Camden and Amboy Railroad" (9/18/1855, p. 4). Nor did Stockton enter into a literary duel with Henry C. Carey whose half dozen critical pamphlets had bedeviled Stockton five years earlier [6, p. 165; 40].

However, Stockton and Van Rensselaer knew each other [6, pp. 66, 174; 41; 42; 43; 44, p. 95; 45]. Both were supporters of Princeton University and its seminary, residing but a few miles away, in the case of Rensselaer, and directly across the street, in Stockton's. Cortlandt's cousin, Robert Schuyler Van Rensselaer, was superintendent of the Camden and Amboy railroad at this time and became general superintendent after the Civil War. Both Stockton and Van Rensselaer were great admirers of Daniel Webster, and, in his 1852 *Eulogy on Daniel Webster,* three years before this combative newspaper dialogue, Van Rensselaer had even called Stockton a "high-soul-ed Senator":

> Our own honored Richard Stockton [Robert's father], too, was his intimate, personal friend; and the equally distinguished son, New Jersey's high-soul-ed Senator in Congress [a reference to Commodore Stockton] [46, p. 3].

Moreover, they were not just mutual admirers of Webster's; they also shared a number of Webster's values:

1. Belief in the innate goodness of technological improvements [47, 48]. Webster wrote:

> It is an extraordinary era in which we live. It is altogether new. The world has seen nothing like it before. I will not pretend, to discern the end; but for scientific research into the heavens, the earth, and what is beneath the earth; and perhaps more remarkable still for the application of this scientific research to the pursuits of life [49].

Figure 32. The Rev. Dr. Cortlandt Van Rensselaer.

Van Rensselaer echoed this observation when he wrote in *Signals from the Atlantic Cable. An Address delivered at the Telegraphic Celebration:*

> Fellow-citizens of Burlington, it is becoming to the dignity of this ancient city, and to its educational and industrial spirit, to unite with other cities in this and in distant lands, in celebrating the successful laying of the Atlantic Telegraph. This is one of those leading happy events in human history, which, when it occurs first, anticipates the emotions and honors of future triumphs of the same kind. Now is the time and the hour! Our celebration, on the appointed day, brings us into heartfelt connection with the general joy and praise; and the

telegraphic poles of Burlington exchange signals with the wires on Albion's cliffs, and return the festival dashes, which pulse with the power of life, from our commercial metropolis to the outstretched boundaries of this great Republic [50].

Stockton also echoed Webster's sentiments when he explained why he invested so much money in the Delaware and Raritan Canal:

> I was importuned for aid. I was assured that if the canal failed now it was lost forever; and, deeming the canal of infinite importance to the State and the nation, I subscribed the balance of the stock necessary to preserve the charter, amounting to over four hundred thousand dollars [51, p. 2].

2. Strong opposition to slavery and hopes for colonization in Africa [47, 48, 52, 53]. In the American Society for Colonizing the Free People of Color of the United States, Webster was listed as one of the founders and as a vice president of the national society, along with Van Rensselaer, from 1841 [54] until Webster's death in 1852, at which time Stockton was elected a vice president of the society. Both Stockton and Van Rensselaer were vice presidents of the national society from 1852 until 1860, when Van Rensselaer died [55]. Moreover, Stockton had helped to obtain the lands that became Liberia [4, p. 332; 23, pp. 59-60; 56, p. 165], and, in 1825, he helped establish the New Jersey branch of the organization, becoming its manager in 1838.

What they did not share, however, was the sense of corporate liability for accidents, and knowing each other drew passions that none of the Carey-Stockton encounters ever did [57].

Van Rensselaer first published a pamphlet, "Review of the Camden and Amboy Company's Report" [58], a closely reasoned rebuttal to Stockton's report, and signed it "A Burlingtonian," quite similar to Carey's pseudonymous signature in his pamphlets, "A Citizen of Burlington." In fact the pseudonyms were so similar, and the object of their criticisms so parallel, that to this day, libraries mistakenly attribute Van Rensselaer's review to Carey. Perhaps Stockton did so too when he first read it, and the bloody stripes he had endured for years from Carey's pen may have contributed to the vehemence with which Stockton responded.

Van Rensselaer's "Review of the Camden and Amboy Company's Report" began by examining three systemic management problems of the Camden and Raritan that led to the accident:

- A single-track system with express trains [58, p. 4].
- Conductors failing to wait until the train in the opposite direction actually arrives, rather than strictly adhering to a printed time schedule [58, p. 4].
- Going backwards at 15 mph [58, p. 6].

Once these three systemic management problems were addressed, Van Rensselaer commented on some specific points of defense offered by the company in its report, using testimony drawn from the coroner's jury.

However, in the midst of this careful, logical critique, Rensselaer added parenthetical combative comments, such as:

> Twenty-four human beings were killed, and from eighty to a hundred were more or less severely wounded, under circumstances of great aggravation; and yet all is passed by without a syllable of kindly notice or commiseration. Even an Indian could scarcely have been trained to such unnatural indifference. This painful feature of the Report, which will be remembered against the Company, at least during the present generation, can scarcely be accounted for except on the maxim that "Corporations have no souls"—a maxim recognized only at law [58, p. 3; 59; 60, pp. 54-55].

> These suggestions in regard to the defective management of this great railroad will, I doubt not, commend themselves to the great mass of intelligent and observing persons. The Amboy Company, however, show in their late Report a tenacity of preconceived rules, and an obstinacy of opinion, rarely to be encountered. . . . Oh, gentlemen, do you point in proof the wisdom of your rules, to your bleeding and dying victims? Do you add insult to injury and mockery to massacre? So it seems to me well that corporations have no souls, if such are their specimens of rationality and evidences of existence [58, p. 7].

At this, Stockton lashed out with his retort magnified by the wounds he had endured from all the other critics in this case. His open letters and Cortlandt Van Rensselaer's responses were printed in the *Public Ledger and Daily Transcript* [61]. Some of the emotional aspects of Stockton's first letter on October 11 included:

> The assassin of character as well as of life "loves darkness rather than light," and as your designs were incompatible with the character and propriety of a Christian gentleman and minister, you have, in some measure, properly assumed the anonymous mask, rather than disgrace a time-honored ancestry by affixing your name to a production replete with slander and misrepresentation. You ought to have known, however, in perpetrating so unusual an outrage upon others, that your clandestine disguise would be torn away, and that your name and clerical character would be revealed [9, p. 23].

> . . .

> Your pamphlet seems likewise to indicate that you are on the popular side, in your labors to criminate the Companies; and that notoriety is another object of your most unexpected and puerile attack. I am not at all indisposed to aid your itching in this way; and, whilst I have no intention, at present, of replying to the various perversions of facts and special pleadings of your publication, [9, p. 23].

> . . .

But before I proceed to do even that, I may be permitted to say that I am not aware of any particular qualification possessed by the clergy, which enables them to instruct railroad companies with regard to the construction and management of railroads. Where have you, reverend sir, obtained that information which justifies your setting up your *ipse dixit* against the experience and knowledge of those who have devoted the best part of their lives to the consideration of railroad subjects? If it belongs to your professional duties to give instruction on those subjects, I must be permitted to express the hope that the General Assembly of your Church will assign that duty to someone who can perform it with better temper, more wisdom and discretion, and in a more Christian spirit.

You make it a matter of enormous crime that, in the Report of the Executive Committee, "sympathy is not expressed for the unfortunate sufferers." You call it a *"painful feature"* of the Report; *"unnatural indifference,"* and multiply epithets of reproach for this omission. . . . You, sir, who make this accusation, are a professional sympathizer general; it may he natural, therefore, for you to insist on its public and ostentatious manifestation on all occasions, without regard to the proprieties of time and place. And it ought, perhaps, to be considered as equally natural for you to magnify your own merit as a sympathizer, by contrasting your profuseness in that particular, with the deficiency of others [9, pp. 23-24].

. . .

And now, reverend sir, in conclusion, permit me to hope that this letter may not be considered "arrogant or defiant" [9, p. 24].

Five days latter, Van Rensselaer wrote a signed response that also joined in Stockton's combative tones:

. . . The only difficulty I have in answering it is that of engaging in a controversy with a person who seems to be so unscrupulous an adversary [9, p. 25].

. . .

If the Company's Report was a blunder of the brains, the Commodore's Letter is a blunder of the passions, So far as relates to its various epithets and insinuations, freely used in a rough, marine, and thoughtless manner, it might be allowed to pass off with its own noise [9, p. 25].

. . .

The personal abuse you have seen fit to lavish upon me, can do no harm. If your reputation can bear giving the abuse, I venture to hope that mine can bear taking it . . . [9, p. 25].

. . .

You conclude with expressing the hope that your letter "may not be considered arrogant or defiant." No, Commodore; it is too humiliating to be "arrogant," and too harmless "to be defiant" [9, p. 28].

The next day, Stockton published in the paper:

> In writing to a person so industrious in hunting up falsehoods, and attributing bad motives, it seems to be proper that I should make this additional remark—I have an habitual respect for all clergymen whose practice corresponds with their profession. It is not the clergy that I write against, it is only those who violate the sanctity of their office, by making it instrumental in casting unjust odium upon their fellow-citizens [9, p. 29].

To which Van Rensselaer replied two days later:

> . . .

> You are among the last men, sir, who ought to complain before the public of severe language from an opponent. You appear to be unable to appreciate the difference between calling hard names, and dealing in hard things. Whilst abuse glances off into the air, keen truth pierces to the bones. I am not belligerent, believe me, sir; although, perhaps you may think me like the non-combative Quaker, who was opposed to taking life, but who thought it no great harm to let a considerable stick of timber fall on the head of his adversary [9, p. 29].

> . . .

> Sir, your Company is in a most serious position at the present time. They have incurred already the condemnation of two juries, one of whom has indicted an engineer for the crime of manslaughter. The decisions of other juries will follow; and, if the facts of the case are weighed with the same care that they have been by Burlington County juries, the Company will begin to learn wisdom. In fact, all the railroads in the country are suffering, in various incidental ways, from the bad management of the New Jersey single track. People are beginning to get afraid to invest their funds in railroads, or to ride on them, or to be associated in their directorship, especially when public developments are impressing upon them the conviction that the chief managers of some companies are destitute of the common sense and practical skill which are the only basis of confidence [9, p. 30].

> . . .

> The object of your coming before the public is sufficiently discerned. It was undoubtedly for the purpose of affecting an escape, if possible, from the condemnation incurred by issuing the unfeeling Report of September 10th. Like the Russian General, Gortschakoff, who, in order to avoid pursuit and capture, went to work *springing mines,* so the Commodore has sought to make a noise, in the vain hope of drawing off the attention of a watchful public [9, p. 30].

An unpublished biography of Stockton was titled, "Fighting Bob: The Life and Exploits of Commodore Robert Field Stockton, United States Navy." The nickname "Fighting Bob" has been variously attributed to Stockton's martial actions aboard the *President* in the War of 1812 [62, p. 79], as well as to his propensity to challenge British officers to duels in defense of his country's honor when he was stationed in the Mediterranean [6, pp. 38-41; 23, p. 56; 44, p. 108; 63]. His acquaintances acknowledged that he had an "imperious temper," and that he was "proud, impetuous, headstrong, frank, and sincere" [6, p. 167; 44, p. 108; 63]. A biographer called him "the navy's problem child" [44, p. 88]. Yet the nickname could just have easily been awarded for this combative exchange of letters with Cortlandt Van Rensselaer—the natural outcome of an investigation without the "disinterestedness" of science in the conversation.

IN THE END

After all the rhetorical sound and fury, nothing was accomplished; everyone vehemently declared their feelings and never changed. It is true that the stock of the road fell off quite rapidly after the accident [20, p. 785]. However, no one was found guilty in a court of law, no money was given to victims, and, worst of all, the single-track system of the Camden and Amboy was not corrected for another decade. With justice unavailable in the political or judicial system of New Jersey, *Colburn's Railroad Advocate* spoke of hopes for satisfaction to be gained with national intervention:

> If there is any hope, it is in the action of Congress. That body might authorize a post route through the state of Stevens, Stockton & Co., and thereby give the country the means of safe and decent communication between the two greatest cities of the western continent [64, p. 2].

During the Civil War, when the Camden and Amboy single track proved a bottleneck to the movement of troops and the goods of war, Congress did indeed try this maneuver, but it was unsuccessful [65, p. 1; 66-70].

Sadly, the accidents on this line also continued. Not two months after the accident, *Colburn's Railroad Advocate* had this piece on the Camden and Amboy, which sounded remarkably like Carey's quadrille criticism seven years earlier:

> Camden and Amboy Amusements.

> It has become a standard diversion on the Camden and Amboy line to see at how fast a rate the trains may be driven *backwards*. A few evenings since, the Belvedere train was being made to contribute in this manner to the amusement of the engineer and conductor, when a little circumstance occurred which doubtless heightened the interest of the performance, and which will of course lead to renewed devotion to that innocent and exhilarating sport. The skipper of a schooner, on the canal alongside, had put his jib boom across the track,—intending no doubt to make a comfortable perch for the owl train,— when the Belvedere train, as above mentioned, tripped over the obstruction and went sprawling over the sleepers,—narrowly escaping a plunge, with all its passengers, into the canal. The rear car, no doubt, made an interesting wreck,—its ends broken in, seats thrown into confusion, the passengers more

or less bruised,—besides the agreeable excitement due to the recollection of a recent event, occurring under nearly the same circumstances, at a place called *Burlington.*

The able managers, assisted probably by the master mechanic of the road, have with great effort given to the world, a contrivance which promises to do away with all future "accidents," besides furnishing a rich musical enter-tainment for passengers. We have not seen it, but we have *heard it.* Its name was not announced to us, but we should say it would be called a patent *Heineken frightener, owl-signal and harum scarum.* It appears to be an asthmatic steam whistle, worked by an eccentric on the driving axle making with each revolution a distressing hoot, and, at 30 miles an hour, a din similar to the uproar of a Chinese musical convention, or of an owl serenade. We had the satisfaction, the other day, of listening to this choice entertainment between Bordentown and New Brunswick. Of course we felt *safe* with *such* a protection.

But seriously,—here is a road, denying all responsibility to public opinion,—and which openly and daringly violates the very first and essential rules of safety,—killing two dozen or more human beings one day, and the next, recklessly and defiantly *backing* its trains at full speed,—without signal, without flagmen, without thought, with care.

Think one moment what it is to back a train. With every foot of rail passed over in going forward, the train loses *all right* to that part of the road, The switchman can put his switch wrong, the track gang can take out a rail, a gravel or freight train can come out of a turnout,—*anything* can be done to the track, avoiding only all trains *following* the first.

The moment a train commences backing, it loses all the protection of the police of the road,—all claim upon the lookout or care of any one else upon the line,—it is bound to take care of itself and cannot safely *move* without having a man out, 300 yards on each side. What then is to be thought of a company which allows its trains to be backed at any point at 30 miles an hour?

What is to be thought of a body of railroad managers with the blood of 28 human beings fresh upon their hands,—who will trifle with themselves, the public and common sense, with such a contemptible abortion as the perpetual hooting apparatus just noticed? Surely these men have adopted public opinion and hoot themselves from one end of their road to the other [21, p. 3].

Commodore Stockton died in 1866, and, when his line was leased to the Pennsylvania Railroad Company in 1871, the line died too. But, as evidenced by the bitterness and acrimony between the Companies and their critics and the coroner's jury, the combative methods of assigning blame offered no relief to any party.

ENDNOTES

1. *Brooklyn Eagle,* November 15, 1852, p. 1.
2. *Harper's New Monthly Magazine,* 12 (68), January 1856.
3. Robert B. Shaw, *A History of Railroad Accidents, Safety Precautions and Operating Practices,* Binghamton, N.Y.: Vail-Ballou Press, Inc., 1978.

4. Wheaton J. Lane, *From Indian Trail to Iron Horse: Travel and Transportation in New Jersey, 1620–1860*, Princeton N.J.: Princeton University Press, 1939.
5. Descriptions of these five separate accidents can be found in the *Brooklyn Eagle*.
6. Alfred H. Bill, "Fighting Bob: The Life and Exploits of Commodore Robert Field Stockton, United States Navy." Unpublished manuscript, Princeton University Library: AM 18536, CO144, Folder 21.
7. *The New York Times*, August 11, 1853, pp. 1, 4; August 12, pp. 1, 4; August 13, p. 3; and September 13, p. 4.
8. Donald R. Sinclair, "Railroad Accident at Burlington in 1855," *The Journal of the Rutgers University Library*, 10 (2), June 1947.
9. *Hear Both Sides: Documents and Papers Related to the Late Camden and Amboy Railroad Accident, at Burlington, NJ.* Philadelphia, Penna.: Joseph M. Wilson, 1855.
10. Thomas C. Cochran, *Railroad Leaders: 1845-1890—The Business Mind in Action.* Cambridge, Mass.: Harvard University Press, 1953. Sadly, there is some precedence and logic to this, in that company executives were afraid that compensating those injured would establish precedents for the assumption of liability. Six years after the Burlington accident, the president of the Michigan Central, Henry Ledyard, responded to calls to aid a boy who had lost two legs in an accident with the following: "Our legal officers . . . advised that no liability whatever can rest against this company. While regretting the sad circumstances of this accident. . . . I cannot see my way clear to authorize compliance with your request" p. 207.
11. Compare the harsh tone of this report to that responding to Lardner's, which attributed the explosion to a lightning strike even though there has been no record in all of science history to support such a claim. However, rather than harshly correct Lardner, note how the following in the use of passive voice and self-deprecation make the criticism of Lardner's conclusion quite gentle: "In the first accounts of this explosion much stress was laid upon the fact of its having occurred during a thunderstorm, and the agency in the accident has been attributed to electricity; but in what manner it may be conceived to have acted; whether by heating the boiler or the steam, within it, or in what other way, it increased the tension, of the steam or diminished the strength of the material, the committee cannot conjecture. If there are any experiments, or observations, on record, tending to show the power of electricity to produce such effects in a good continuous conductor, as a locomotive engine, running too be it observed, upon a wet rail, the committee are in ignorance of them; and, independently, of this, the evidence to the contrary is as plain as could be desired" [12, p. 29].
12. Robert Frazer, "Explosion of the Locomotive Engine *Richmond*," *Journal of the Franklin Institute*, 3 Series (9), January 1845.
13. Thomas Ewbank *Journal of the Franklin Institute*, 13, 1834. Or consider Ewbanks's opening line to his criticism of the *New England* report in the first chapter: "Although the explosion of these boilers is, as I believe, justly attributed to an excessive pressure of steam, there is room to suppose that one remote source of the calamity may be found in the inferior quality of a portion of the copper of which they were formed" [p. 289].
14. "Short Notices," *Princeton Review*, 27 (4), October 1855, which used the religious texts of the Hindu Vedas as "furnishing the text."
15. "Mrs. Abigail Adams," *Ladies Repository*, 4 (1), July 1876. Abigail is said to "furnish the text for a sermon."

16. In the *Teacher's Institute* (1867), a letter is said to "furnish the text" for a lesson about evils in school discipline.
17. *The 4 Gospels* (1872), *Theology of the New Testament* (1871) and in *Christian Pamphlets* (1868).
18. H. A. Boardman, *God's Providence in Accidents*, Philadelphia, Penna.: Parry McMilliam, 1855.
19. *Public Ledger and Daily Transcript*, 9/24/1855. Cited in [9, p. 21].
20. "Camden and Amboy Railroad," *American Railroad Journal*, Second series, 11 (50), December 15, 1855.
21. "Camden and Amboy Amusements," *Colburn's Railroad Advocate*, October 13, 1855.
22. "Camden and Amboy Annual Accounting," *American Railroad Journal*, 1041 (29), March 29, 1856.
23. Glenn W. Price, *Origins of the War with Mexico: The Polk-Stockton Intrigue*, Austin, Texas: University of Texas Press, 1967.
24. This profitability continued over the next decade so that Stockton could point out that in 1853, the annual expenses of New Jersey government amount to $90,000 and the payment from the company had been $91,000.
25. M. K. Medbery, "The New Jersey Monopolies," *North American Review*, 104 (2), April 1867. "As New Jersey was already an owner of a thousand shares in the Camden and Amboy Railroad by a provision of the charter of the company, she would thus be in possession of two thousand shares of stock without the payment of a single mill. But the companies were ready to be even more liberal. If the State would insure them against all danger of competition, they would pledge themselves to pay into the treasury an annual revenue of not less than thirty thousand dollars, in transit dues and dividends, from the day the works were completed" (p. 439).
26. Samuel John Bayard, *A Sketch of the Life of Commodore Robert F. Stockton*, New York: Derby & Jackson, 1856. In fact, Bayard's book, published in 1856 just in time for the American Party convention, was standard political laudatory biography fare of the time. Bayard himself was Stockton's cousin, close friend, and political writer in his camp.
27. *New Jersey Books: 1801-1860—The Joseph J. Felcone Collection*, Princeton, N.J.: Joseph Felcone, 1996.
28. *The New York Times*, 5 (1509), June 17, 1856.
29. Henry C. Carey, *Letters to the People of New Jersey, on the Frauds, Extortions, and Oppressions of the Railroad Monopoly.* Philadelphia, Penna.: Carey and Hart, 1848.
30. *The New York Times*, August 11, 1853.
31. J. A. Anderson, Library of Congress railroad map, 256.
32. "The Camden and Amboy Affair," *American Railroad Journal*, September 15, 1855.
33. "The Calamity on the Camden and Amboy Railroad," *American Railroad Journal*, 1012 (28), September 5, 1855.
34. For example, the Silliman/Redfield/Olmsted report only suggested that the copper boiler was improperly constructed, and Lardner emphasized that lightning caused the explosion in Reading, not that Norris Brothers' workmanship and materials were all proper.
35. "The Camden and Amboy Disaster," *American Railroad Times*, 7 (42), October 18, 1855.

36. "The Pacific Railroad Catastrophe," *American Railroad Journal,* Second series, 11 (48), December 1, 1855.
37. "Railroad Accidents," *Journal of the Franklin Institute,* 30 (5), November 1855, pp. 347-351. The Companies's report is printed in total in this issue just before the critique. It is unclear if this was the specific work of the Committee of Science and the Arts, since the report on the Camden and Amboy Railroad is not listed in either Percy A. Bivins's *Index to the Reports of the Committee on Science and the Arts of the Franklin Institute, 1834-1890,* Philadelphia, Penna.: Franklin Institute, 1890 nor in A. Michael McMahon and Stephanie Morris, *Technology in Industrial America,* Wilmington, Del.: Scholarly Resources, 1977.
38. It is interesting that in Chapter 6, which examines the Revere accident in 1871, the failure to use the telegraph to maintain safe order on a railroad was a main reason for the accident.
39. *An historical discourse on the occasion of the centennial celebration of the Battle of Lake George, 1775,* Philadelphia, Penna.: C. Sherman & Son, print., 1856. It is interesting that two days before the company produced its report on the accident, on September 8, Cortlandt was at Lake George giving a speech on the history of the battle of Lake George.
40. Stockton was not totally unemotional in his retorts to Carey, for he did call him and his compatriots "socialists, speculators and demagogues."
41. "Puseyism or Newmania, Exhibited from the Diverse Writings of Bishop Doane," Burlington, N.J.: J. L. Powell, 1843.
42. Cortland Van Rensselaer, "The Apostasy of Mr. Newman, and Some Traces of Newmania on New Jersey Soil," Burlington, N.J.: J. L. Powell, 1845.
43. One possible source of friction that is quite apart from railroads, Webster, or the anti-slave movement, had to do with their diametrically opposed feelings on the effects of the Oxford Movement (a.k.a. puseyism or the High Church or Anglo Catholic movement) in America. As a reformed Presbyterian, Van Rensselaer was opposed to such popist influences and wrote a highly critical piece [41, 42]. Stockton, on the other hand, as a founder and vestry member of Trinity church (Episcopal) in Princeton, was a friend and frequent correspondent of Bishop Doane, and, helped to later redesign the church from a pulpit-centered design to an altar-centered design—an architectural effect of the Oxford Movement.
44. Alfred H. Bill, *A House Called Morven: Its Role in American History,* Princeton, N.J.: Princeton University Press, 1954.
45. The Rev. Dr. Cortlandt Van Rensselaer, "The Late Camden and Amboy Railroad Accident: A Review of the Camden and Amboy Company's Report," in [9, p. 11] "Personally acquainted with all the gentlemen, who sign this Report [the Company's Executive Board report], except two, and well acquainted with some of them. . . ."
46. The Rev. Dr. Cortlandt Van Rensselaer, *Eulogy on Daniel Webster,* Philadelphia, Penna.: C. Sherman, 1852.
47. The Rev. Dr. Cortlandt Van Rensselaer, *A Discussion on Slaveholding: Three Letters to a Conservative,* Philadelphia, Penna.: J. M. Wilson, 1858.
48. *God Glorified by Africa: An Address Delivered on December 31, 1856, at the Opening of the Ashmun Institute, near Oxford, Pennsylvania,* Philadelphia, Penna.: J. M. Wilson, 1859 (Van Rensselaer directly discusses the Society pp. 11-18).

49. "Daniel Webster: Economic Nationalism Continued," in *Jacksonian America, 1815–1840, New Society, Changing Politics,* Frank Otto Gattell and John M. McFaul (eds.), Englewood Cliffs, N.J.: Prentice-Hall, Inc., 1970.

50. The Rev. Dr. Cortlandt Van Rensselaer, *Signals from the Atlantic Cable. An Address delivered at the Telegraphic Celebration, September 1st, 1858, in the City Hall, Burlington, New Jersey,* Philadelphia, Penna.: J. M. Wilson, 1858.

51. Robert Field Stockton, *Appeal of Commodore R.F. Stockton to the People of New Jersey in Relation to the Existing Contracts between the State and the United Delaware and Raritan Canal and Camden and Amboy Railroad Companies, September 24th, 1849,* Princeton, N.J.: J. T. Robinson, 1849: "I was importuned for aid. I was assured that if the canal failed now it was lost forever; and, deeming the canal of infinite importance to the State and the nation, I subscribed the balance of the stock necessary to preserve the charter, amounting to over four hundred thousand dollars," p. 2.

52. *Slaveholding and Colonization: a Reply to George D. Armstrong, D.D., of Norfolk, Va., on Slaveholding and Colonization,* Philadelphia, Penna.: J. M. Wilson, 1858. (Van Rensselaer directly discusses the Society on pp. 71–77).

53. Robert Field Stockton, *Letter of Commodore Stockton on the Slavery Question,* New York: S. W. Benedict, 1850.

54. The same year he gave the ninth installment of $100 to the state organization. This followed on the footstep of his father, Stephen Van Rensselaer, who was one of the largest contributors to the national organization in 1838.

55. *Annual Reports of the American Colonization Society* (1841–1860), Volumes 24-43. (Facsimile reprint, New York: Negro Universities Press, 1969): see annual lists of vice presidents.

56. Lee M. Pearson, "The *Princeton* and the *Peacemaker*: A Study in Nineteenth-Century Naval Research and Development Procedures," *Technology and Culture,* 7, Spring 1966.

57. Just as the *American Railroad Journal* presented both investigative reports in the case of the *Richmond* explosion so as to "give our readers both sides of the question," so too now a publication was offered, entitled, *Hear Both Sides,* which encompassed the verdict of the coroner's jury, the company's internal report, and the Stockton-Van Rensselaer exchange of letters.

58. C. Van Rensselaer, "Review of the Camden and Amboy Company's Report," Burlington, N.J., 1855.

59. "Subsidies And Public Morals," *Harper's Weekly,* (March 5, 1859, p. 145) June 24, 1876, p. 506. The criticism that corporations had no souls was a somewhat common reaction in the mid-nineteenth century to such highhanded management actions. Consider these two quotes from *Harper's Weekly* concerning railroad company management: "Twenty years ago most of the steamers plying between New York and neighboring ports were owned by powerful corporations, who enjoyed a monopoly of the traffic, and whose wealth and obvious 'soullessness' were a terror to steamboat men" (March 5, 1859) ". . . But surely the evils of a plutocracy could not be felt more sorely than in the control of legislation by "soulless" corporations of immense wealth" (June 24, 1876).

60. Wu Jie, "The Public Reaction to Railroad Accidents in the United States: 1850-1900," Master of Arts Thesis, History Department, University of Massachusetts, Boston, 1982.

61. *Public Ledger and Daily Transcript*, September 4 to October 18, 1855.
62. Harold D. Langley, "Robert F. Stockton: Naval Officer and Reformer," in *Quarterdeck and Bridge: Two Centuries of American Naval Leaders*, James C. Bradford (ed.), Annapolis, Md.: Naval Institute Press, 1997.
63. Stockton wrote in 1851: "I must have my own way in the matter. I cannot be bothered with the interference of others."
64. "The Camden and Amboy Tragedy," *Colburn's Railroad Advocate*, September 15, 1855.
65. See the following for discussions of this during the Civil War: John P. Jackson, *A general railroad system for New Jersey: by free legislation for local railroads for every part of the state: and a main trunk double-track railway for the nation: and an examination of the alleged monopoly of the Camden and Amboy Railroad Company: being a correspondence between citizens of New Jersey and John P. Jackson, with legal opinions of Hon. A. Dutcher, Hon. Peter D. Vroom, Hon. Joseph C. Hornblower: and a railroad map of New Jersey*, Newark, N.J.: A. S. Holbrook, Printer, 1860.
66. *Free legislation for railroads: a history of the railroad conflict in the Eighty-fourth Legislature of New Jersey: and the opening of free legislation for railroads*, Trenton, N.J.: Murphy & Bechtel, printers, 1860;
67. *Review of the N.J. Railroad Co.'s pamphlets, on a system of free railroads*, Trenton, N.J.: Printed at "True American" Office, 1861.
68. William Allen Butler and Edwards Pierrepont, *Railway Communication Between New York and Washington. Remarks and Opinion of Counsel*, New York, 1864.
69. *Reasons Why the Raritan & Delaware Railroad Company Should Not Be Destroyed by the Camden and Amboy Monopoly*, Washington, D.C.: Gibson Brothers, 1864.
70. Charles Sumner, *Rail-road Usurpation of New Jersey. February 14, 1865,* New York: New York Young Men's Republican Union, 1865.

CHAPTER 5

The Gasconade Bridge Accident, November 2, 1855

Fly by steam-force the country across
Faster than jockey outside a race horse,
With time-bills mismanaged, fast trains after slow,
You shall have danger wherever you go!
To the tune of Ride a Cock-Horse,
"The Railway Nursery Rhymer" [1, p. 1]

A CELEBRATION WITH POLITICAL EFFECTS

A few weeks before the Camden and Amboy disaster, the Pacific Railroad of Missouri finally reached Hermann, eighty-one miles west of St. Louis, on its way to the Pacific. It had taken four years of construction to reach this point, so a celebration was in order. At the celebration, chief engineer O'Sullivan noted that "The press of the state, after the Legislature, were the next best help to railroad enterprises"[2, p. 2].

This put the best spin on the fact that the Pacific Railroad of Missouri was, at that very moment, under investigation by the state legislature for construction delays, cost overruns, and profiteering. By the time of the August celebration, although the charges had been cleared, the railroad and the Legislature both knew that they would meet again in November when the Legislature reconvened in Jefferson City to consider the railroad's request for additional capital to complete the road [3, p. 2].

By mid-October 1855, O'Sullivan felt sufficiently confident that the line would be complete to Jefferson City (forty-four miles beyond Hermann) so that he supported the Board of Director's idea of a special, invitation-only, excursion train from St. Louis to Jefferson City for November 13 [4, p. 252]. O'Sullivan then issued the following invitation:

PACIFIC RAILROAD

FIRST DAY of NOVEMBER 1855

Pass _____

On invitation of the citizens of Jefferson City. To and return. Good for return on 1st or 2nd November.

THOS. S. O'SULLIVAN
Eng'r & Sup't.

Trains leave 7th Street, St. Louis, at 8:30 a. m., and reach Jefferson City at 3:03 p. m.

Returning, leave Jefferson City at 6:o6 p. m., and reach St. Louis at 12:30 A. m.; and leave Jefferson City on 2nd Nov. at 6:oo a. m. & 3:00 p. m.

Show this ticket on entering cars. Not transferable.

Once the guests reached Jefferson City, a grand banquet in the Capital Building awaited them. The five hundred guests included legislators, former mayors of St. Louis, and the president of the Pacific Railroad of Missouri himself, Hudson E. Bridge. The company wanted press coverage and got it by inviting all these celebrated guests. When O'Sullivan issued the invitations, the road itself was progressing well. But as the date of the celebration drew near, the truss bridges over the Gasconade and Osage rivers still remained to be completed.

RAILROAD TRUSS BRIDGES

When railways began moving across America, the question of bridge construction became crucial. Early on, a few major masonry structures were created, but they proved too costly, and so wooden bridges became the most viable alternative. In the 1830s, Town, Long, and Pratt took out patents for various wooden bridge designs [6, p. 110; 7, pp. 1-58, 566-607], but it was a timber and iron truss bridge design patented in 1840 by William Howe of Massachusetts that achieved the most widespread popularity. Howe's design became the principal bridge design for railroad bridges on the western roads, from the Pacific Railroad of Missouri in the 1850s to the post-Civil War construction of the Union Pacific.

The Howe truss, illustrated in Figure 34, consisted of a horizontal timber upper or "through" chord and a lower or "deck" chord. To prevent sagging, diagonal wooden braces were added. These braces would be in *compression* (squeezed), but since they were formed into triangles, the braces tended to hold their shape under a load. Bridges with chords and braces in triangles had been built before, but what Howe did to improve on such bridges was to combine all these timber pieces with vertical *tension* (pull or stretch) members made of

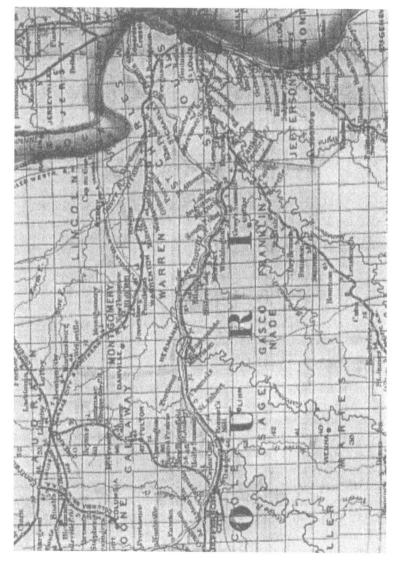

Figure 33. Railroad map of route between St. Louis and Jefferson City. Note the road's intersection with the Gasconade and Osage Rivers both of which emptied into the Missouri River just north of the train route [5].

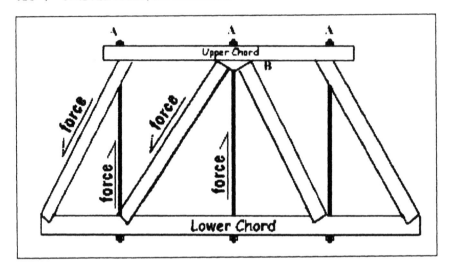

Figure 34. A through-Howe-truss as originally designed with stresses
distributed across diagonal compression members with vertical
iron rods in tension connecting the upper and lower chords.

wrought iron. The ends of the iron tension rods (Figure 35) were threaded and
secured to iron shoes at the panel points of the web. By taking a long truss and
fitting it with wrought-iron vertices, Howe created an economical bridge that
was easy to manufacture and simple to assemble [8, pp. 112-124]. All of the
components could be loaded on flat cars and delivered to the bridge site.
Moreover, since the railroad construction gangs could not wait for properly
seasoned wood for the bridge, the Howe truss could be adjusted over time using
bolts, washers, nuts, turnbuckles, and rods so that the shrinkage of the green timber
could be accommodated. Moreover, Howe truss bridges could bear the heavy,
concentrated weight of moving locomotives without being crushed. A good
demonstration of the design's strength was that in 1853-56, it was a Howe truss
bridge that first successfully spanned the Mississippi River.

Howe himself was "content to be just the inventor, a friendly man who
liked music and the good things in life that his bridge royalty payments brought
him" [7, pp. 112-124]. But his brother-in-law, Amasa Stone, was more ambitious
and, in 1841, bought exclusive rights for building Howe truss bridges in New
England [9, pp. 63-67]. In 1849, at the age of thirty-three, Amasa Stone moved
to Cleveland, where, with two partners, he contracted to construct the Cleveland,
Columbus, and Cincinnati Railroad, and made the line a showcase for the
Howe truss. Amasa Stone's brother, Andros, joined with Lucius Boomer to
create Stone & Boomer, Co., which built the Howe truss prefab pieces in
Chicago—receiving and processing 3.5 million feet of timber in their first year

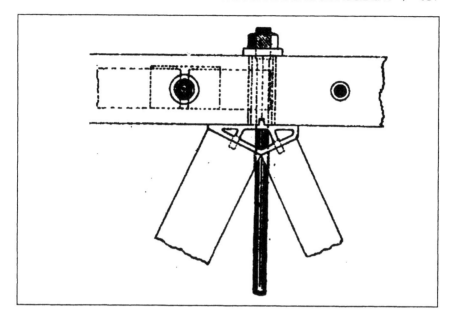

Figure 35. Example of a cast wrought iron joint where timber and iron
are joined by threads and bolts [7, Plate 11].

of operation [11, p. 115]. In fact, with 400 employees, they completed 11,887
linear feet of bridges in 1854 and had another 7,000 feet to complete [12,
pp. 26-27]. Stone & Boomer, Co. had so many bridges to build and were using
so much timber that they established a company town, Castle Rock, under the
management of Lucius's brother, George Boardman Boomer, on the Osage River
in Missouri—the next river between the Gasconade River and Jefferson City
to the west on the Pacific Railroad line. A letter described how busy Castle
Rock was in 1855:

> At that time (1855) his saw-mill was in active operation, going day and night,
> turning out vast quantities of lumber, and he also shipped large quantities to
> St. Louis. He employed a great many men . . . [12, p. 6].

All this building and work made Lucius one of the richest men in Chicago [13].
However, Stone & Boomer, Co. was also experiencing some hard financial
times in 1855; George had written of the ramifications of a general financial
downturn in the economy: "times were hard and every mail and telegraph
dispatch brings bad news" [12, p. 6]. Worse, on September 30, their bridge
works in Chicago burned to the ground with a loss of $100,000 [13]. Stone
& Boomer, Co. needed the contracts for constructing bridges for the Pacific
Railroad of Missouri in 1855 [14, p. 713], but had fallen behind schedule on
the Gasconade Bridge when O'Sullivan's special excursion train for November 1
was announced.

UNFINISHED BRIDGES WERE ROUTINELY USED

In the 1850s, the standard procedure for constructing truss bridges was to first build a "falsework" upon which the bridge superstructure would be laid. The falsework itself included piles driven into the riverbed about 14 feet apart along the line of the bridge, with extra-long horizontal beams on them upon which the superstructure would be laid. Once the truss bridge was sufficiently strong, the "falsework" would be removed, and the bridge left freestanding.

The bridge over the Gasconade River for the Pacific Railroad included eight spans: two of 180 feet, two of 140 feet, and two of 92 feet, and the abutment spans at either end of 130 feet. Although the abutments and the five piers were completed by November 1, the superstructure was not [15, p. 3].

A. J. Carter, superintending the trestlework for Stone & Boomer, Co. [15, p. 9], testified that the posts of the falsework were doweled into the caps on the span with two-inch wooden dowel pins. The caps on the piles were tied together, each to the one adjoining, with two-inch planks that were spiked. However, none of the superstructure was finally bolted and finished on the day of the excursion train. Julius W. Adams, a civil engineer for twenty-three years and principal engineer of the Lexington and Danville Railroad, later testified that:

> there is scarcely a Railroad in the country, I know of none, where these structures [falseworks] have not been called into use . . . but, not to delay the opening of the road, the contractor undertook to strengthen his scaffolding, so that trains might pass in safety, without waiting for the completion of the bridge. This is by no means an unusual occurrence, and one that I have frequently witnessed [15, pp. 14-15].

To test the unfinished bridge, Stone & Boomer, Co. ran a full gravel train over the structure on the day of the excursion train and watched carefully to see if it exhibited any weaknesses. Thomas Ross, engineer on that gravel train, later testified:

> I ran the gravel train which first passed over the bridge on the morning of the accident. There were ten loaded, gravel cars, well loaded with gravel, and three empty cars in my train. We went at the rate of about five miles an hour. Going over when the cars were loaded, we were backing the train. I noticed no unusual motion of the bridge when crossing. It seemed to be firm. When we returned across the bridge the cars were empty, and we increased our speed to twelve miles an hour [15, p. 5].

THE ACCIDENT

The *St. Louis Missouri Republican* described what happened next when the excursion train approached the Gasconade Bridge:

> The train, consisting of fourteen cars left the depot on Seventh street, at 9 o'clock, crowded with invited guests, a half hour after the time advertised. By the time it reached Hermann this delay was fully recovered, thus showing the

good condition of the track. After leaving Hermann, the train proceeded with good speed and without the least difficulty until it reached the Gasconade, when one of the most disastrous accidents occurred which has yet thrown this city into mourning. The bridge across that stream gave way, ten of the cars were precipitated a distance of twenty-five or thirty feet. The locomotive, from all appearances, had reached the edge of the first pier when the structure gave way, and in falling reversed its position entirely, the front turning to the east, and the wheels upward. On the locomotive at the time were the President, Mr. H. E. Bridge, Mr. O'Sullivan, the chief engineer of the road, and an additional number of the employees. Mr. Bridge, it is supposed, is the only one saved of the individuals named.

An hour after the disaster, voices from beneath the wreck of the locomotive were heard asking for assistance, and when we left the scene of disaster active efforts were making to relieve the sufferers. It is possible—nay it is to be hoped probable, that many of these unfortunates may have been rescued.

The road enters the bridge with a curve, and this circumstance, perhaps, prevented the disaster from being more fatal, as the cars thereby were diverted, and thus prevented from falling directly in a general melee, enough of injury, however, was accomplished. The baggage car, next the engine, went down, to use the expression of one who was in it "extremely easy," without causing any serious casualty. The first and second passenger cars followed, and in these several were killed, and a great number more or less mangled. In the third, one or two were killed, only. This car, although in a dangerous position, and almost entirely demolished, was less fatal to life and limb. In the fourth and fifth cars a great many were fatally injured, and several instantly killed. The balance of the train followed swiftly on their fatal errand, and the loss of life, with contusions more or less severe, was dreadful.

Some of the cars plunged on these beneath them with their ponderous wheels, and crushed or maimed the unfortunate persons below. Others hung upon the cliff, in a perpendicular position, and two or three turned bottom upward down the grade. Only one—the extreme rear car—maintained its position on the rail [16, p. 2].

The thirty-one fatalities included two state representatives, two formers mayors of St. Louis; the president of the St. Louis City Council; Thomas O'Sullivan, the road's chief engineer; the secretary of the road; the treasurer of the road; and the president of the road, H. E. Bridge, who died later of injuries received at the time [18, p. 38]. As the bodies returned to St. Louis, the mayor issued the following proclamation:

TO THE CITIZENS OF ST. LOUIS—In view of the awful and inscrutable dispensation of Providence, by which so many valuable lives were lost on Thursday last, I have deemed it proper to recommend, and as the mayor of the city I do hereby recommend and set apart Monday next, the 5th inst., and ask that it be observed universally as a day of cessation from all labor, as a tribute of respect to those who are most deeply stricken by this terrible blow, and a day of heartfelt thankfulness and gratitude to God by and on account of all who are saved from death.

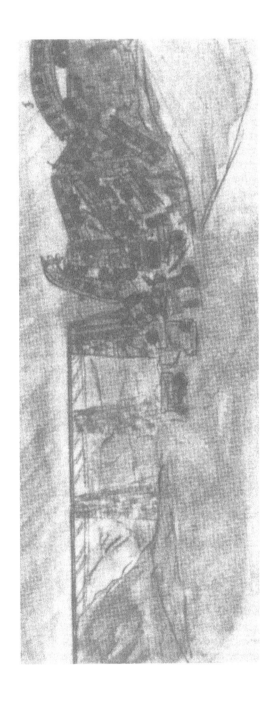

Figure 36. Eyewitness sketch of the wreck [17].

I recommend that all business houses be closed, and that all secular pursuits go unobserved on that day. I also request that the churches of all denominations be opened for religious worship on that day.

Washington King, Mayor.
Mayor's Office, St. Louis, Nov. 3, 1855 [19, p. 1161]

The Pacific Railroad of Missouri received the widespread publicity that it sought in inviting all the dignitaries, arranging the banquet, and notifying the press. However, it was not the publicity attendant to a disaster that it sought and received from the front pages of the St. Louis papers to, among others, the *Brooklyn Eagle, The New York Times,* the *National Observer* [20], and *Scientific American* magazine [21, p. 78; 22, p. 97]. A week later, when Professor Silliman, the chief investigator of the *New England* explosion described in Chapter 1, took the stage in St. Louis to give another one of his scientific lecturers, he "referred in words of tender endearment to the late Railroad catastrophe, which he spoke—especially to the aged—of the brevity of life and the certainty of death" [23, p. 2].

THE CORONER'S INQUEST

In the customary first step of a disaster investigation, the coroner of Gasconade County held his inquest in Hermann on November 2. Only one witness, however, was called, Erastus Wells [24, p. 3]. His testimony, not later a part of the company report, was as follows:

> ... I started from St. Louis in the train of the Pacific Railroad Company, and we proceeded in safety until we reached the crossing of the Gasconade River about eight miles beyond the town of Hermann, Gasconade County, Mo. We reached that point about two o'clock P. M. of that day and the train proceeded to cross the bridge over the Gasconade River, the cars at a speed of about twenty miles per hour as far as I can judge. After crossing the first abutment the timbers of the bridge gave away, and the locomotive and a number of the passenger cars were precipitated a distance of about twenty-five or thirty feet to the East Bank of the Gasconade River. This caused the death of ____ and the twenty-five other persons now in view of the jury [25, p. 3].

[What follows appears to be responses to jury members' specific questions, but only Wells's answers were recorded.]

- I do not know which car I was in. It must have been about the center of the train. There were ten or twelve cars composing the train.
- I should not consider the bridge a safe one to cross with a train of cars at the speed at which we were going.
- I do not think that the cars were overloaded. I was sitting down at the time.
- I thought we were going at the same speed that we made between Hermann and the bridge. I suppose it could not have been more than a minute or two from the time the accident happened until I was out of the car. The car bursted open at the top and I went out the opening thus made [25, p. 3].

The verdict of the jury after viewing the bodies and hearing Wells's testimony was: "the above named person came to their death by the breaking of the Gasconade Bridge on the 1 day of November 1855" [25]. Once again, the coroner's jury proved less than insightful into the cause of the accident.

THE PRESS WEIGHS IN

As in the cases of the *Moselle* and the *Camden and Amboy*, rumors and accusations immediately began circulating through the press. On Tuesday, November 7, *The New York Times* exclaimed: "We know nothing of the causes of the falling of the bridge across the Gasconade, but it is enough to know that it fell; and it could have fallen only from some defect in its construction" [26, p. 3]. The following day, November 8, it continued:

Piecrust Bridges.

We made some remarks yesterday on the remarkable circumstance of the giving way of two bridges on the Pacific Railroad, by the fall of one of which a great number of human lives was sacrificed, and a large amount of property destroyed; and the St. Louis Democrat of the 5th inst. brings us the intelligence of another bridge having fallen on the same road; this third tumble was of the bridge which crossed the Morean at Jefferson. A fearful judgment awaits the incompetent architect to whose incapacity these disasters must be attributed. Such a calamitous commencement of the great enterprise of a Pacific Railroad is a bad augury for the continuance or completion of that stupendous work. The further we go from the great centers of commerce and civilization, the more imperfect and unreliable do all works requiring scientific knowledge and mechanical skill become; and, if such accidents can happen as the falling of these three bridges on a road so near to St. Louis, what disasters might not be expected on a railroad constructed in the deserts and wildernesses between that point and the Pacific! Of all the products of civilization, there are none which, demand such care, such accuracy of mechanical knowledge, such skill and integrity, as railroads; the slightest deviation, the most trifling carelessness, the most inconsiderable neglect often leads to disasters of fearful magnitude, as we are almost daily receiving proofs of; but in the case of the falling of the piecrust bridges on the line of the Pacific Railroad, there must have been the grossest miscalculations and errors of construction; they crumbled away at the first touch as though they had been built of cards or loose boards. The bridge across the Gasconade, it appears, was a single span, but the other two were carried away by the current of the river [27 p. 4].

In defending the local railroad, the *St. Louis Missouri Republican* pointed out that despite the fact that three bridges had indeed fallen, *The Times* failed to note that all three were incomplete structures still under construction [28, p. 2]. Against these incomplete structures, the heavy storm mentioned in the narrative of the Gasconade Bridge collapse continued sending driftwood and strong floodwaters against the other two structures, causing them to collapse. Moreover, if the bridges collapsed because of the want of proper engineers, as *The Times* suggested—"The further we go from the great centers of commerce and civilization, the more imperfect and unreliable do all works requiring scientific knowledge and mechanical skill become"—then the *Republican* reprinted a testimonial given to the Pacific Railroad's chief engineer, Thomas O'Sullivan, eight years earlier when he left New York City. The testimonial was published in the *New York Evening Post* (November 1847) and in part said:

> We the undersigned, a committee appointed by your friends employed in the United States Dry Dock of this city [Brooklyn Navy Yard], have the gratification to present you with this transit, as a testimonial of their high regard. We are desired to express, at the same time, the respect and esteem they bear towards you for your skill as an engineer, and deportment as a gentleman, and to add that while under your charge they viewed with pleasure the easy and agreeable manner in which you performed the duties assigned to your office [28, p. 2].

A week after the coroner's verdict was delivered, and a day after *The New York Times* issued its verdict on the cause of the accident even though, "We know nothing of the causes," a committee was "invited and requested" on November 9, by the Directors of the Pacific Railroad to investigate the "immediate" causes of the accident. It began its work a week later and completed its investigation, issuing its report and a minority report within two weeks.

THE COMPANY'S REPORT—
DOES NOT FULLY EXONERATE THE COMPANY

The members of the committee who wrote the report included officials from competing railroads serving St. Louis:

- Maj. R. Walker, late of the Ohio and Mississippi Railroad
- W. W. Morris, of the North Missouri Railroad
- James H. Morley, of the Iron Mountain Railroad

and several St. Louis engineers:

- J. B. Moulton, present City Engineer
- C. Robert Campbell
- Capt. J. C. Swon (recall that West Point was one of the premier centers of civil engineering at this time)
- R. M. V. Kerchaval
- Gerard B. Allen
- Z. T. Knott
- Henry Kayser, former City Engineer, who was both an official from a competing company and a St. Louis engineer.

None were employees of the Pacific Railroad, and the report, for the first time, presented a critical minority report from Henry Kayser—this is the first time that a company-sponsored report had ever spoken with contending voices.

The report was sixteen pages long, and prefaced by a summary of the Committee's charge and general findings. The remainder of the report was largely composed of witness testimonies. The testimonies reveal no overall order of presentation, with employees of the railroad mixed in with those of Stone & Boomer, Co., and workers on the bridge mixed in with conductors and engineers of the gravel train and the excursion train. No analysis of the testimonies is presented because the fact that a heavier gravel train preceded the excursion train seemed to be the primary verity noted by everyone. Thus, the majority summary concluded:

> After a critical examination of the portion of the structure now standing, the Commission proceeded to examine in detail the witnesses brought before them, and, from the evidence adduced, which was reduced to writing, and accompanies this report, combined with the result of their observation of the structure itself are of the opinion that although they consider it unsafe for general use, yet that its strength might have been sufficient for the passage of the train at a speed not exceeding five miles per hour. This is sufficiently proved by the passage of a heavily loaded gravel train at about five miles per hour, which recrossed empty at about twelve miles per hour, the weight of which when loaded was one hundred and fourteen net tons for the length of the broken span, whilst the weight of the passenger train, which would have covered the same span, was but seventy-one net tons; and although the engine of the passenger train weighed on the drivers three net tons more than did that of the gravel train, yet the testimony goes to show an excess of strength for a dead weight more than equivalent to this difference.
>
> We are therefore of opinion that the immediate cause of the disaster was the high rate of speed at which the train was moving at the time of the accident [16, p. 760].

The culprit was the engineer, William Tucker, and this conclusion reached the national press. However, the company and its report were under unusual scrutiny from the legislature and the public because:

• a number of state legislators and St. Louis mayors had been killed in the accident
• the road was dependent upon the largesse of the state for its completion, and
• the road had just come out of an intense investigation by the legislature.

Thus, the company could not ignore a critical minority report written by Henry Kayser.

HENRY KAYSER—
A CRITICAL SCIENTIFIC VOICE OF THE COMPANY

Kayser was one of the leading civil engineers in St. Louis before the Civil War. An example of his early expertise can be seen in his work on the port of St. Louis. In the mid-1830s, the Mississippi shifted its current at St. Louis to the Illinois side of the river, creating a sandbar off the port that would eventually block traffic [29, p. 25]. The chief of the U.S. Corps of Engineers appointed Lieutenant Robert E. Lee to construct a diversion dike, and in 1837, Lee made Henry Kayser his assistant. In August 1839, further national appropriations for the project stopped, and Lee had to leave the work. At this juncture, however, Kayser was named by the city as City Engineer and hired to carry on the dike work at the city's expense [30, p. 2]. Kayser served as City Engineer for sixteen years and was elected City Comptroller in 1871 and 1873.

Kayser and his brother Alexander were also involved in the railroad business [32]. Henry was a member of the St. Louis and Iron Mountain Railroad Company's initial Board of Directors [31, Vol. II, p. 1153; 33; 34, p. 49], and in 1855, was completing some grading work awarded to Messrs. Kayser & Co. for a three-quarters of a mile section of the railroad [34]. From the dike and grading projects, Kayser turned his attention to the Gasconade Bridge failure when he was invited to join the committee.

Rather than relying on the witness testimony, as did the majority report and all the corporate reports in the earlier investigations, Kayser relied on his analysis of the structure at the scene of the accident. He noted that:

- "They [the piles] stand irregularly hardly any of them plumb, but overhanging in every direction."
- "That they [the piles] were not driven to a final resistance, is stated in the testimony given by Mr. Connel, who superintended the work of driving, How deep these piles were driven into the mud and alluvial soil, and what an insecure foundation they constitute may be judged from the fact, that I found two rows of them gone in one of the western bays."
- "In a number of instances the tops of the posts do not even reach to the caps, but open gaps are left between them."
- "The only timber connections between the piles are the sills, and between the posts are the caps, and these connections are effected merely by dowel pins; and likewise, that there is no timber connection at all between the different rows of piles and posts, called bents."
- "Bracing connections . . . are not uniform; on the contrary, they are omitted in many places, and only partially to be found in others."
- "Two of said bents in one of the middle bays were entirely gone, and others had so much settled, sunk and inclined under the weight of the bare superstructure that the railway thereon presented wave-lines, more than two feet out of grade and out of line, while the testimony attests that but ten days before it had been laid pretty fair and true" [15, p. 12-14].

Figure 37. Henry Kayser [31, Vol. II, p. 1150].

Relying "mainly upon my own observation and judgment," Kayser concluded:

The cause of said disaster was the breakage of the wooden structure in, and the superstructure over the bay between the eastern abutment and next pier west, a consequence of their entire insufficiency in foundation, material and construction, to bear the pressure of the locomotive and car running over the same.

And further: The attempt of running a locomotive and cars carrying human life over a river like the Gasconade upwards of thirty-five feet above its bed, upon such frail structures, can only be ascribed to incompetency, recklessness, or infatuation.

And, lastly: The fact of the said attempt having been made, and particularly at a speed of about fifteen miles per hour, can only be ascribed to a management of the affairs of the company—defective in system, supervision and responsibility [15, p. 14].

From Kayser's perspective, the engineer of the train was doomed no matter what speed he crossed the bridge, and the real cause of the disaster, the remote cause, was a management problem. Only the scientists at the Franklin Institute and Professor John Locke had ever used their own analysis and judgment, and they quite often were able to point to more important remote causes of accidents—Ewbank in the case of the *New England* to the inability of copper boilers to handle high pressures; the Committee of Science and the Arts in the case of the *Richmond* that looked at the fractures of the bridge-bar, and Locke to the lack of training given to engineers and to the infatuation with speed by the general public.

Kayser's minority report was two pages long, of which the first one and a quarter pages are spent in very specific description of what he observed at the site in a fairly disinterested manner, as illustrated above. However, his tone changed as he moved to a conclusion, and he began to employ a variety of rhetorical figures of speech [35]. He used rhetorical questions, "do you wonder," to begin each sentence:

> And, do you wonder, if such frail "false works," evidently erected without plumb or square, which as a whole, or in their different sections, or in their component parts, present to the eye not one continuous horizontal or perpendicular line, and resemble more a field of cornstalks after corn gathering, than anything in the way of building,—I ask, do you wonder if such frail "false works," under the pressure of a heavy weight moving on them, sink, give way or break? particularly when I have to add that, already at the time of the inspection by the commission, two of said bents in one of the middle bays were entirely gone, and others had so much settled, sunk and inclined under the weight of the superstructure that the railway thereon presented wave-lines, more than two feet out of grade and out of line, while the testimony attests that but ten days before it had been laid fair and true? [14; 15, pp. 13-14].

He continues his rhetorical scheme of anaphora and parallelism in his next paragraph by beginning each successive sentence in nearly identical ways:

- Or, is it necessary,
- Or, is it essential,
- Or, is it material,
- Or is it of avail [15, p. 14].

This series of parallel rhetorical questions reaches a climax with the question:

> Or, in short, is it compatible with commonsense to resort to any scientific or mathematical calculations to prove a mere scaffolding a Railroad bridge? [15, p. 14].

To this final question he writes: "I say, No!" [15, p. 14].

Kayser realized he was in a peculiar position as a critic of the very company that invited him to be on the Commission. He also realized he was in a peculiar position by criticizing the rest of the Committee members, who felt they were not authorized to investigate beyond the immediate causes. The realization of just these peculiar rhetorical positions would have been sufficient to motivate him to express himself passionately, directly addressing his audience, and being transparently persuasive rather than scientifically dispassionate. He also took responsibility for his findings by frequently referring to himself: "I shall proceed to state to you the facts collected by me"; or to repeat a number of times "I found. . . ." He was also the first on the Committee to allude to the loss of "human life" in the disaster, and perhaps this too motivated him to employ so many persuasive rhetorical features.

Kayser's unusual minority report received national notice in the *Scientific American* [22, p. 97] and the *Brooklyn Eagle* [36, p. 2], among others. A most telling comment came four decades later in the *Encyclopedia of the History of St. Louis:*

> After the memorable Gasconade bridge disaster he was appointed a member of the commission to inquire into the cause of the accident, and made a report, which at the time attracted general attention, evincing the thoroughness of his knowledge as a civil engineer and his fearlessness in exposing carelessness and incompetence [31, Vol. IV, p. 1153].

JULIUS ADAMS'S REBUTTAL

In an unusual move, another member of the committee, Julius Adams, offered a rebuttal to Kayser's criticisms in the final two pages of the report. Adams had been a civil engineer for twenty-three years and was principal engineer of the Lexington and Danville Railroad. Once Kayser shifted to a passionate tone, Adams felt obliged, evidently, to respond with a similar passionate tone. He criticized Kayser for going beyond the charge of the Committee to find the "immediate" cause of the accident and attacked his creditability as an engineer who "in all probability never was called upon, either to design or build a temporary structure for the passage of a thirty ton engine" [15, p. 14]. Adams's key point was that the "false-work" and the passage of a train over it was "an every day affair in the experience of the undersigned [Adams], and to this day, without an accident of any kind" [15, p. 14].

Adams then proceeded to offer a scientific analysis, returning to the dispassionate tone of the initial majority report and Kayser's initial section of his minority report:

> We may infer with certainty that either the vibration or undulation caused by a new and consequently rough track, traversed at a high speed, or a sudden blow, such as would take place were the engine to leave the track, were

necessary in order to cause a failure of the floor beams, the fracture of any one of which would be followed by the instant destruction of the bridge. Whether the engine left the track or not, we have no means of determining—my own opinion is that it did.

. . .

I would not presume to attempt an explanation of the probable movement or action of the engine, but there were known causes present, sufficient to produce a high percussive effect, which the structure never was designed to encounter, and which proved its destruction [15, p. 16].

From a quantitative basis different from that of the witness testimony, Adams returned to the conclusion of the majority and restated:

The proximate cause of the failure of the bridge was, as above stated, the too rapid speed of the engine and train attributable in the opinion of the undersigned, to an error in judgment on the part of the engine man who drove the locomotive [15, p. 16].

IN THE END

Despite the death of two of its members in the bridge accident, the Missouri State Legislature voted a month later, December 10, 1855, for further funding to the Pacific Railroad [37, p. 149]. However, settlements to the Gasconade accident victims and families took a sizeable chunk of this new funding.

Work on the Pacific Railroad line continued with the money from the legislature, and in December 1855, the *Leader* printed a short article as follows:

OPEN TO HERMANN.—The Pacific Railroad is again open to Hermann, trial trains having passed over the road on Wednesday. The locomotive and the passenger cars saved from the wreck at the Gasconade Bridge will now be brought down for repair and in a day or two passenger cars will be placed on the route for travel. The bridges have been, and will be, subjected to the severest tests, before passenger cars cross over but the builders have every confidence that they will resist any weight that can be put upon them [38, p. 7].

And, in March 1856, the line was opened to Jefferson City with the simple advertisement, "Wednesday, March 12, this road will be open to Jefferson City, for the transportation of passengers and freight, through without change of cars" [10, p. 3].

That following year, 1856, Stone & Boomer, Co. built the first bridge across Mississippi River using Howe trusses. It also built the Illinois Central Railroad Passenger Depot in Chicago, whose roof was the largest span ever constructed—and it too was built on the principle of the Howe truss [11, pp. 49-50]. Stone & Boomer, Co.'s financial statements show that it completed

5 percent more linear feet of bridges in 1855 than in 1854, and had another 114 percent over the 1854 bridge feet to complete [11, pp. 26-27]. The financial statements also show that the value of the Stone & Boomer, Co. manufactures in 1855 was $950,000, an increase of $115,000 over 1854. Thus, the bridge company fared very well in 1855.

Also in 1856, Henry Kayser finished the Mississippi dikes [29, p. 31]. Robert E. Lee had written congratulatory words in an 1844 letter to Kayser on his reappointment as City Engineer. Lee's words also rang true for Kayser's work in the Gasconade Report:

> I am very glad to hear that you have been reappointed City Engineer & that it has been done in a manner so satisfactory & complimentary to yourself. It shows that your good works speak for themselves and are properly appreciated [30, p. 35: letter of June 30, 1844].

The collapse of the Gasconade Bridge was not to be the last time a Howe truss bridge failure entered railroad history. In 1858, Andros Stone of Stone & Boomer, Co. left Chicago and moved to Cleveland, where he became president of the Cleveland Rolling Mill Company, supplying iron I-beams to his brother Amasa's bridge across the Ashtabula River in 1865 (see Figure 38). The Ashtabula Bridge was the largest, all-iron, truss railroad bridge in the United States.

The report on the Gasconade Bridge accident was an example of the new scientific investigations that were part and parcel of the investigation process rather than being a peripheral element appearing only late on the scene in scientific journals. On this occasion, standard legal procedure was followed. The coroner's jury report proved to be of a superficial nature, like all the previous ones. Luckily, however, there was a competent scientist/engineer who could go beyond the mere testimony of witnesses and beyond proximate causes of the accident. Here was a man willing to examine the root causes of the accident and the complex systemic problems, And, rather than assign blame to a scapegoat like the engineer of the excursion train, Kayser was able to question the standard construction process of railroad bridges, which often required mere scaffolding to perform the task of finished structures. Kayser more than any other member of the committee realized that the Pacific directors were only the immediate audience of the report, and that the ultimate audience was the general public, since the report was to be printed as a pamphlet and the newspapers would comment on its findings. Only one of the others on the committee held public office, and Kayser—who in 1871 was elected City Comptroller—had perhaps the best political instincts of anyone on the Committee. Unfortunately, there is no evidence that either the bridge construction industry or Boomer & Stone changed its process of building bridges and using half-finished bridges for railroad traffic.

CLEVELAND

ROLLING MILL CO.

MANUFACTURER OF

Bessemer Steel Rails, Axles,

Plates, Bars, Rods, Forgings, etc,

IRON RAILS, BEAMS, GIRDERS,

Merchants' Bar, Boiler Rivets, Fish Plates,

Track Bridge Bolts, Hot Pressed Nuts, and

Rail Road Supplies.

———

OFFICE AND WAREHOUSE:

99 and 101 Water Street,

CLEVELAND, OHIO.

A. B. STONE,   H. CHISHOLM,   D. O. COLE,

President.   V. Pres. & Gen. Supt.   Secretary.

Figure 38. Advertisement for Cleveland Rolling Mill Co. from the *American Railway Times*.

ENDNOTES

1. *Brooklyn Eagle,* November 15, 1852, p. 1.
2. *Missouri Republican,* August 7, 1855.
3. "The Railroad Disaster," *The Leader,* November 10, 1855: "The passenger train which left Hermann on the first of November for Jefferson City, was the first to pass that portion of the road. The Legislature was about to convene, and further Legislative aid was necessary for the prosecution of the enterprise. It was desirable to show the representatives of the State the advantages of the improvement, and the energy which characterized the directors," p. 9.

4. *Centennial History of Missouri: One Hundred Years in the Union, 1820–1921. Vol. 2,* St. Louis, Mo.: S. J. Clarke Publishing Company, 1921.

5. *New Commercial and Topographical Rail Road Map & Guide of Missouri,* New York, 1872 Library of Congress Geography and Map Division Washington, D.C.

6. Dirk J. Struik, *Yankee Science in the Making,* Boston, Mass.: Little, Brown and Company, 1948.

7. Theodore Cooper, "American Railroad Bridges," *Transactions of American Civil Engineers,* 21 (418), July 6, 1889.

8. Richard Sanders Allen, *Covered Bridges of the Middle West,* New York: Bonanza Books, 1952.

9. Sara Ruth Watson and John R. Wolfs, *Bridges of Metropolitan Cleveland: Past and Present,* Cleveland, Ohio: s.n.

10. *The Western Journal,* March 10, 1856.

11. *Fourth Annual Review of the Commerce, Manufactures, and the Public and Private Improvements of Chicago, for the Year 1855. Complied from Several Articles Published in the Daily Democratic Press,* Chicago, Ill., 1856. Western Historical Manuscript Collection—Columbia, Missouri.

12. Frank F. Fowle, "Memoir of General George Boardman Boomer, Bridge Builder and Soldier," An unpublished typescript "Compiled from Private Sources for the Engineering History Division of the Western Society of Engineers," Folder 492, Western Historical Manuscript Collection—Columbia, Missouri.

13. Obituary of L. B. Boomer, *Chicago Tribune,* March 8, 1881.

14. "Terrible Catastrophe on the Pacific Rail Road," *American Railroad Journal,* 11 (45), November 10, 1855.

15. *Report of the Committee Appointed by the Directors of the Pacific Railroad Investigate the Causes of the Accident At Gasconade Bridge,* St. Louis, Mo.: Republican Book and Job Office No. 11 Chestnut Street, 1855.

16. Cited in "The Pacific Railway Disaster," *American Railroad Journal,* 11 (45), November 8, 1855.

17. Reprinted from Karl Roider's "Eyewitness: Letters about the Gasconade Bridge Disaster," *Railroad History,* 184, Spring 2001, p. 63. The drawing was in a letter to Miss Lizzie W. Marsh from W. S. Eager, a Pacific Railroad of Missouri employee.

18. William H. McKenzie, *Opening the Rail Gateway to the West: Constructing the Pacific Railroad of Missouri,* St. Louis, Mo.: St. Louis Chapter, National Railway Historical Society, 2001.

19. J. Thomas Scharf, *History of Saint Louis City and County,* Vol. II, Philadelphia, Penna.: L. H. Everts, 1883.

20. *National Observer,* November 29, 1855.

21. "Railroad Bridges—Terrible Accident," *Scientific American,* 11 (10), November 17, 1855.

22. "The Gasconade Bridge Disaster," 11 (13), December 8, 1855.

23. "Prof. Silliman in St. Louis," *Missouri Republican,* November, 8, 1855.

24. *St. Louis Missouri Republican,* November 6, 1855.

25. *Return of Coroner Proceedings,* County of Gasconade, Archived at the Gasconade County Historical Society, P.O. Box 131, Hermann, Mo. 65041.

26. *The New York Times,* November 7, 1855.

27. *The New York Times,* November 8, 1855.

28. "The Late Disaster," *St. Louis Missouri Republican,* November 13, 1855. This and subsequent *Republican* articles defended the line also against rumors in a) the Chicago papers, which printed the fact that Bridges, president of the line, expressed his worries about the bridge to O'Sullivan before they began crossing the bridge; b) the *Railroad Record,* which suggested false economies caused the bridge to be made of shoddy material; c) the *New York Journal of Commerce,* which stated that the collapse was caused because the line was bankrupt "broken down in means and credit" (November 22, 1855, p. 2).

29. Frederick J. Dobney, *River Engineers on the Middle Mississippi: A History of the St. Louis District, U.S. Army Corps of Engineers,* Fort Belvoir, Va.: U.S. Army Corps of Engineers, 1978.

30. Stella Drumm, "Letters of Robert E. Lee to Henry Kayser, 1838-1846," *Glimpses of the Past,* 3, January-February, 1936.

31. *Encyclopedia of the History of St. Louis,* William Hyde and Howard L. Conard (eds.), New York, Louisville, St. Louis: The Southern Company, 1899.

32. Evidence of their common financial doings can be observed in the *St. Louis Missouri Democrat,* November 3rd issue, which advertised a lot for sale in St. Louis County "Trustee's Sale."

33. Kayser, though not on the board in 1855, was evidently still powerful enough in the company to move in the annual meeting of the stockholders on November 8, 1855 that the annual report of 1855 be published in its entirety in the papers, *St. Louis Missouri Republican,* November 7, 1855, p. 2.

34. Article V1, "Third Annual Report of the Board of Directors of the St. Louis and Iron Mountain Railroad Company, to the Stockholders," *The Western Journal and Civilian,* 15 (1), December 1855. It is rather odd that Kayser was both a member of the road's Board of Directors as well as being a member with his brother Alexander of a company with contracts for construction of the line. However, such financial maneuvers were exactly what enriched the board members of the Central Pacific and the Union Pacific a decade later and finally resulted in the Crédit Mobilier scandal during the Grant Administration in 1873.

35. In the subsequent paragraph he used rhetorical questions, parallelism, polysyndeton, climax, and anaphora among others.

36. *Brooklyn Eagle,* November 25, 1855.

37. "Article 1, Missouri and Her Railroads," *The Western Journal and Civilian,* 15 (3), February 1856.

38. *The Leader,* December 22, 1855.

PART THREE

The Antebellum Period of Disaster Investigation: Transformation Ends and a Constellation of Roles and Reports Becomes Normal

Updated and more effective interstate steamboat regulations became law in 1852. Initially, there was hostility to the inspections, but, within a decade, the Board of Supervising Inspectors could report to the Secretary of Treasury that:

> A general admission of the great utility of the laws and expressions of satisfaction at the results which have followed its observance, which to those interested in such property is now fully apparent, has now taken the place of the original opposition with which the inspectors were met in many instances; and incomplete as this law may be, in some respects, the cause of almost every accident to passenger steamers which now occurs can be readily traced to a violation of its provisions, or of the regulations of this board made pursuant thereto [1, p. 5].

As of 1852, therefore, the investigation of steamboat accidents moved out of the hands of coroners, cities, and states to the federal government. Thus, in this third and final part of the book, we will focus only on railroad accident investigations, since they were still in the hands of coroners, cities, and states and investigative procedures were still being worked out. The interstate steamboat regulations did, indeed, set a precedent in regulating railroads. However, interstate regulation of railroads in the Interstate Commerce Commission Act would take another thirty-five years to become law (1887). And even then, it was only with the turn of the century and the presidency of Theodore Roosevelt that the commission began to be a powerful regulatory force [2, pp. 5-10].

However, as seen in the case of the *Moselle* and the Pacific Railroad of Missouri, the power of private corporations to stand against the public will in the West was much less than in the East, and the "disinterested" expert began to play more of a central role in the investigations—even leading them in Locke's case. The last two accident investigations of this part return to the East, but now the "disinterested" expert begins to take over the entire process and not by fluke, as in the case of the *Moselle,* nor by sheer bravado, as in the case of the Gasconade accident.

The role of the "disinterested" expert grew because scientific expertise—once centered in the Franklin Institute and its loose association of scientist volunteers in the Committee of Science and the Arts—greatly expanded through the Civil War and became more widely dispersed. For example, so many people became civil engineers that a professional society, the American Society of Civil Engineers, was founded in 1852 and began to play a role in investigations.

This post-Civil War/pre-Interstate Commerce Commission Act period of railroads was also the time of state investigative commissions, which used the investigation reports rhetorically to mold public opinion and to put pressure on the private corporations. In these last two cases not only are the investigation reports taken out of the hands of the companies being investigated and put into the hands of state commissions, but even coroner's juries began to utilize experts and to produce much more penetrating findings.

Finally, most of the discourse communities that arose prior to the Civil War in response to these technological catastrophes were essentially transitory, with little rhetorical knowledge carried over from one instance to the next. True, there were some general standard procedures for coroner's juries, but little direction regarding the role of scientists: Were they defenders of the company, working for the public welfare, or peripheral critics? Part Two's transition period reflected the provisional nature of these roles. In Part Three, however, a consistency to the reports emerges, especially about the role of scientists. This occurs primarily because of the national involvement of Charles Francis Adams, Jr., chairman of the Massachusetts Railroad Commission. Adams' 1879 book, *Notes on Railroad Accidents,* for the first time made widely available to general readers the lessons to be learned not only from American investigations, but also from those established overseas by the British Board of Trade and its Railroad Inspectorate.

THE ROLE OF THE NEWSPAPERS IN
THE INVESTIGATIVE PROCESS

Proceeding through this history of railroad and accident investigations, the role of newspapers evolved from simply serving as a location for printing coroner or company reports to acting as a subtle tool to mold public opinion. In the first two cases, the *New England* explosion in 1833 and the *Richmond* locomotive explosion in 1844, newspapers reported the facts of the explosions when they occurred, and, in the case of the *New England* explosion, the *Hartford Courant* printed the verdict of the coroner's jury. The "disinterested" investigators published their findings in limited-circulation journals such as the *Journal of the Franklin Institute*, and the company defensive reports were made public in this and other limited-circulation journals. The audience that the authors hoped to affect was relatively small: investors and future industrial customers of engines from either the West Point Foundry Association or Norris Brothers Locomotives. In these two cases, public opinion did not need to be molded.

In the case of the Amboy and Camden accident, Stockton and the company had been publicly assailed for some years in

- small circulation booklets by Henry Carey
- the railroad trade newspapers
- the newspapers of New York (especially Horace Greeley in the *New York Tribune*, who attacked Stockton and his company for its monopoly status)
- in sermons by various clergy.

So the attacks on the Camden and Amboy were public. Moreover, the monopoly that was the cornerstone of the company's profits had been granted by the state legislature, and the legislature had endeavored to take it away. Thus, it was for the first time in these investigations that a defendant company tried to mold public opinion, and it was done by using personal letters printed in Philadelphia's *Public Ledger and Daily Transcript.* It was done openly and without much finesse by attacking the credibility of the critic, as if this were a private exchange of letters. Stockton did not give much thought to the rhetoric of public opinion.

Locke worked to publish his findings and did use letters publicly addressed to the newspapers to get the Cincinnati City Council to release the report. However, he evidently did not attempt to mold public opinion. Rather he hoped to influence ship owners, steam engineers, those who would train engineers, and Congress in creating regulations. Locke's report was never printed in large numbers, nor was it reprinted in any newspapers or scientific journals. Neither was the report from the *Pacific Railroad* on the Gasconade accident reprinted in any newspapers or scientific journals. True, the company had been assailed by the New York papers for "piecrust bridges," but such remarks from the East only moved the local Missouri papers to defend the company. Moreover, the real audience for the company's report was the members of the state legislature, which was soon to meet to consider further funding for the road. So in neither case did newspapers play a crucial role, because in these cases the audience was limited.

All of that changed with the Revere and the Ashtabula investigations in this section. Adams made it clear that his purpose was to mold public opinion, and he attempted to do that in his

- Commission's report on the Revere accident in 1871, which was widely circulated and reprinted

• his Lowell Institute Lectures, which were well attended and whose content showed up in various magazines
• his *Atlantic Monthly* articles
• his book, *Notes on Railroad Accidents.*

The Eastern Railroad Company even tried to steal the march on Adams, apparently, in the "Justice" series of magazine articles, which attempted to defend the upper echelon of management and blame the accident on a lower echelon, and they did it secretly with some attempt at finesse, rather than using Stockton's rather blunt, public name-calling.

INTERNATIONAL INFLUENCES IN THE UNITED STATES INVESTIGATIVE PROCESS

Charles Francis Adams was the American ambassador to Great Britain during the Civil War and, much of this time, his son Charles Francis Adams, Jr. was an officer in the Union Army. However, after the war he visited his parents in London, where his father remained as ambassador until 1868, and there is an excellent possibility that he came across the work of a fellow army officer in the British Board of Trade's Railroad Inspectorate. Captain Henry Whatley Tyler, later Sir Henry Whatley Tyler, joined the inspectorate from the Royal Engineers in 1853 and became its Chief Inspecting Officer in 1871. Tyler reported on railroad accidents in England for some twenty-four years before retiring from the inspectorate in 1877. Thus, for most of the 1870s, while Charles Francis Adams, Jr. was the Chief of the Massachusetts Railroad Commission, Tyler was chief of the British Railroad Inspectorate.

Whether they personally met or not, they knew of each other's work. Tyler was cited by Adams twenty times in his *Third Annual Report of the Board of Railroad Commissioners 1872,* in which Adams reported on the Revere accident [3, pp. 117, 130, 150-154], as well as in the later versions of the accident published in the *Atlantic Monthly* (1876) and the *Notes on Railroad Accidents* (1879). Most telling of all, however, was that after the Revere investigation, in 1876, when Adams was working with congressman and soon-to-be-president James A. Garfield to introduce national legislation for the government inspection of railroad accidents, Adams specifically modeled his proposals on Tyler's British bureau:

> The British Board of Trade inspectors are an exactly similar body. They have done good work, and to all appearances greatly hastened the introduction of well-tested and approved appliances in Great Britain and reduced the number of accidents and lessened the losses by them. Our engineer officers are quite as well qualified for such work, and there certainly is plenty of it to be done [4, p. 74].

In the final chapter, one of Tyler's railroad inspectorate reports will be compared to the two Interstate Commerce Commission (ICC) reports with which this book began, and the apparent similarities will clearly demonstrate the British influence on the rhetoric of U.S. accident investigation reports.

ENDNOTES

1. Lloyd M. Short, *Steamboat-Inspection Service: Its History, Activities and Organization,* New York: D. Appleton and Company, 1922.
2. Richard D. Stone, *The Interstate Commerce Commission and the Railroad Industry: A History of Regulatory Policy,* New York: Praeger Publishers, 1991.
3. Tyler and his Board of Trade reports (representing perhaps the whole of the Inspectorate to Adams) was cited throughout Adams' annual Massachusetts Commission Reports, *Third Annual Report of the Board of Railroad Commissioners 1872,* Boston, Mass.: Wright & Potter, State Printers, 1873.
4. "Government Inspection of Railroad Accidents," *Railroad Gazette,* February 16, 1877.

CHAPTER 6

The Eastern Railroad Accident at Revere, Massachusetts, August 26, 1871

Smashery, mashery, crash!
Into the "Goods" we dash:
The Express we find,
Is just behind—
Smashery, mashery, crash!
To the tune of Dickory, Dickory, Dock,
"The Railway Nursery Rhymer" [1, p. 1]

THE ACCIDENT

Though by 1871 the Eastern Railroad Company line was handling up to 110,000 passengers per week, it was handling this volume with an outdated and inefficient infrastructure better suited to the 1850s. Like the Camden and Amboy Railroad of 1855, the Eastern Railroad Company of 1871 had only a single-track line with side-spur tracks for trains to await passing trains. Moreover, like the Camden and Amboy, this single-track arrangement was prone to accidents:

- on November 3, 1848, six people were killed and forty wounded at Castle Hill in Salem; and
- on September 17, 1862, five were killed and thirty-five wounded at Hamilton [2, p. 7].

The Directors of the Eastern Railroad became so worried about its liability for employee injuries that in 1871 the company required all employees to certify they would not seek damages in court if they were injured while working on the railroad [2, p. 23].

The telegraph could have coordinated the movement of trains over the system since there were instruments at nine of their stations. However, the mid-level superintendents were unaccustomed to telegraphy and chose instead to give verbal orders to engineers or conductors as they passed through stations—another method utilized by the Camden and Amboy in the 1850s and prone to problems.

Air brakes were available; the Westinghouse brake had been used on another New England line for a year. However, the Eastern Railroad had recently spent large sums experimenting with an alternative air brake system, the "Creamer Safety Brake," which had proved practically useless and was given up...and no other type of brake was investigated after this expenditure [3, p. 72].

Part of the Eastern Railroad Company system formed a loop between Everett on the south about five miles out of Boston and Lynn to the northeast, and it was on August 26 that an accident happened on this loop:

> Across the salt marshes and skirting the seashore north of Boston, lay the single-track main line to Portland, operated solely "by schedule." Eight miles from Boston, a parallel line branched off to serve the settlements to the west. Revere, where the accident occurred, was situated on the main line, no more than two miles north of the junction.
>
> According to the timetable, two belt line trains, an accommodation, and a fast Portland train, were scheduled to depart in the order named from Boston to the North, within a space of ninety minutes. On this occasion however, the schedule was disarranged to the extent that the four trains were dispatched within a period of one hour, the time interval between the "Limited" and the preceding local being reduced from the customary forty-five minutes to no more than fifteen or twenty. Pending no further confusion of movement, the

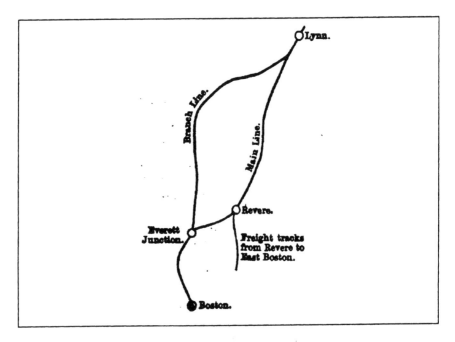

Figure 39. Railroad map of tracks north of Boston [4, p. 276].

simple case was presented of a fast train following a local for eighteen miles, with twenty minutes headway.

Were a southbound local train due at the junction point, the operating rules required that "all northbound move-merits should await its arrival before crossing the junction". In the absence of a passing siding, such trains were compelled to occupy the single main track. With utter disregard of the rules that were admittedly ill-conceived, it was the practice of the operating crews to clear the main track for the "Portland Limited" by occupying the branch in the event of delay.

On this summer evening in 1871, however, the employee in charge of movement of trains at the junction was unfamiliar with the customary operating procedure, but he did know and abided by the rules. The southbound train off the branch had not reached the junction when the northbound locals arrived. Minutes passed with three trains occupying the main track. Locomotive disorders had detained the southbound local. The "Limited" plunged through the dark with the assurance that its way would be cleared, bearing closer and closer upon the preceding, helpless trains. At last, the southbound train arrived. The belt line locals were shunted to the branch. The accommodation proceeded north on the main track, the distance between its last coach, occupied by seventy passengers, and the fast approaching locomotive rapidly diminishing. The engineman of the "Limited" glanced for a moment to observe the station signals at Revere, then turned his eyes quickly to the track to see the tail lights of the accommodation, eight hundred feet ahead.

Frantically, he whistled "Brakes." The brakemen responded quickly but the delay in reaching their posts and the further delay in drawing up the slack chains consumed too many of the precious seconds. With brakes grinding, the locomotive of the "Limited" penetrated the crowded coach for a distance of two-thirds its length. Impact, fire, and escaping steam claimed the lives of twenty-nine persons. Fifty-seven others were dreadfully injured. No person in the last car of the accommodation escaped fearful injury or death [5, pp. 14-15].

INSTANT ANALYSIS, *THE RAILROAD GAZETTE,* SEPTEMBER 2, 1871

The Railroad Gazette, reporting new advances in technology, annual reports, and also accidents, was mostly produced and endorsed by the management of the railroads. Thus, this was its analysis of the accident:

. . . The terrible calamity at Revere on the Eastern Railroad of Massachusetts seems directly traceable to what we must call the diabolical carelessness and disobedience of a railroad employee, who, being warned that a train was ahead of him behind time and charged to take extraordinary care to keep out of it, drove his train at full speed into the train ahead just where it was to be looked for—at a station where it stopped regularly. It is not easy to see how the company's officers could have made their orders clearer or better; the road is

Figure 40. Revere Station, scene of accident [4], looking south: freight tracks to left; tracks to Everett Junction to right (compare to Figure 39).

Figure 41. The Revere accident, August 26, 1871 [4].

one of the best in the country and has a reputation for exceptionally good management; the superintendent, Mr. Prescott, has served the company for twenty years or more with distinguished ability and his recent appointment as General Superintendent of the Northern Pacific Railroad has been considered a very wise one; the fault of the officers, if fault there was, lay in the choice of such an employee as the engineer; but here again the testimony, so far, is that he was a sober man and therefore reckoned careful during his term of service. If the facts reported are true, and they seem confirmed beyond a doubt, the sole responsibility for the disaster lies with the engineer of the express train, who was criminally careless, criminally disobedient, and therefore deserves prosecution, conviction and punishment as a criminal—an offender against the peace of the commonwealth, and not solely delinquent to his employers.

. . .

Such an accident suggests that it should be one of the first cares of a railroad officer to ascertain by all practicable tests the carefulness and accuracy of his subordinates. If no special effort is made to this end, a man may run a train safely enough for months while everything is regular and there is no occasion for extraordinary care and watchfulness, yet on the very first occasion demonstrate his unfitness for his place by sacrificing lives and limbs through carelessness. It is not everyman—not every intelligent man—who is fit for such duties, as trainmen have to perform, and it is of great importance that companies should use the utmost pains to ascertain their fitness. It will not do to prove a man in a situation where his failure to sustain the test will cause death and destruction [6, p. 252].

Once again, the very first analysis of the situation looked to only proximate causes and to offer a scapegoat low in the company structure. But something unique happened when the official enquiry of the coroner took place.

CORONER'S JURY VERDICT, SEPTEMBER 10

Two coroner's juries met to consider criminal charges in the Revere accident, one at Revere that began and ended first and a second at Lynn [7]. The former took most of the limelight because Charles Francis Adams, Jr., chairman of the Board of Railroad Commissioners of Massachusetts, not only made suggestions to the jury but also actually led in the questioning of witnesses [7]. The result of this involvement of Adams was that *The New York Times* called the jury's verdict—in contrast to all previous ones that were castigated as being inadequate—"a fair and righteous statement of the responsibility for the disaster" [8, p. 4].

Like the *Railroad Gazette* eight days earlier, the coroner's jury criticized Nowland, the conductor, but also added Lunt, the station-master, to the list of culprits:

And the jurors further find that the direct cause of said collision was the negligence of John S. Nowland, conductor of the Beverly train, upon which said persons were killed, and Ashbel S. Brown, engineer of the colliding Pullman train. The former failed to notify the latter, by signals or otherwise, that his, the said Nowland's train had been delayed on the road after starting about twenty minutes, and said Nowland would have known, had he consulted his watch that the Pullman train had an unobstructed view of at least one-half of a mile of the Beverly train as it stood at the depot at Revere directly before the collision, and could and should have seen the tail-light of said train in season to avoid the collision. The jury further find that Samuel O. Lunt, depot-master at Boston was remiss in duty in not correctly transmitting the order of the Superintendent to the engineer of the Pullman train to lookout for trains ahead, thus depriving the engineer of information that might have enabled him to avoid the Beverly train [8, p. 1].

Simply criticizing Nowland and Lunt would have been typical of all previous coroner's juries. However, this one, considering more remote causes, also accused the President and Directors of being remiss and contributing to the disaster by having:

- inadequate "rolling stock necessary for the safe and timely transit of passengers on said road";
- "frequent delays in the time of starting, occasioned by extra or excursion trains";
- "telegraphic communication with trains on the road that needs their consideration";
- "the need of improved appliances for the safety of trains" [i.e., air-brakes];
- "the risk attending the use of explosive burning fluids";
- "the want of a siding at the Saugers Branch" [8, p. 1].

The New York Times report on the coroner's jury further pointed out that Adams offered the following line of reasoning from the testimony of President Browne of the Eastern Railroad Company in the final session of the inquest:

> That the rolling stock of the road has been taxed to its utmost capacity; that the road though having ninety miles of single track, is conducted without telegraph line; and that with every opportunity and every obligation to know the real condition of the road, the only excuse offered by the President for the deficiency in cars was his own ignorance of the need of them [8, p. 4].

Thus, for the first time in all the investigations examined in this book, the findings of the coroner's jury offered insights into systemic problems and criticized those beyond the proximate culprits to those high up in the corporate structure.

REPORT OF THE COMMITTEE OF THE DIRECTORS, OCTOBER 20, 1871, AND "JUSTICE" IN THE *AMERICAN RAILROAD TIMES*, OCTOBER 21 TO DECEMBER 23

By 1857, there were already 352 employees in the Eastern Railroad [3, p. 61], and the corporation was structured in the following way:

- Board of Directors (nine members)
- President
- Superintendent
- Conductors and Engineers.

The management of the Eastern Railroad was split into a couple of power centers or "rings." Charles Wilson Felt in *The Eastern Railroad of Massachusetts; Its Blunders, Mismanagement & Corruption* described these different management rings controlling the railroad—a major one made up of the Hooper family and a minor one made up of "a few officers." Felt continued: "But the Revere disaster made more impression [more than the Hamilton accident], and the chief ring charged the minor ring with leading them into difficulty" [2].

Upper-level management not only blamed the conductor in the accident, Nowland, but also the more formidable superintendent Prescott of the minor management ring [3, p. 17]—the very man about whom the *Railroad Gazette* a month earlier had said:

> [Prescott] is one of the best in the country and has a reputation for excep-
> tionally good management; the superintendent, Mr. Prescott, has served the
> company for twenty years or more with distinguished ability and his recent
> appointment as General Superintendent of the Northern Pacific Railroad has
> been considered a very wise one [6, p. 4].

At the time of the accident in 1872, Prescott had been promoted from conductor in 1851 to superintendent [3, p. 51] despite being involved in near-accidents and fatal accidents. In 1856, Prescott issued an order endangering several trains that luckily produced nothing more than delays; one freight was delayed twelve hours [2, p. 12]. However, in the 1862 accident at Hamilton, Prescott again had issued an order to the conductor of one train but forgot to caution other trains about the unusual route of the first. The verdict of the coroner's jury blamed Prescott for the accident. He immediately resigned, but President Browne did not accept his resignation [3, p. 68].

Prescott also had a known antipathy to the use of telegraph [3, p. 69]. When Charles Francis Adams, Jr. interrogated Prescott during the coroner's investigation, Adams asked Prescott if he did not think that the use of the telegraph might have prevented the accident:

> No, he didn't think so; it might work well under certain circumstances, but
> for himself he could not be responsible for the operation of a road running

Figure 42. Jeremiah Prescott, Superintendent of Eastern Railroad,
1855-1875 [3, p. 102].

the number of trains he had charge of in reliance on any such system!
[3, pp. 70, 89].

The Board of Directors' report was twenty-three pages long and organized chronologically. Like the *Gazette* and the coroner's jury verdict, the board of directors blamed conductor Nowland for his actions.

However, the report took care to point out the following management mistakes and laid them all at the feet of Prescott. The company report:

• Noted the lack of a siding at the Saugus Branch junction, and that its presence would have greatly aided in avoiding the accident. However, the company report noted that Prescott as superintendent should have called attention to the need of such a siding. He never did [36, p. 7].

- Observed that telegraphic instruments were in place on the road. However, Prescott chose not to use them [36, p. 7].
- Conceded that additional rolling stock would have helped in handling the large volume of passengers. Yet the company report noted that Prescott, as superintendent, should have requested the necessary additional stock. However, in 1871, he had asked for only ten additional cars, and the board itself increased that purchase to twelve [36, p. 20].
- Agreed that the Westinghouse brake would have helped, but noted again that it was Prescott's job to bring such safety appliances to the board's attention. He had not [36, p. 20].
- Pointed out that Prescott asked the stationmaster at Boston to warn one train of possible problems with a delayed train, but had not told the stationmaster to warn the second train [36, p. 12].

An unusual aspect of the Revere accident investigation was that on the day following the release of the company's report the first of five articles signed by "Justice" appeared in *The American Railway Times* (published in Boston) [9]. The first two of the articles were so popular that the issues sold out, and the articles were reprinted in the November 18 issue [10].

In the articles, "Justice" pointed out the differences in management responsibility in the Eastern Railroad Company and repeatedly noted that Prescott, as superintendent, was remiss, just as did the company's report. The first article also wondered aloud:

> Mr. Prescott being very popular with the newspapers, whatever comes from his mouth is certainly reported as true, and this accounts for the abuse of the directors who appeared in the papers of the week following the accident [9, Oct. 21, 1871, p. 330].

The first two articles by "Justice" criticized the coroner's jury verdict and pointed out individuals whose testimony had been omitted or facts that had not been properly understood. However, where "Justice" criticized the coroner's verdict, "Justice" appeared to highlight the company report's findings:

> Of the irrelevant matters brought up in the investigations before coroner' juries it may be well for us to take some notice. They are The Telegraph System; the Westerhaus [a.k.a. Westinghouse] Brake; Signaling; Uniforming the Operatives; and The Want of a Sufficient Number of Cars.
>
> First, the *Telegraph System*. There is a telegraphic instrument in the superintendent's office at Boston. There are also instruments at Lynn, Salem, Beverly, Wenham, Ipswich, Newburyport, Hampton, and Portsmouth; and the only reason we can find in our mind why the telegraph is not used is that the superintendent himself has never studied up the matter; and no testimony is given that even on the night of the disaster any call was made for Lynn to answer if the 6 p. m. train had started, or what was the delay. We cannot believe that the directors prevented Mr. Prescott from adopting any mode of

telegraphic signals he chose, for *prima facie* the having of instruments at every important station is proof to the contrary. But if the superintendent has not a genius for getting up a system of telegraphic signals, perhaps he would like to be commended for not using any. After all, the telegraph must be operated by clerks, and we do not believe that operators are more likely to be correct than conductors or locomotive engineers.

The *Westerhaus* [a.k.a. Westinghouse] *Brake* is an apparatus said to be capable of setting all this wheels in the train almost immediately, so as to slide on the rails. The happy thought of the inventor seemed to be to make use of compressed air housed in a reservoir underneath the locomotive. Air is compressed by a pump worked by steam, under the eye of the locomotive driver. The compressed air is conveyed to a cylinder and piston attached to each car in the train, and by this means every brake can be set at once. Gutta purcha or india-rubber hose must be used with coupling joints at each connection of car or engine. This is all machinery, and the certainty of its operation depends on its being air tight always through all its connections. All the duties of brakemen are thrown on the locomotive driver. This mode of braking is not so old as to be established and accepted as the best mode of braking. Many other plans have been brought forward for years past to secure the application of brakes more rapidly than can be done by manual power, and none have proved practicable. But whose business is it to take the initiative—the superintendent's, or the directors'?

Still after all that may be said, it must be operated by a human being, and one too who is already charged with the heavy responsibility of being the pilot and engineer of the train. Of all human beings we admire the daring and heroism of a good locomotive engineer . . . his path, which at full speed he can pass over in ten or eleven seconds; only one inch of metal flange between him and eternity. A bad joint, a broken rail, a switch misplaced, and it is the end of all things to him. He relies with the utmost confidence upon the rules and orders laid down by his superintendent, and takes his chances. He seldom, if ever, makes a mistake, or forgets himself. Alone and silently, throughout midnight darkness, he performs his whole duty, houses his engine, and retires to his home, asking no praise nor reward other than his daily pay. But let his superintendent deceive him by misplacing the trains, so that in darkness, and without the slightest warning, he finds himself driving at full speed upon a crowded train,—no time to think, to prepare himself. Will he be ready to sound the whistle, shut his throttle, throw over his reversing lever, and apply the Westerhaus brake? Perchance he will; and it is but a chance. We have summered and wintered with some of such men, and we know that it is rare that they are off guard. All they require behind them is a cool, clear headed superintendent, one whose head is set square, and is always level.

Signaling. A very simple mode of signaling for trains running in the same direction on one track is to have a white board, on which black figures denote the time preceding train left the station. This could be illuminated at night, and placed so as to be plainly visible to time engineman. We believe that Mr. Prescott could at any time have adopted any mode he chose.

. . .

The Want of a Sufficient Number of Cars, or Rolling Stock. That it appears
to be a fact that more cars were needed the week previous to the accident may
be true; but is that a sufficient explanation for the superintendent's forgetful-
ness to provide for a block of trains at the junction in Everett, which resulted in
smashing one car and burning two at Revere? This pretended deficiency of
rolling stock is the weapon used by the superintendent to turn public attention
and condemnation away from himself, and toward the directors. But testimony was finally brought out, showing Mr. Prescott's own estimate of the
number of new cars needed for the year, and that time directors supplied him
with two more in addition. It is unfortunate for him that he made such a statement, for it amounted to a confession of guilt in the case of the accident, and
gave that as an extenuating circumstance, so as to throw the blame on the directors. Mr. Prescott being very popular with the newspapers, whatever comes
from his mouth is certainly reported as true, and this accounts for the abuse of
the directors who appeared in the papers of the week following the accident.

The Eastern Railroad has been abused as an antiquated concern, with no
improvements for many years. And pray whose fault is it? Has Mr. Prescott's
time been consumed in courting popularity, in preference to studying up
signals, brakes, and the use of the telegraph? We as a stockholder care but little
for that kind of popularity which supplies flattery, and so intoxicates a man as
to unbalance his head [11, p. 343].

The final three articles critiqued the Report of the Committee of the Directors
of the Eastern Railroad Company:

Mr. John J. Robinson's testimony is given on page 8 of the report, and it
appears from that that he has operated the road in the vicinity of the signal post
at the junction in Everett for several years, without the knowledge of the
other superintendent whose office is in Boston. This is a curious case to be
developed that an important official should have been left for years without
reporting, or being called upon to report the occurrences at his station.

Mr. Prescott says he never felt the want of a sidetrack at the junction.
Mr. Robinson says that an outward branch train was frequently delayed
there, waiting for the inward train, and without the knowledge of the other
superintendent, he has passed trains to and from on main tracks to prevent a
block of trains. Mr. Robinson was taken sick the day before the accident, and
Mr. Crimmins, assuming his duties carries out the very letter of the law, and
no trains are allowed to shift from one main track to the other, and thus the
road is blocked. The more we investigate this matter, the more we become
convinced of a total lack of discipline from the superintendent's office, a total
neglect of ordinary precaution, and that many of time subordinates knew
better how to manage than the "super" as they knew him [11, p. 407].

Although Eastern Railroad management came in for some criticism, the criticism was very selective. "Justice" targeted Prescott, a second echelon manager,
rather than the President or Board of Directors, suggesting that, in fact, "Justice"

could have been the nom de plume for a member of Eastern's board of directors, the major circle.

Thus, in the usual investigation documents that have included the coroner's report, the company report, and the technical expert report, this case included the interloper of mass media in the articles of "Justice." "Justice" seemed to comment in the newspaper on the investigation from the position of "disinterested" expert, thus gaining creditability. However, "Justice" largely promulgated the same points as the director's report, pointing the finger at Prescott and his management mistakes. Thus, for the first time, participants in the investigation used newspapers to publicize their points of view and to mold public opinion.

THE MASSACHUSETTS RAILROAD COMMISSION REPORT, JANUARY 1872

Each year since 1870 when the Massachusetts Legislature created it, the Massachusetts Railroad Commission produced a report that discussed the finances, management, and accidents of railroads within the state of Massachusetts. It was well-known that Charles Francis Adams, Jr., the Chairman of the Committee, wrote most of the annual reports, and each year he would add to these rather mundane lists an extended commentary on national topics of railroad finance, management, or safety, etc. The reports were of such high quality that requests for them came from across the United States, occasionally requiring additional printings [12, p. 23]. Moreover, newspapers not only published summaries of the reports, but "once the Chicago *Tribune* not only carried the entire report as an item of general interest but also reprinted and distributed 10,000 copies on its own initiative" [12, p. 23].

In its report on the Revere Accident in their 1872 report, the Commission described its legal boundaries:

> The Commissioners do not understand that it in any way belongs to them to apportion responsibility among those immediately implicated in the occurrence of the Revere or any other railroad accident. That duty the law devolves upon other public officials. The understanding of the Commissioners as to their province in this and all similar cases was expressed in their *Second Annual Report* (pp. 25-6): "The object of the legislature in directing all accidents to be reported to this Board, and an examination into them to be made by it, was undoubtedly twofold: 1st, to provide for the enforcement of any penalty prescribed in case the accidents arose from the failure of a corporation to obey the laws of the Commonwealth; and 2d, in all cases where it should appear that the existing laws were insufficient to provide for the security of the traveling public, to make provision for supplying such deficiency" [13, pp. xcv-cv].

It is interesting to observe that the head of the commission, Adams, hardly worked within these guidelines. When Adams played such a large role in the coroner's investigation—beyond the commission's legal boundaries—*The New York Times* wrote:

> ... the public has reason to be thankful that its interests have been defended by Mr. Charles Francis Adams, Jr. This gentleman is Chairman of the Board of Railroad Commissioners of the State, and he has conducted the examination with great patience and perseverance [8, p. 1].

When Adams questioned Prescott concerning the comprehensibility of the rules for the running of trains issued under Prescott's signature three years earlier, Adams had Prescott himself read aloud the particular rules related to the running of trains on the Eastern Loop where the accident occurred:

> 4. At the junction of the Saugus Branch at South Malden Two Balls or Two Red Lanterns at the mast head, give the track to trains on the main line, and One Ball or Lantern allows Branch Trains to enter or leave the main line.
>
> . . .
>
> 6. At the Junction of the East Boston Branch with the Main Road, at North Chelsea, One Ball or Lantern at masthead allows Branch Trains to enter or leave the Main Road; but when no Ball or Lantern is seen at masthead, Trains of Main Road may pass.
> 7. At the Junction of the Saugus Branch at West Lynn, the target or two lanterns crosswise, allows the trains on the main road to pass; but if the target or lights are perpendicular the trains can enter or leave the Branch.
>
> . . .
>
> 22. Trains coming from any of the branch tracks on to the main track, if behind time, will keep clear of all regular trains on the main track; if in coming to a station a train is receiving or discharging passengers, the approaching train must stop back [14, p. 1; 15, pp. 1, 4].

In response to Prescott's reading, Adams remarked that he "thought it a rather complicated process for the employees to understand, as it was difficult to understand it himself" [14, p. 1].

Moreover, Adams not only worked with the duly constituted coroner's jury, but also—beyond the Commission's legal boundaries—with a committee of five appointed by the citizens of Swampscott, Mass. to meet with President Browne of the Eastern Railroad and present him with nine requests to improve the future safety of passengers on board the Eastern Railroad. The meeting that drafted the requests became dangerous for a time:

> Hardly had he ceased speaking, however, when Mr. Wendell Phillips was noticed among the audience, and immediately called to the platform. His remarks were a most singular commentary on the chairman's injunction to calmness. He began by announcing that the first requisite to the formation of a healthy public opinion in regard to railroad accidents, as other things, was absolute frankness of speech, and he then proceeded as follows:—" So I begin

by saying that to my mind this terrible disaster, which has made the last thirty-six hours so sad to us all, is a deliberate murder. I think we should try to get rid in the public mind of any real distinction between the individual who, in a moment of passion or in a moment of heedlessness, takes the life of one fellow-man, and the corporation that in a moment of greed, of little trouble, of little expense, of little care, of little diligence, takes lives by wholesale. I think the first requisite of the public mind is to say that there is no accident in the case, properly speaking. It is a murder; the guilt of murder rests somewhere" [16, p. 142; 17, p. 1].

Luckily, Adams had a hand in the citizens' committee's petition:

During the earliest stages of the investigation, therefore, this Board was invited by members of the citizens' committee to advise them as to what additional safeguards to travel on the Eastern railroad seemed to be of immediate necessity. The Commissioners in reply submitted in writing such changes and precautions as their examinations so far suggested. Those were subsequently incorporated with others into a body of requests which were submitted by the committee to the president of the Eastern road, who at once complied with them upon all material points [16, p. 142; 17, p. 1].

And finally, before the commissioners had even officially met and offered a report, Adams "and the Board" issued a circular—beyond the Commission's legal boundaries—calling for the officers of Massachusetts railroad companies to meet on September 19 in Boston to consider methods to prevent the "causes" of the Revere accident from re-occurring [18, p. 1]. The New York Tribune stated that the circular maintained the cause of the disaster was "wholly unnecessary," and that it had been described in the circular as:

. . . the attempt of the company to operate a single track branch road without the aid of telegraph led immediately to the collision, which might have been avoided by the application of this, one of the oldest, and most ordinary, and least expensive appliances in operating railroads. The second fact established in the evidence was that the colliding train discovered the train ahead of it in ample time to have prevented the disaster had the train been equipped with brakes operated instantaneously from the locomotive, instead of the old fashioned hand-brake [18, p. 1].

Thus, rather than waiting for the official report to be issued four months later at year's end, Adams began molding public opinion and directing the investigation, unlike any previous "disinterested" expert.

Four months later when the official report was printed at year's end, in the first two-thirds of the report, the commissioners tried to present the facts of the accident in a chronological fashion without the accusatory asides directed at Prescott or the Board of Directors [13, pp. xcv-cii]. Eventually, however, they described the cause of the collision at Revere as "a combination of causes and defects of management, all of a preventable nature, but some of them peculiar to the Eastern Railroad, while others were common to it with almost all other

Figure 43. Charles Francis Adams, Jr., Chairman of the
Massachusetts Railroad Commission.

members of the railroad system" [13, pp. cii-civ]. They then offered these five
suggestions on the causation:

1st. To a laxity of discipline, running throughout the organization, which had
apparently resulted in a very considerable confusion not only in the movement
of trains but in the carrying out of the rules for operation the road generally,
and which was especially noticeable in the confusion prevailing in and around
the station in Boston.

2d. To a deficiency in rolling stock adequate to meet the demands of the
average summer business.

3d. To the want of siding at the Saugus branch junction.

4th. To the want of the telegraphic communication with the stations on the
Saugus branch road, which would have enabled the company to move its
trains over that road without the necessity of unlimited delays at fixed points
of passing, the happening of one of which caused the delay which resulted in
the collision.

5th. To the attempt at doing an excessive amount of excursion and extra business, thus imperiling the safety of the regular travel.

[Finally] . . . the overcrowded condition of the Eastern railroad during the week ending the 26th of August was the immediate cause of the disaster. The company was trying to do more than it had the means of doing. This arose fully as much from the active competition it was then carrying on with the Boson & Maine road on its through business, as from its exceptional summer travel [13, pp. 57-58].

The commissioners suggested in their report that if the lines combine "the properties and tracks of two of the four roads entering there it would get rid of one vexatious and dangerous grade crossing; it would enable the two roads to greatly reduce their number of officials, to combine their machine shops, both reduce and simplify their train movement, and by combining rolling stock, to use it much more effectively. Finally, it would extend one equable and responsible management over all the north-eastern portion of the State, which has for years been a species of battle-ground for these contending companies" [13, p. civ]. So, the commissioner's report does not discriminate between the levels of management, as did the Company Directors or "Justice."

CHARLES FRANCIS ADAMS, JR.'S ACCOUNT OF THE REVERE ACCIDENT, *ATLANTIC MONTHLY*, JANUARY 1876 [19]

Adams expanded on the Commission's Report four years later on February 5, 1875, first in a lecture in the famous Lowell Institute lecture series [20, p. 1] that was then picked up and first reprinted by the *Railroad Gazette* [21] and then in an article for the *Atlantic Monthly* in January of 1876 [19, pp. 92-103]. This was the third in a series of articles on railroad accidents for the magazine that Adams wrote and later collected in book form in 1879, called *Notes on Railroad Accidents* . . . the subject of the final chapter of this book.

Where the earlier Commissioner's Report suggested that the root cause of the accident lay in the competition between the Eastern Railroad and the Boston and Maine, this article suggested that the accident was the "inevitable calamity of an antiquated and insufficient system" [19]. However, Adams ended his article's short introduction by noting that the numbers of accidents in New England have gone down with the use of new safeguards and safety appliances such as the Westinghouse brake. He returned to this "happy conclusion" at the end of his article to suggest that those who died in the accident did not die in vain.

In the rest of his article, Adams used much of the Commission's Report for setting the context of the accident, giving a chronological description of the events. However, he was much more descriptive and specific when describing the effects of the accident and the moment it occurred. He also broadened the scope of his discussion to:

• Discuss the attempts to find a scapegoat by local citizens groups reacting to the accident:

> Grave men—men who ought to have known better—indulged in language which would have been simply ludicrous save for the horror of the event which occasioned but could not justify it. A public meeting, for instance, was held at the town of Swampscott on the evening of the Monday succeeding the catastrophe. The gentleman who presided over it very discreetly, in his preliminary remarks, urged those who proposed to join in the discussion to control their feelings. Hardly had he ceased speaking, however, when Mr. Wendell Phillips was noticed among the audience, and immediately called to the platform. His remarks were a most singular commentary on the chairman's injunction to calmness. He began by announcing that the first requisite to the formation of a healthy public opinion in regard to railroad accidents, as other things, was absolute frankness of speech, and he then proceeded as follows:—"So I begin by saying that to my mind this terrible disaster, which has made the last thirty-six hours so sad to us all, is a deliberate murder. I think we should try to get rid in the public mind of any real distinction between the individual who, in a moment of passion or in a moment of heedlessness, takes the life of one fellow-man, and the corporation that in a moment of greed, of little trouble, of little expense, of little care, of little diligence, takes lives by wholesale. I think the first requisite of the public mind is to say that there is no accident in the case, properly speaking. It is a murder; the guilt of murder rests somewhere." Mr. Phillip's definition of the crime of "deliberate murder" would apparently somewhat unsettle the criminal law as at present understood, but he was not at all alone in this bathos of extravagance. Prominent gentlemen seemed to vie with each other in their display of ignorance [19, pp. 97-98].

• Show how accident reporting is handled in England and to give some examples of their accidents, as well as an earlier one on the Camden and Amboy.

At the end of his piece, Adams returned to the topic of the need for more safety devices and safeguards and how they have improved the situation:

> There is, however, another and far more attractive side to the picture. The lives sacrificed at Revere were not lost in vain. Four complete railroad years passed by since that catastrophe occurred, and during that time not less than one hundred and thirty millions of persons were carried by rail within the limits of Massachusetts. Of this vast number not a single one has been lost through any causes for which any railroad company is responsible. This certainly was a record with which no community could well find fault; and it was due more than anything else to the great disaster of August 26, 1871. More than once, and on more than one road, accidents occurred which, but for the improved appliances introduced in consequence of the experience at Revere could

hardly have failed of fatal results. Not that these appliances were in all cases very cheerfully or very eagerly accepted. Neither the Miller platform nor the Westinghouse brake won its way into general use unchallenged. Indeed, the earnestness and even the indignation with which presidents and super-intendents then protested that their car construction was better and stronger than Miller's; that their antiquated handbrakes were the most improved brakes, better, much better, than the Westinghouse; that their crude old semaphores and targets afforded a protection to trains which no block-system would ever equal,—all this certainly was comical enough, even in the very shadow of the great tragedy. Men of a certain type always have protested and will always continue to protest that they have nothing to learn; yet, under the heavy burden of responsibility, learn they still do. They dare not but learn [19, p. 102].

Thus, where the reports on the accidents in other cases were concluded within months after the accident, the discussion of the Revere accident went on five and even eight years after the event in articles and books by Adams because:

The worst of it is . . . that if the blood of the martyrs thus profusely spilled is at all the seed of the church, it is a seed terribly slow of germination. Each step in the slow progress is a Golgotha. In the case of railroad disasters, however, a striking exception is afforded to this rule. The victims of these, at least, do not lose their lives without great and immediate compensating benefits to mankind. After each new "horror," as it is called, the whole world travels with an appreciable increase of safety. Both by public opinion and the courts of law the companies are held to a most rigid responsibility. The causes which led to the disaster are anxiously investigated by ingenious men, new appli-ances are invented, new precautions are imposed, a greater and more watchful care is inculcated. And hence it has resulted that each year, and in obvious consequence of each fresh catastrophe, travel by rail has become safer and safer, until it has been said, and with no inconsiderable degree of truth too, that the very safest place into which a man can put himself is the inside of a first-class railroad carriage on a train in full motion.

The study of railroad accidents is, therefore, the furthest possible from being a useless one, and a record of them is hardly less instructive than interesting. If carried too far it is apt, as matter for light reading, to become somewhat monotonous; though, none the less, about these, as about every-thing else, there is an almost endless variety. Even in the forms of sudden death on the rail, nature seems to take a grim delight in infinitude of surprises [16, final page].

IN THE END

No one went to jail for the Revere accident, a conclusion foreshadowed in a *New-York Daily Tribune* observation in September 1871:

The Massachusetts law relating to railway accidents is this: The corporation may be assessed not over $5,000 for killing a passenger. A careless servant of the road may be punished by imprisonment for a term not exceeding one year in length, and by a fine of not more than $1,000. Well, here's your Eastern Railroad case; here are your careless servants, your murders, and your laws; and yet we question whether either the corporation or its careless servants will have much trouble, except from personal suits, which may be economically compromised. As for the year's imprisonment, we doubt if either conductor is shaking much in his shoes at the prospects of that [22, p. 3].

However, the accident did wreak financial havoc for the Eastern Railroad; according to its own figures, there was $510,600 in damages. President Browne, who had not accepted Prescott's resignation for the Hamilton accident, had his own resignation quickly accepted by the Board of Directors. The stock price for the road began a rapid descent from an average of $120.81 in 1870 to $114 in 1871 to $9.25 in 1875, the lowest in its history. It merged with the Boston and Maine in 1884.

Prescott remained as superintendent on the Eastern Railroad until 1875, when he was nominated by the governor and received confirmation to become general manager of the Hoosac Tunnel [24, p. 699]—then the longest tunnel in North America and a high point of nineteenth century civil engineering. Prescott held his new job for five years [25, p. 389], and it was a plum position, since the salary was as high as the governor's, and yet all the intricate management problems surrounding the tunnel's construction over two decades had been completed by the time he arrived. Ironically, Adams indirectly became Prescott's boss by being one of the "corporaters" for Massachusetts when the state took over the tunnel from the private railroad firm. Adams is shown visiting the tunnel in 1876 in Figure 45, with Prescott somewhere in the middle. (Charles Felt, Prescott's former subordinate, claimed in *Nuts for Butler to Crack,* that this position was a *quid pro quo* with Congressman Butler, who had needed Prescott's free railroad passes for voters in 1868, 1870, and 1872 [26; 27, p. 1].)

However, before Prescott left his Eastern Railroad position, he got his comeuppance late one night when, having advertised a train to leave at 11 P.M., he failed to issue orders for it to start. Passengers found a horse and buggy, drove to Prescott's house, woke him, and took him to Boston to issue appropriate orders [2, p. 24].

Charles Hatch of the Lake Shore and Michigan Southern Railway, the road that is the subject of the next chapter, was brought in as president in 1872 and perfected telegraphic coordination of trains, introduced Westinghouse air brakes, installed automatic electric signal blocks—in fact, all the improvements recommended by the commission [29, p. 23]. The annual report of the railroad commissioners a year after their Revere report had this to say about Mr. Hatch's efforts:

> On no railroad in the United States probably has such vigilance to prevent accidents been exercised during the last year as upon the Eastern Railroad. The best appliances [e.g., Westinghouse air-brakes] and modes of

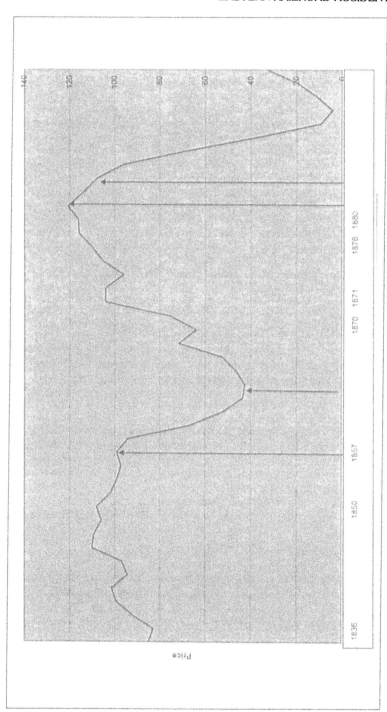

Figure 44. History of Eastern Railroad stock price fluctuations from 1836 to 1884 [23]. Notice the precipitious drop in value after the 1871 accident.

Figure 45. Adams (A on the extreme right) and Massachusetts railroad commissioners visiting Hoosac Tunnel in the spring of 1876 [28, p. 81].

constructing rolling stock had been adopted without regard to expense; a most thorough system of electric signals to warn all trains of their proximity to each other had been put in use on the more crowded parts of the line; nothing which suggested itself to their minds as a precaution against accident had been neglected by the officials [30, p. 17].

It is also quite interesting to consider how the new management rewrote the rules for the running of trains that Adams with his law degree and long experience in the railroad industry had found so difficult to understand:

• Where the earlier instructions were very location specific in the use of signals, e.g., "At the junction of the Saugus Branch at South Malden Two Balls or Two Red Lanterns"; "At the Junction of the East Boston Branch with the Main Road, at North Chelsea, One Ball or Lantern"; "At the Junction of the Saugus Branch at West Lynn, the target or two lanterns crosswise" is replaced by general rules for the use of bells, whistles, lamps, flags, draws, and colors throughout the system. Thus, the amount of information on signals is greatly reduced and simplified, i.e., "4. One bell, when running, is a signal to stop. This is the only bell signal." "A lantern raised and lowered vertically is a signal for 'starting;' when swung at right angles, or crossways of the track, 'to stop.' When swung in a circle, 'back the train'" [31, p. 1].

• Where the earlier instructions were very time-specific because the coordination of the system was done only by timetable, a new ten-page section is included for the "Telegraph Department" and the "Rules for Running Trains by Telegraph."

• The former list of 137 rules scattered among the reproduction of state ordinances and schedules and beginning with a new number "1" ten times now grows to include 368 rules numbered sequentially throughout the book and not interrupted by the reproduction of state ordinances, which are segregated to a different part of the manual.

• Whereas in the earlier list a whole page is devoted for the conductor on the "Rules for the Punching of Tickets," those are deleted in the new set of rules and much more emphasis is placed on safety, such as, "They must ascertain where the air-brakes are in proper working condition; and see that the Brakemen are properly stationed, where the train is equipped with air-brakes or not" [31, p. 22].

• President Rockwell signed these rules, rather than the superintendent as was done earlier—thus signifying the level of importance the company attached to the new set of rules.

Sadley, despite all these improvements, an accident on October 22, 1872, killed two and wounded twenty near Seabrook. The week following this incident three minor accidents occurred, causing the *Boston Advertiser* to write: "If there is such a thing as ill luck, surely the Eastern Railroad has fallen into it" [32].

The reports issuing from the coroner's jury, the company, the newspapers, and the "disinterested experts" exemplify the new paradigm of accident investigation. Now it is clearly the "disinterested experts," Adams and the Railroad Commission, who participate on the coroner's jury and give direction to a public petition—both outside the legal boundaries of their commission. The company appears to have used the "Justice" columns of the *American Railroad Journal* to project blame onto Prescott . . . who seems to have his own journalistic connections with the *Railroad Gazette,* and the *American Railroad Journal,* which in 1875, upon his appointment as manager of the Hoosac Tunnel, described Prescott in the following manner:

> Mr. Prescott brings great experience and ability to his new position, his knowledge of railroad matters and acquaintance with business men eminently fitting him for the duties of this important trust [24, p. 699].

Adams, by working with the coroner's jury, the petitioning group, and then having a version of the commission's investigation into the accident reprinted in his *Atlantic Monthly* piece five years later, had hoped for some national action along the lines of the British, who would collect statistics on accidents on a

national level, analyze them, and come up with some organizational, technological, and/or operational corrections:

All that is necessary is that provision should be made its connection with the
Department of the Interior for a bureau of railway statistics. It should include
two officers, the one accountant and statistician, the other a railroad expert and
engineer. The first should collect and put in shape for reference this vast
amount of information connected with the interior commerce of the country,
which is now practically inaccessible. The last should make a study of all
railroad accidents, and specially investigate those that present unusual
features, or the cause of which is difficult of attainment. The public would
then know what the railroad companies are now under the strongest inducement to keep to themselves.

In the first place, it would know—what now it does not—how many
railroad accidents take place, and how many lives are lost or injuries sustained
in them. In Great Britain last year—carrying on their railroads at least twice as
many travelers as we did on ours—they reported but 17 passengers killed.
No one can say how many were killed during the, same time in this country—
probably 10 times 17. But apart from mere statistics, we should then know
to what causes—whether carelessness, or defective material, or imperfect
appliances, or poor construction, or natural agencies each disaster was due
[33, p. 5; 34; 35, p. 207].

However, this did not happen. Thus, six years later, with no national changes
being made, he would write despairingly:

... the railroad company can, and probably will, investigate it thoroughly in its
own interest. The public cannot. It has no machinery better than a "crownur's
'quest" for doing so. Yet, in this matter, the interest of the public and the
interest of the corporation are far from identical. In a case of manslaughter, we
do not generally leave the investigation into the circumstances wholly in the
hands of those responsible for the killing. Practically, this is exactly what we
habitually do in this country when the killing is done by a railroad company
[33, p. 5; 34; 35, p. 207].

Adams got another chance to introduce his national railroad board when he
became involved in 1877 with the Ashtabula Bridge accident, the subject of
our next chapter.

ENDNOTES

1. *Brooklyn Eagle,* November 15, 1852, p. 1.
2. Charles Wilson Felt, *The Eastern Railroad of Massachusetts; Its Blunders, Mismanagement & Corruption,* Liverpool, Lancashire, England: Miss J. Green, 1873.
(Felt was the assistant superintendent under Prescott.)
3. Francis B. C. Bradlee, *The Eastern Railroad: A Historical Account of Early Rail-
roading in Eastern New England,* Salem, Mass.: Essex Institute, 1922.
4. *Every Saturday,* September 16, 1871. Cited in [3, p. 88].

5. L. K. Sillcox, "Safety in Early American Railway Operations," *A Newcomen Address*, 1936.

6. *The Railroad Gazette*, September 2, 1871.

7. *Boston Daily Advertiser*, 118 (62), September 12, 1871, p. 3; 118 (56), September 5, 1871, p. 1.

8. *The New York Times*, 20 (6232), September 11, 1871.

9. *The American Railroad Times*, 1871 issues: October 21 (p. 330); October 28 (p. 343); December 9 (p. 391); December 16 (p. 399); and December 23 (p. 407).

10. "The Eastern Railway Disaster at Revere," *American Railroad Times*, November 11, 1871.

11. Justice, "The Late Accident at Revere Station," *American Railroad Times*, October 28, 1871.

12. Thomas K. McCraw, *Prophets of Regulation*, Cambridge, Mass.: Belknap Press, 1984.

13. *The Massachusetts Railroad Commission Annual Report*, January 1872.

14. "The Railroad Accident," *Boston Daily Advertiser*, 118 (54), 1871.

15. *Rules and Regulations of the Eastern Rail Road, for Running Trains, &c*, Commencing December 7, 1868, No. 88. Issued by J. Prescott, Superintendent.

16. *Notes on Railroad Accidents*, New York: G. P. Putnam's Sons, 1879.

17. *The New York Times*, 20 (6231), September 10, 1871.

18. "Railway Reform in Massachusetts," *New York Tribune*, September 14, 1871.

19. Charles Francis Adams, Jr. "The Revere Catastrophe," *Atlantic Monthly*, (37), January 1876.

20. "Lectures," *Boston Evening Transcript*, 48 (14658), February 3, 1875.

21. Charles Francis Adams, Jr. "The Railroad Problem," *Railroad Gazette*, 1875.

22. *New-York Daily Tribune*, September 14, 1871.

23. Developed from financial figures in *A Brief History of the Eastern Railroad*. Website.

24. *American Railroad Journal*, 31 (22), May 29, 1875.

25. *American Railroad Journal*, April 16, 1881.

26. Charles Wilson Felt, *Nuts for Butler to Crack*, Boston, N.P. 1879. It is interesting to note that when Butler was asked on the campaign trail for governor of Massachusetts about the Revere accident, and what he would offer as a remedy, he suggested raising the salaries of the engineer and brakeman to be the highest-paid on the road so that really qualified men would fill the positions. He also thought the whole idea of the coroner's jury was "an invention of our ancestors, and had gone by," p. 8.

27. "General Butler in Lynn," *Boston Daily Herald*, 118 (56), September 5, 1871.

28. Henry Ward Photo, North Adams Public Library Collection. From Carl R. Byron, *A Pinprick of Light: The Troy and Greenfield Railroad and Its Hoosac Tunnel*, Shelburne, Vt.: New England Press, 1995.

29. William A. Crafts, "Ten Years Working of the Massachusetts Railroad Commission," in *The Railroad Gazette*, New York: State Railroad Commissions, 1883.

30. *Fourth Annual Report of the Board of Railroad Commissioners*, Boston, Mass.: Wright & Potter, State Printers, January 1873.

31. *General Rules and Regulations of the Eastern Railroad Company, for the Government and Information of Employees Only, April 1878*. Boston, Mass.: Franklin Press, 1878.

32. *Boston Advertiser*, October 1872.

33. *Iron Age*, 19 (3), January 18, 1877.

34. Also *New York Tribune,* January 13, 1877.

35. *Atlantic Monthly,* 1877.

36. Report of the Committee of the Directors of the Eastern Railroad Company Appointed to Investigate the Causes of the Accident at Revere on the Evening of August 26, 1871. Boston, Mass.: Henry W. Dutton and Son, 1871.

CHAPTER 7

The Ashtabula Railroad Disaster, December 29, 1876—The State and the Professionals Take Over

Little Bo-Peep
Is fast asleep,
In th' Excursion train you'll find him:
Oh! It's ten to one
If he ever gets home—
For a 'Special' is close behind him!

To the tune of Little Bo-Peep,
"The Railway Nursery Rhymer" [1, p. 1]

Stone & Boomer, Co. was hired by the Pacific Railroad of Missouri to build the Gasconade Bridge in 1855, on which the Chief Engineer and thirty others were killed [2, p. 713]. Three years later, Andros Stone left the firm and moved to Cleveland, where he became president of the Cleveland Rolling Mill Company. Five years earlier, his brother, Amasa, had also turned from bridge building to become president of the Lake Shore and Michigan Southern Railroad [3, p. 122]. In 1863, the executives thought that the wooden bridge used by the Lake Shore and Michigan Southern Railroad over a deep gorge of the Ashtabula River needed to be replaced. Still considering himself a bridge designer, Amasa Stone sketched out a new bridge on the pattern of a tried-and-true Howe truss such as that used on the Gasconade Bridge and elsewhere through the West. However, this was to be "Mr. Stone's Pet Bridge" [4, pp. 63-67], and it was to be the longest span and an all-iron Howe truss bridge [5, p. 88], using wrought-iron I-beams supplied by his brother Andros' mill.

FOUR VARIATIONS ON THE TRIED-AND-TRUE HOWE TRUSS DESIGN

In designing the bridge, Amasa made four important variations on the tried-and-true Howe truss design. The first two variations had to do with length

Figure 46. Sculpted head of Amasa Stone, architect of
the Ashtabula Bridge [6].

and materials. Amasa had earlier built an all-iron Howe truss bridge, as the first all-iron bridge in Ohio in 1850, over the Ohio Canal in Cleveland [7, p. 36]. However, it was only five feet high; this bridge was to be 70 feet high. Moreover, his earlier bridge was 25 to 30 feet long; this was to be 154 feet long. To achieve this length and height, all of the components of Stone's new bridge were to be made of wrought iron. Since bridge loads were nearly doubling [8, p. 97], wrought iron's strength was certainly needed for the Ashtabula's bridge, even though it would cost dearly [9]. However, with the added strength came added weight of the bridge itself, the dead weight, and thus the bridge would have to support more weight just from itself. When a civil engineer and railroad-employed designer, Joseph Tomlinson, finished his original design of the new bridge, he objected to Stone's demands for an all iron-bridge [10]. He was fired. Subsequently, when the road's chief engineer, Charles Collins, was asked to take over the construction, he refused. And so, in the end, Stone replaced these engineers with his own designs and a carpenter—a carpenter who had never built a bridge of any sort, let alone long, high, iron bridges.

A third variation on the tried-and-true Howe truss design involved turning the traditional "through" design upside down so that the upper chord was the roadbed and all the support trusses were below rather than above (contrast Figure 34 with Figure 49). This particular variation of the Howe design had a known tendency to buckle where the braces supported the chord. And, indeed, the bridge's braces buckled at the first trial of the bridge. This problem was then compounded by the fact that the I-beams at the chords had been placed on their sides rather than, as shown in Figure 47, on a vertical. To correct this, the problem was further

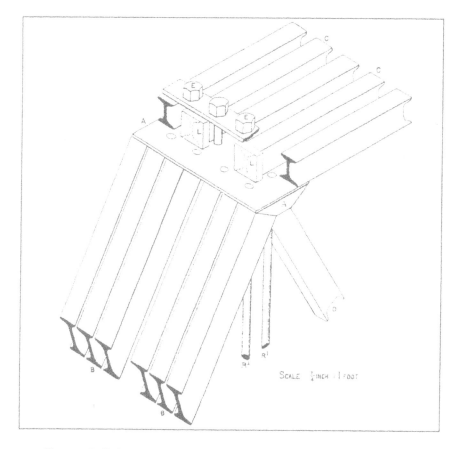

Figure 47. Point at which braces were attached to cast-iron angle joint. Points (A) is where a lug protruded from the angle joint taking the compression stresses of the roadbed and transferring them to the braces.

complicated yet again by the addition of more iron I-beams as braces, increasing the already large dead weight. However, when it was found that the additional braces would not fit cleanly into the angle-iron block, to the problem was compounded yet even more, portions of the I-beams were cut away to fit (see Figure 48), thus weakening their ability to transfer compression.

Stone's fourth variation on the tried-and-true Howe truss design was that he designed the Ashtabula Bridge to be a "Single Howe" truss design. Most Howe trusses in the East and Midwest had two diagonal braces and one counterbrace in each panel, with two vertical rods between (see rebuilt version of the bridge, which had this typical bracing for a Howe truss, Figure 54). Often the end panels had three rods. Only five Eastern bridges were not so designed, and they were called "Single Howe," because they had but one diagonal brace and one or more panel rods. The Ashtabula was like these singular bridges.

Erected in 1865, according to orders and patterns given by Stone [12, pp. 15-17], the bridge had panels 11 feet long, and between these the strength of the chords depended on three iron beams 6 inches thick and 8 inches wide. The whole width of the bridge was 19½ feet; its height between chords 20 feet; its length 165 feet, and all in a single span. Moreover, the bridge was not cheaply made—it cost $75,000, a rather large sum for a bridge at that time [8, p. 97]. The *Railroad Gazette* in February wrote: "All engineers who have examined the bridge agreed that there was a superfluous amount of material in it; that no expense was spared to make it as safe as possible" [13, p. 86]. In later testimony, Tomlinson, the fired civil engineer and railroad-employed designer, was asked if he thought that frugality was a consideration in the erection of the bridge. For a man fired by Stone, his answer was quite telling: "I think not. I think it was Mr. Stone's intention to make a first-class bridge" [14, p. 111]. For eleven years the bridge was in constant service on the mainline of the Lake Shore and Michigan Southern.

THE ACCIDENT

Then, on December 29, 1876, the bridge gave way, and the disaster was described in the following article from *Harper's Weekly:*

> Our illustration shows the scene of the terrible railroad accident at Ashtabula Creek on the night of December 29, 1876. The train, consisting of eleven cars drawn by two engines, reached the bridge over Ashtabula Creek about eight o'clock, and was moving at a low rate of speed. The engines had crossed in safety, when the bridge, without warning, gave way, and the whole train, with the exception of the leading engine, the couplings of which broke, was precipitated into the ravine, a distance of seventy-five feet. The banks are steep, and the furious snow-storm that had been raging for several hours rendered it difficult for those who hastened to the scene of the disaster to reach the wreck. To add to the horror of the situation, the cars took fire from the stoves, and many passengers who were not killed outright by the fall were

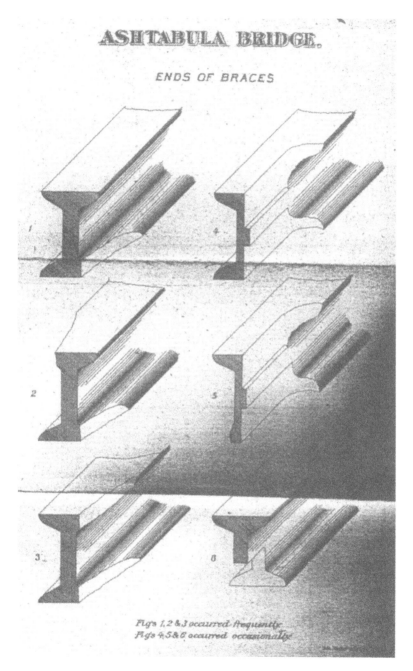

Figure 48. The cutaway bridge braces attempt to correct a
construction mistake [11].

Figure 49. The bridge as built and depicted in an article
in *Harper's Weekly* [15, p. 48].

burned to death. Imprisoned by heavy fragments of the broken cars, or unable
to move on account of injuries, men, women, and children met death in this
agonizing form. Some, it is supposed, were drowned.

Help arrived early from Ashtabula village, but nothing could then be done
to save life, except to remove the wounded, who had already been taken from
the cars, to places where they could have surgical attention. The heat from the
burning wreck was intense, and in the confusion of the moment the means
which might have been used to extinguish the flames were not thought of until
too late. At the water-works, within 150 yards of the burning cars, lay 500 feet
of hose, the coupling of which exactly fitted a plug within pistol-shot of the
fire, the plug being connected with a powerful pumping apparatus, and there
being sixty pounds of steam in the pump boiler. The hose could have been
pouring a stream on the fire within five minutes but for somebody's fault or
stupidity.

Figure 50. Photograph of locomotive on end of
Ashtabula Bridge as originally built.

A survivor of the disaster, Mr. BURCHELL, of Chicago, describes the
scene in vivid colors: "The first thing I heard was a cracking in the front part of
the car, and then the same cracking in the rear. Then came another cracking in
the front louder than the first, and then came a sickening oscillation and a
sudden sinking, and I was thrown stunned from my seat. I heard the cracking
and splintering and smashing around me. The iron-work bent and twisted like
snakes, and every thing took horrid shapes. I heard a lady scream in anguish,
'Oh! help me!' Then I heard the cry of fire. Some one broke a window, and
I pushed the lady out who had screamed. I think her name was Miss
BINGHAM. The train lay in the valley in the water, our car a little on its side,
both ends broken in. The rest of the train lay in every direction, some on end,
some on the side, crushed and broken. The snow in the valley was nearly to my
waist, and I could only move with difficulty. The wreck was then on fire. The
wind was blowing from the east, and whirling blinding masses of snow
over the terrible ruin. The crackling of the flames, the whistling wind, the
screaming of the hurt, made a pandemonium of that little valley, and the water
of the freezing creek was red with blood or black with the flying cinders.
    The number of persons killed can not be accurately stated, as it is not known
exactly how many there were on the train, and it is supposed that some bodies
were entirely consumed in the flames. The official list of the killed and those
who have died of their injuries, gives the number as fifty-five, but it is
supposed to be somewhat higher.

Figure 51. The destruction of the bridge from *Harper's Weekly*. Notice the terrible conditions of snow, ice, and fire.

Figure 52. The destruction of the Ashtabula Bridge from *Daily Graphic.*

On this page we give a diagram showing the construction of the bridge, which was of iron. [See Figure 49.] It was built about eleven years ago, and was supposed to be a structure of great strength. It had been, tested with the weight of six locomotives; heavy trains had crossed on both its tracks at the same time; it was believed to be well constructed of the best materials. Yet suddenly it fell under a weight far below its tested strength. No wonder that the traveling public anxiously inquire, "What was the cause?" Was it improperly constructed? Was the iron of inferior quality? After eleven years of service, had it suddenly lost its strength? Or had a gradual weakness grown upon it unperceived? Might that weakness have been discovered by frequent and proper examination? Or was the breakage the sudden effect of intense cold? If so, why had it not happened before in yet more severe weather? Is there no method of making iron bridges of assured safety? And who is responsible (so far as human responsibility goes) for such an accident—the engineer who designed the bridge, or the contractor, or the builders, or the railroad corporation? Was the bridge, when made, the best of its kind, or the cheapest of its kind? Was the contract for building "let to the lowest bidder," or given to the most honest, thorough workmen? These and a hundred similar queries arise in every thoughtful mind, and an anxious community desire information and assurance of safety. The majority of people can not, of course, understand the detailed construction of bridges, but they do desire confidence in engineers, builders, contractors, manufacturers, who have to do with the making of them, and in the railroad companies, into whose hands they are constantly putting their own lives and the lives of those dearest to them [15, p. 48].

THE INVESTIGATIONS

As in all the previous investigations, the first group to investigate the disaster was the local coroner's jury. And, as usual, from across the country, the expectations were very low:

- the *Iron Age* journal flatly declared "we do not expect much from Coroner's Jury" [16, p. 14];
- the *Railroad Gazette* was even more scathing:

    Coroner's juries are proverbial for their stupidity, and when the subject to be investigated involves some of the most abstruse facts involved, or draw correct conclusions from premises involving profound mathematical and scientific questions. It is very rare that either coroners or coroners' juries have any special training which would qualify them for investigating intelligently the causes of ordinary railroad accidents, and when such inquiries involve some of the most profound questions of engineering science, the average coroner and his jury are as helpless and imbecile as so many children would be in dealing with the facts or in drawing conclusions therefrom [17, p. 6].

- even *The New York Times* joined the critical chorus in an editorial:

    Two investigations into the cause of the Ashtabula disaster are now going on—one conducted by the local coroner and one by a committee of the Ohio Legislature; neither of them, however, promises any satisfactory result. It is quite evident, from the testimony so far taken, that there was loose management of the affairs of the Lake Shore Road, a dozen years since, when the bridge was built, and that confusion, jealousy, and want of system prevailed among the officers of the company. But, while it will be very easy to make unpleasant impressions on the public mind by the reproduction of the quarrels of that time, the questions involved in the case of the disaster are not solved by such evidence [18, p. 4].

Moreover, as in all previous investigations except that of the *Moselle,* everyone expected the company to investigate itself. Again, from across the country, the expectations were very low:

- from the *Railroad Gazette:*

    On the other hand if such investigations are delegated to the officers of railroads themselves, then we have judge, jury, and counsel deliberating on a case in which each is or may be vitally interested: in which some are possibly or probably culpable; and in rendering a verdict, if "the truth, the whole truth and nothing but the truth" is told they may be imposing enormous penalties on the company to which their fealty and from which their salaries are due, Even without such selfish motives, the temptation is great to shield a companion officer, or to lay or not lift the mantle which would or does cover some fact which would reveal the true cause of the disaster, and which would be a verdict of condemnation of a superior officer whose voice might be potent to certain or dismiss the very people who pronounce the decision [17, p. 6].

The *Railroad Gazette* despairingly concluded:

Now this being the case, what shall be done? Must such investigation be entrusted to the bungling and stupid inquiries of mere local coroners without any special qualifications for such work, or must we accept only such information as railroad officials may choose to give to the public? In the present condition of things, this is undoubtedly the only alternative. The only courts which represent the interests of the public, at least so far as investigation into the causes for the purpose of preventing similar accidents are concerned are coroners' juries, and the voluntary verdicts which the railroad companies may choose to render. After an accident, among the first things usually done by the companies themselves, who are prima facie the culprits, is to remove all evidence indicating the cause of accidents usually without reference to finding out the cause of the reason for their occurrence.

The moral which we wish to suggest should be drawn from the late sad calamity is, that there should be some competent authority created by the state whose duty is to make a thorough investigation of all railroad accidents which result in loss of life. The Board of Trade in England is such an authority, and accidents are there carefully investigated and full reports thereon made, giving all the facts and conclusions relating thereto. Competent engineers are employed by the board for this work. A board or railroad commissioners might act in such a capacity here, if they were made entirely independent of political influences.

If the terrible sacrifice of human life which is made each year on our railroads is to have any meaning at all, it is to teach us how to avoid accidents in future. To disregard entirely such costly lessons and to allow the victims to be carried to their graves and leave no warning to those who are left behind, is to add to the crime of our own ignorance or carelessness that of indifference to a warning which is made more which attended the fall of the Ashtabula bridge [17, p. 6].

• in a *New York Times* editorial on January 21, 1877, a few weeks after the investigations had begun:

In what has so far been done, there is little reason for hope that the actual and complete causes of the awful disaster at Ashtabula will ever be known. The investigation from which most was to have been expected, that of the Ohio Legislature, though better by far than the Coroner's inquest made under local authority, cannot, in its result, be accepted as final. The only adequate means for reaching the exact and whole truth—if, indeed, that has at any time been within reach—was a careful inquiry by competent engineers free from the bias of previous employment by the Lake Shore Railroad or its associate companies, yet aided by that road. Such an investigation the officers of the Lake Shore Road could have had if they had desired it, and to have secured it would have been an act of great service to the public and some compensation for the calamity at Ashtabula. But as the company did not choose to secure the investigation, and as there was, unfortunately, no means of compelling them to provide or submit to it, the disaster must remain a sort of vague horror in the history of railway travel, unrelieved by any practical and valuable warning, conveyed for the future [19, p. 4].

Within a week of the disaster, the central figure of the Revere disaster, Charles Francis Adams, Jr., chairman of the Massachusetts Railroad Commission, reappeared and wrote to the congressman who represented the Ashtabula, Ohio, district, James A. Garfield (Garfield would be elected president three years later). Adams's letter was published in *Iron Age*, the *New York Tribune,* and the *Atlantic Monthly.* He also had very definite expectations of how the accident investigation of the Ashtabula Bridge would take place:

My Dear Sir:

You, I believe, represent the Ashtabula district in Congress. For this reason, and this reason only, I apply directly and personally to you in the hope, by so doing, of securing some good public results from the deaths of the hundred victims of the recent Ashtabula railroad accident. As respects the number of those killed, it leads, I believe, the whole ghastly record. Before, its details, then, wholly disappear from the press, and the impression made by it from the public mind, I want to call attention to one great want which it revealed in our public system All the world in America travels, and the traveling is necessarily done by rail. In that way the intercourse, as well as the commerce between the states of the Union is kept up. Now, it is perfectly true that this travel is wonderfully secure now, making the Union as a whole, as secure as it is in Europe, but still its security is marvelous. Allowing all credit to those to whom credit is due on this account, it still remains true that during the last four years there have been, upon an average, 1100 reported railroad accidents a year, resulting in the death of 250 persons and the injury of 1000 persons annually. There also are the cases of accidents, deaths and injuries that we know of, without any system of official reports. How many more have occurred of which no record has been made, we have no means of ascertaining. Now, very likely it may be said that this is not a large price on human life and limb to pay for such an enormous amount of transportation at much a great rate of speeds This may well be so and yet, unquestionably, even this amount would admit of great reduction. It can, however, be reduced only by a careful study of its causes and by distinctly placing the responsibility for each accident just where it belongs.

In the case of the Ashtabula accident, for instance, the railroad company can, and probably will, investigate it thoroughly in its own interest. The public cannot. It has no machinery better than a "crownur's 'quest" for doing so. Yet, in this matter, the interest of the public and the interest of the corporation are far from identical. In a case of manslaughter, we do not generally leave the investigation into the circumstances wholly in the hands of those responsible for the killing. Practically, this is exactly what we habitually do in this country when the killing is done by a railroad company. Here in Massachusetts, every railroad accident which occurs is at once investigated by the Railroad Commissioners, and, if it presents any features of importance, a formal report upon it is published. These reports always specify exactly how and why the accident occurred, and who, if anyone was responsible for it. The annual report of the board for the last year will include eight of these special reports, each one of which closes with a district statement that "this accident was due" to such and such causes.

. . .

All that is necessary is that provision should be made in connection with the Department of the Interior for a bureau of railway statistics. It should include two officers, the one accountant and statistician, the other a railroad expert and engineer. The first should collect and put in shape for reference this vast amount of information connected with the interior commerce of the country, which is now practically inaccessible. The last should make a study of all railroad accidents, and himself specially investigate those which present unusual features, or the cause of which is difficult of attainment. The public would then know what the railroad companies are now under the strongest inducement to keep to themselves.

In the first place, it would know—what now it does not—how many railroad accidents take place, and how many lives are lost or injuries sustained in them. In Grèat Britain last year—carrying on their railroads at least twice as many travelers as we did on ours—they reported but 17 passengers killed. No one can say how many were killed during the, same time in this country— probably 10 times 17. But apart from mere statistics, we should then know to what causes—whether carelessness, or defective material, or imperfect appliances, or poor construction, or natural agencies each disaster was due. The experience of one railroad would be made the experience of all. Now each official is limited to his own narrow range of observation. Finally, and most important of all, through such an agency the use of improved appliances could be hastened. An official report stating with unpleasant precision the conclusion that "this disaster would not have occurred had the train been equipped" with some well known appliance—this conclusion exercises a wonderfully quickening influence on every railroad official who reads it. It is a form of words, also, which would often have to be used.

The lives lost at Ashtabula will not have been thrown away if, through you, they should arouse Congress to a sense of the propriety of creating some machinery through which other and similar holocausts may be intelligently investigated. I feel very confident that if you would introduce and now urge forward the necessary measure to bring that about, you would satisfy a strongly felt public demand, and the law would be passed with opposition from no one.

With great respect . . .
Charles F. Adams Jr.
Boston, January 9, 1877 [20, p. 5; 21; 22, p. 207; 23]

Adams fully expected the company would investigate itself in its own interest just as in the case of the *New England,* the *Richmond,* and the *Camden and Amboy.* Moreover, he anticipated that the public could not and would not investigate because the public had no machinery better than a "crownur's 'quest" for doing so.

Such criticism is odd coming from someone who had so orchestrated the coroner's jury in the Revere case that it received such accolades as *The New York Times* description of the verdict in that case as "a fair and righteous statement of the responsibility for the disaster" [36, p. 4]. Adams had been able to achieve something with a coroner's jury, so why was he, of all people, so critical? Could it be that his intimate knowledge of railroad accident investigations suggested to him that, if he were not intimately involved, it wouldn't work.

However, this coroner's jury also received accolades such as:

- *The Railway Gazette,* which had termed coroner's juries "bungling and stupid" and "helpless and imbecile as so many children," said about the Ashtabula coroner's jury:

  We doubt whether there has ever been a more thorough investigation of a railroad accident in this country . . . due to the fact that the accident was so interesting to experts in bridge-building . . . and more wonderful than all, it has presented its conclusions in a calm, clear, judicial statement not unworthy of a judge on the bench, and certainly not to be expected of a jury, not to say a coroner's jury [24, pp. 123-124].

- and *The New York Times,* which had said nine months earlier that there was "little reason for hope that the actual and complete causes of the awful disaster at Ashtabula will ever be known" also discovered a similar unexpected quality in the coroner's investigation: "The verdict of the Coroner's Jury on the Ashtabula disaster is unexpectedly clear, precise, and full" [25, p. 4].

Moreover, the company decided not to investigate itself. Only in the *Moselle* investigation had there ever not been a corporate defense report:

  A *Times* reporter inquired of Mr. William H. Vanderbilt yesterday whether or not the Lake Shore Railroad Company, of which he is President, proposed to make an investigation into the cause of the Ashtabula disaster. Mr. Vanderbilt replied that the railroad company, by itself, had not contemplated making an investigation for the reason that its officers believed the investigation now in progress on the part of the Ohio Legislative Committee would probably develop all the facts that could be obtained. The railroad company itself would be far less able to conduct a thorough examination than a committee of the legislature which had power to summon witnesses and compel them to testify [25, p. 4].

No only did the coroner's investigation confound expectations, and the company withdraw the usual defensive report, but the two public investigations were joined by a unique one performed voluntarily by a civil engineer, Charles MacDonald, whose findings were read in a paper to the American Society of Civil Engineers [26].

THREE UNIQUE INVESTIGATIONS

Three different investigations of a dramatically different quality from all previous investigations began immediately, overlapped, used the same experts [27], and confounded expectations (see Table 2). The first, as in all the other cases, was the coroner's investigation beginning on December 30. It sought to assign legal responsibility for the disaster preliminary to indictments and a trial. Civil engineer Charles MacDonald performed the second investigation, and published his findings in a paper read to the American Society of Civil Engineers on February 21, 1877, and printed in their transactions. He sought to generate interaction and discussion with other civil engineers to avoid those design problems he found. The third investigation, by a Joint Committee of the state

Table 2. Investigation Schedules

	Coroner's Jury	ASCE-MacDonald	Ohio Legislature
Accident Occurs 12/29/1876	Begins Investigation 12/30/1876	Begins Investigation 1/3/1877	
Week 2			Begins Investigation 1/12/1877
Week 3			
Week 4			
Week 5-7			
Week 8		Ends Investigation 2/21/1877	
Week 9			
Week 10	Ends Investigation 3/8/1877		
Week 11			
Week 12			Ends Investigation 3/22/1877

legislature, began two weeks later on January 12, 1877, and reported its findings on March 22. It sought to design legislation to prevent such accidents.

What made the difference in the quality of the coroner's report and the withdrawal of the company's effort to investigate? In all the Ashtabula investigations, a number of out-of-town engineers traveled to the site at their own expense, studied it, and relayed their findings [28]. The experts were drawn to investigate this disaster, provoking responses from as far away as Boston because this bridge design was thought to be the future of bridge building since it was created wholly from iron. Moreover, the bridge's Howe truss design represented the current status quo in bridge design . . . and in dozens of bridges already created for railroads clear across the country: "The failure of the Ashtabula Bridge not only alarmed the general public, but also shook the blind confidence of railroad companies in their existing bridges" [8, p. 97].

All the experts worried that the collapse of this bridge was a symptom of a prematurely short life expectancy for all iron bridges. Moreover, the Failure Rate Curve suggests that most cases of failure in complex mechanical systems happen early in their life cycle—such as occurred in the *New England* steamboat, the *Richmond* locomotive, the *Moselle* steamboat, and the Gasconade Bridge, which all failed within one month of their creation. Such early failures were predictable. However, the Ashtabula Bridge had been in service for eleven years. What, then, did this failure mean?

It is also interesting to consider that Charles Francis Adams, Jr., the gifted amateur railroad expert, who had never studied engineering, thought his legislative commission was the only way to proceed in these investigations. Indeed, when the Interstate Commerce Commission (ICC) took shape in the 1880s, it followed Adams's lead. However, the Ashtabula investigation represented another line of successful investigations in the tradition of the *Moselle* report by Locke and Kayser's minority report in the Gasconade disaster. Unlike the legislatively sanctioned approach of Adams, these reports came from engineers actively engaged in steamboat and railroad technology, and their audiences were other engineers. Rather than wait for laws, this line of "disinterested" investigation put pressure on the future work by engineers because they had to meet professional standards of work. In a country that prided itself on its gifted-amateur quality, this reliance on specialist professionals was something new.

The Coroner's Jury

A jury was assembled on Saturday, December 30, 1876, the day following the accident. Seven Ashtabula citizens, mostly merchants, were chosen, along with the justice of the peace who was the acting coroner [29], and a jury's counsel. The investigation lasted sixty-eight days.

As already pointed out, this coroner's jury had bridge experts advise them in the general conduct of the investigation, and a number of out-of-town engineers traveled to the site at their own expense, studied it, and relayed their findings to the jury [28].

The actual report from the coroner's jury was eight pages long and was broken into eight succinct points:

First. That at about 7:30 in the evening of Friday, December 29, 1876, the iron bridge in the railroad of the Lake Shore and Michigan Southern Railway Company, spanning Ashtabula creek near Ashtabula station, on said railroad, gave way under the two locomotives and express car forming the forward portion of the west bound passenger train on said railroad known as No. 5, and fell as the leading locomotive passed on to the west abutment, leaving a chasm about sixty feet in depth between the abutments of said bridge, into which the baggage and passenger cars in said train following said express car were precipitated.

Second. That in their fall, the cars were partially destroyed by crushing, and their destruction was completed by a conflagration immediately following, kindled by fire from their stoves.

Third. That the fall of the bridge was the result of defects and errors made in designing, constructing, and erecting it; that a great defect, and one which appears in many parts of the structure, was the dependence of every member for its efficient action upon the probability that all or nearly all the others would retain their position and do the duty for which they were designed, instead of giving to each member a positive connection with the rest, which nothing but a direct rupture could sever. The members of each truss were, instead of being fastened together, rested one upon the other, as illustrated by the following particulars: the deficient cross-section of portions of the top chords and some of the main braces, and insufficient lugs or flanges to keep the ends of the main and counter braces from slipping out of place; in the construction of the packing and yokes used in binding together the main and counter braces at the points where they crossed each other in the shimming of the top chords to compensate deficient length of some of their members; in the placing, during the process of erection, of thick beams where the plan required thin ones, and thin ones where it required thick ones.

Fourth. That the railway company used and continued to use this bridge for about eleven years, during all which time a careful inspection by a competent bridge engineer could not have failed to discover all these defects. For the neglect of such careful inspection, the railway company alone is responsible.

Fifth. That the responsibility of this fearful disaster and its consequent loss of life rests upon the railway company, which, by its chief executive officer, planned and erected this bridge.

Sixth. That the cars in which said deceased passengers were carried into said chasm were not heated by heating apparatus so constructed that the fire in it will be immediately extinguished whenever the cars are thrown from the track and overturned. That their failure to comply with the plain provisions of the law places the responsibility of the origin of the fire upon the railway company.

Seventh. That the responsibility for not putting out the fire at the time it first made its appearance in the wreck rests upon those who were the first to arrive at the scene of the disaster, and who seemed to have been so overwhelmed by the fearful calamity that they lost all presence of mind and failed to use the means at hand, consisting of the steam pump in the pumping house and the fire engine *Lake Erie* and its hose, which might have been attached to the steam pump in time to save life. The steamer belonging to the fire department and also *Protection* fire engine were hauled more than a mile through a blinding snow storm and over roads rendered almost impassable by drifted snow, and arrived on the ground too late to save human life; but nothing should have prevented the chief fireman from making all possible efforts to extinguish what fire then remained. For his failure to do this he is responsible.

Eighth. That the persons deceased, before mentioned, whose bodies were identified, and whose bodies and parts of bodies were unidentified, came to their deaths by the precipitation of the aforesaid cars, in which they were riding, into the chasm in the valley of Ashtabula creek left by the falling of the bridge as aforesaid, and the crushing and burning of said cars aforesaid; for all of which the railway company is responsible [30].

Later, the coroner himself summed up the corporate culpability in the case in the following way:

Mr. Amasa Stone, President of the company at the time of the erection of this structure, had been for years a prominent and successful railroad contractor and builder of wooden Howe truss bridges. With the undoubted intention of building a strong, safe, and durable wrought-iron bridge upon the Howe truss plan, he designed the structure, dictated the drawing of the plans and the erection of the bridge, without the approval of any competent engineer, and against the protest of the man who made the drawings under Mr. Stone's direction, assuming the sole and entire responsibility himself. Iron bridges were then in their infancy, and this one was an experiment which ought never to have been tried or trusted to span so broad and so deep a chasm. This experiment has been at a fearful cost of human life and human suffering. Unquestionably, Mr. Stone had great confidence in his own abilities, and believed he could build and had built a structure that would prove the crowning glory of an active life and an enduring monument to his name [12, p. 207; 31].

The coroner summed up the technical problem affecting the bridge in the following way:

That a great defect, and one which appears in many parts of the structure, was the dependence of every member for its efficient action upon the probability that all or nearly all the others would retain their position and do the duty for which they were designed, instead of giving each member a positive connection with the rest, which nothing but a direct rupture could sever [12, p. 208]

Like the coroner's jury taken in hand by Adams in the Revere case, this jury with its technical experts was able to look beyond proximate causes and individuals low in the defendant company's chain of command. It also was able to develop a critical technical evaluation of the design. In essence, the Revere's and the Ashtabula's coroner's juries transformed the composition of such juries that had been used since the Magna Carta—twelve average citizens meeting to collect evidence shortly after the accident and usually at the scene of the accident. It may still have been average citizens who signed their names to the jury verdict, but it was the scientific experts who aided the juries in their deliberations, giving them the investigative edge that had formerly been employed in the company's defensive reports when the companies had been able to hire scientific luminaries such as Silliman, Olmsted, and Lardner.

The Joint Committee of the Ohio Legislature Report

However, even before the coroner's jury delivered its verdict, on January 12 the state legislature adopted the following joint resolution:

> Resolved by the General Assembly of the State of Ohio, That a joint committee be appointed, consisting of five on the part of the House and three on the part of the Senate, to investigate the cause or causes of the recent accident by the giving away of a bridge on the Lake Shore road, at or near Ashtabula, on the evening of Friday, December 29 1876, and which was so disastrous to human life and property, and to inquire whether any additional legislation is necessary to render travel by rail more secure [11, p. 2].

Their report was much longer than that of the coroner's jury, thirty-eight pages. It contained an executive summary, three separate reports, and a draft bill filled with design specifications:

- an "Engineers' Report," written by three civil engineers, B. F. Bowen, T. H. Johnson, and J. Graham, twelve pages, three plates of illustrations, and eight tables;
- a "Report of Albert S. Howland, Civil Engineer," ten pages long, one sketch, and five tables;
- a "Report of W. S. Williams," three pages long and five tables.

The executive summary written by the legislators was fairly succinct in its conclusions:

Among the several defects in the original construction, your committee would mention the following:

The members composing each main brace were so constructed as to act separately, instead of acting as one member, thus reducing the carrying capacity of the metal greatly below what it could have carried in safety *if* it had been differently disposed. There should have been diagonals riveted to each member of the brace, or other suitable arrangement to unite the members of each brace so that the brace would have formed a truss and have acted as one member instead of several. No provision was made to prevent lateral buckling or bending of the braces. The longer members were used in compression, and the shorter in tension. If the main braces and counters had been permanently fastened together at their intersection, which they were not, that would have added greatly to the strength of the main brace.

There was the same want of *unity* in the members composing the upper chord as in the main braces. No sufficient provision was made to prevent it from lateral buckling. In fact, at that point in the bridge which first gave way, both the braces and the top chord did buckle laterally. Only a part of the members composing the upper chord received the strain from the braces at each angle block or panel point, and the lugs on the top of the angle blocks, through which the strain was transmitted to the upper chord, it is believed were insufficient for that purpose.

The lateral system between the lower chords was defective in this:

the struts were placed at every other panel point, and the tie-rods extended across two panels, and, instead of being fastened at the ends of the struts, were fastened at alternate panel points, crossing each other at the middle of the strut. The sway braces were too small and too infrequent.

The lateral system between the upper chords had the same defects as that between the lower chords, with this exception; the floor-beams had small lugs united to them, and they acted as struts.

No provision was made for holding the members comprising the braces in their places on the angle blocks, and your committee found that many of them were out of place before and at the time the bridge went down. The braces were greatly weakened by imperfect bearings and having their ends chipped off.

A careful calculation showed that the bridge laid down under a load not greater than was liable to be thrown upon it at any time in the ordinary and usual traffic over it. The south truss at the time of the accident supported only 95 per cent of the weight of the one train on the bridge. The bridge carried a double track. It was so designed, and trains did frequently meet on the bridge. There being but two trusses when trains met, each truss must carry the entire weight of one train; and yet, with only 95 per cent of the weight of the train on the south truss at the time of the accident, it gave way. A careful and patient calculation of the strength of the brace at the point of failure (third panel point from the west end of the south truss), and of the strain upon it under that load, shows that it had a factor of safety of only one and six-tenths (1.6), when ordinary prudence and foresight required it to have a factor of safety of five; and the upper chord from the third panel point to the center of the bridge, numbering from west end, had a factor of safety at the several panel points ranging from two (2) to one and two-tenths (1.2), instead of five.

There was one weight upon the bridge which has been overlooked, and did not enter into the calculation of the engineers, as an inspection of their statements will show, namely, the snow on the bridge at the time of the accident. The proof shows twenty inches of snow on the ground. It is probable that much of the snow had blown off the bridge; but whatever weight of snow or ice there was on the bridge would still further diminish the factor of safety in both the braces and upper chord.

In these calculations no allowance has been made for oscillation, jar, or vibration under a rolling load, but the calculations were made, and the factor of safety arrived at, as if the load was quiescent. The truth is, the bridge was liable to go down at any time during the last ten or eleven years under the loads that might at any time be brought upon it in the ordinary course of the company's business, and it is most remarkable that it did not sooner occur.

It would be needless to say that any engineer would be derelict in his duty who did not provide in the construction of a bridge against wind, snow, ice, and the vibration of a rolling load. They are as much to be anticipated and provided against as the law of gravity.

Your committee is of the opinion that a third or center truss in bridges carrying two tracks would greatly promote safety and security. The material of the bridge was good, and likewise the workmanship, with the exceptions before stated. There was material enough in the bridge and a different disposition of it would have secured five times the strength, and small and comparatively inexpensive additions in the way of diagonals on the braces and upper chord, and a securing of the braces to the brace blocks, would have rendered the bridge secure [11, p. 16].

The "lack of unity" problem mentioned in the executive summary appeared in the "engineer's report" in the following fashion:

If the several groups of beams composing the braces and top chord had each been combined into a single member, by riveting on to their flanges a system of diagonal plates—say three and a half by half inch—running alternately from right to left and from left to right across the entire group, the bridge would have been abundantly safe. This arrangement would have made each group strongest in the lateral direction and weakest in the direction of the webs of the beams; but in this direction the beams offer about five times the resistance that they do laterally. The top chord members could then only deflect in single panel lengths, and, on that account, their strength would have been still further increased—twofold. The result would have been that the factors of safety given in the tables would have been increased five times for the braces and *ten times* for the chord. They would have been so excessively strong that much of the material might have been omitted [11, pp. 15-16].

and in Howland's report in the following way:

Another defect is one that appears in many parts of the structure, namely, the dependence of every member for its efficient action upon the probability that all or nearly all the others will retain their positions and do the duty for which they were designed, instead of giving to each member a positive connection with the rest, which nothing but direct rupture will sever. Instead of being made to *hang* together, the members of the structure rested upon one another. This appears in the bearing of the braces on the plane surfaces of angle blocks with nothing but friction to keep them there; in the bearing of members of the top chord against the plane faces of the lugs on the angle blocks with nothing but friction to keep them in their exact places . . . ; it appears again in the connection of the laterals with the angle blocks, which depends up on the angle blocks and chords always remaining in contact. The bearings of the braces on the angle blocks show displacement in the plane of the truss, varying in amount from half an inch to one and one-half inches in twenty or thirty cases; one beam was half off the angle block. In some cases there was lateral displacement of about one inch [11, p. 25].

In comparing the coroner's jury report and the Joint Committee report, both of which shared witness, calculations, and even sketches, there appeared unanimity of opinion. Both declared that the defects would have been seen by competent later inspections, and that it was the overall design that had gone awry. The problem was that some tunnel vision might have entered into these otherwise laudatory investigations because they shared so much expertise and data. Both missed a key piece to the puzzle that was only seen by an investigation that did not share so many common elements.

MacDonald's ASCE Report

MacDonald's report was eleven pages long, and it was designed to generate interaction and discussion with other civil engineers. It was successful in doing this. Five other engineers commented on and criticized MacDonald's report, including one of the nation's leaders in bridge building, Squire Whipple, who had written one of the few texts in the field.

MacDonald's report added two important pieces to the findings, both of which exonerated Amasa Stone. First, when MacDonald inspected the site, he came across a broken piece of cast iron about 6 inches long and 1 and 11/16s wide. When he tracked down its origin, he was able to discover that the cast-iron angle joint of the second truss—the one all the others had suggested failed first—had a missing cast-iron lug from the top (see Figure 53).

When cast iron cooled, ironworkers knew that there was the constant danger of two different parts of a cast cooling at two different rates, resulting in air bubbles developing along the cooling edge differential. Once the cooling was complete, the air bubbles would leave a void or weak point in the casting.

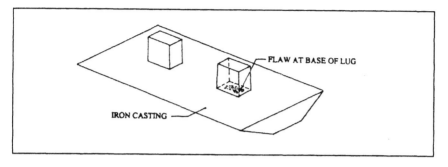

Figure 53. The lug protruding from the angle joint found broken off from the rest of the angle joint because of a fracture at its base— immediate cause of the destruction of the bridge [14].

MacDonald thought this was exactly what had happened to the second truss's angle joint when a foot-thick piece of iron cooled at one rate, and a 1 and 11/16s, six-inch-long piece cooled at another. The resulting void or weak point under years of stress, and the fateful night's extremely cold temperature, propagated a fracture that no inspector would have ever been able to observe, since it was inside the piece of cast iron. This point, according to MacDonald, was the weakest part of the whole bridge and was the immediate cause of its collapse [32]. If the lug had not fractured and failed, he claimed the bridge would have lived out its days without collapsing [33, p. 129].

Having shown that the key point of collapse could not have been observed or prevented, MacDonald went on to put Stone's work in designing the bridge into the context of 1860s engineering:

Twelve years ago, what was the extent of knowledge possessed by engineers on the subject of wrought-iron bridge building,—judge by the work done, rather than what might have been derived from books. On the New England roads there were practically no iron bridges. That great trunk line, the Boston & Albany, still reveled in the security afforded by "the principle of the Howe truss," in wood. The New York Central, under the guidance of a foreign engineer, was experimenting in riveted work, now so much written against. The Pennsylvania Railroad, almost alone in that State, was but in the infancy of the effort which has since resulted in securing to her use some of the finest specimens of bridge architecture in the world. In the West a few scattering efforts had been made, and the subject was beginning to attract the attention of some of the best minds in the country. Squire Whipple, Albert Fink, Shaler Smith, Jacob H. Linville, and Thomas C. Clarke had built bridges at that time, it is true, but such names could almost be counted upon the fingers; and even these would, perhaps, now admit that they then "built better than they knew." If then, the state of knowledge at the time has not been under-estimated, the Ashtabula bridge was the result of an honest effort to improve the bridge practice of the country, undertaken by a man whose experience in wooden bridges warranted him in making the attempt [34, p. 83].

The *Railroad Gazette* concurred with this contextual observation, noting:

> A person who built bridges eleven years ago without such knowledge was much less at fault than he would be now, because such information was less accessible then. The literature at that time was confined within much narrower limits and had not grown into such proportions or assumed the value it has since [13, p. 86].

IN THE END—
MOVE TOWARD LEGISLATIVE ACTION

After giving his testimony before the Ohio Legislature Committee, Charles Collins, chief engineer of the Lake Shore and Michigan Southern Railroad at the time of the bridge's construction, killed himself. He had refused to take part in the building of the bridge, and let a carpenter lead the construction.

Personally and professionally, Amasa Stone was ruined. Six years later, he also committed suicide [35, p. 101]. Tyler Dennett summed up not only Stone's suicide, but the agony of the last twenty years of his life. He had "lived over into a technological age which he did not understand and for which a carpenter's rule of thumb was not sufficient" [35, p. 101].

The bridge was quickly rebuilt (within three months, by the end of March 1877), but with substantially more buttressing underneath the original Howe trusses (see Figure 54). In fact, it was remade as a Pratt truss—and as Professor Robinson of Ohio State University wrote in 1882, "Probably the strongest Pratt truss in the State, so that people need not now go around Ashtabula to avoid a second catastrophe" [37, p. 22].

As part of the investigation by the Ohio legislative committee and as suggested by a report of the American Society of Civil Engineers (ASCE), a bill was introduced in the Ohio legislature "To secure greater safety for public travel over bridges." It never became law.

The ASCE in its reports advocated new specifications for bridge design, which had to wait for over a decade to be enacted [14, p. 123]. However, MacDonald's report was successful in pointing out the dangers of cast iron in bridges, and this material was quickly abandoned in bridge building.

Congressman Garfield responded to Charles Francis Adams's letter by having Adams draft a bill which Garfield, submitted to Congress [39, 40]. *The New York Times* lauded the bill [19, p. 4], but it was not passed. Perhaps Amasa Stone's earlier letter to Congressman Garfield was prescient in this regard:

> I have long known how almost impossible it is for any just claims to receive recognition from Congress, though that august body may respond to any absurd or doubtful one. At the same time, it seemed quite an easy matter when

Figure 54. New Ashtabula Bridge with significantly more underpinning [38, p. 7]. Compare with Figure 49.

properly handed to an engineer. I do not write this letter with any expectation that the claim may still be acted upon, but simply to express my utter disgust with the character of a Congress that can flippantly throw aside the proper business of the people to engage in demoralizing warfare—the great U.S. Congress seems to contain many men most thoroughly versed in the art of "addition, division, and silence" . . . [41, p. 469].

Another decade would pass before Adams's appeal materialized in the form of the Interstate Commerce Commission [42, p. 83].

Three years after the Ashtabula Bridge catastrophe, and the abortive move to national legislation with Garfield, Charles Francis Adams, Jr. tried again to influence national railroad policy with the publication of his *Notes on Railroad Accidents* in 1879 [43, pp. 125-152]. Adams clearly stated in the preface:

> To bring these appliances [the Miller Platform and Buffer, the Westinghouse Brake, and the Interlocking and Electric Signal Systems] into more general use through reports on railroad accidents as they occurred was one great aim with me throughout my official life. I am now not without hopes that the printing of this volume may tend to still further familiarize the public with these inventions, and thus hasten their more general adoption.

ENDNOTES

1. *Brooklyn Eagle,* November 15, 1852,
2. "Terrible Catastrophe on the Pacific Rail Road," *American Railroad Journal,* 11 (45), November 10, 1855.
3. Richard Sanders Allen, *Covered Bridges of the Middle West,* New York: Bonanza Books, 1952.
4. Sara Ruth Watson and John R. Wolfs, *Bridges of Metropolitan Cleveland: Past and Present,* Cleveland, Ohio: s.n.
5. Sarah Katherine Ann Pfatteicher, "Death by Design: Failure and Responsibility in the American Civil Engineering Community Since 1852," Dissertation in History of Science, University of Wisconsin, Madison, 1996.
6. First used as a keystone at the Cleveland Union Railroad Depot; now adorns the Amasa Stone Chapel at Case Western Reserve University.
7. David A. Simmons, "Fall From Grace: Amasa Stone and the Ashtabula Bridge Collapse," *Timeline,* 6 (3), 1989.
8. Henry Petroski, *Engineers of Dreams: Great Bridge Builders and the Spanning of America,* New York: Alfred A. Knopf, 1995.
9. Squire Whipple, *An Essay on Bridge Building,* Utica, N.Y., 1847.
10. George Vose, *Bridge Disasters in America: The Cause and the Remedy* (1880): "An impression exists in the minds of many persons that an iron bridge is necessarily a strong bridge. This is a great mistake. There are good iron bridges and there are also very poor ones. A good iron bridge is the best bridge one can buy; but a poor iron bridge is the worst—much worse than a poor wooden one: for when an iron bridge falls it is apt to go all at once . . . ," p. 7.

11. Ohio General Assembly, Joint Committee on Ashtabula Bridge Disaster, *Report of the Joint Committee concerning the Ashtabula bridge disaster, under joint resolution of the General Assembly*, 1877.

12. Stephen P. Peet, *The Ashtabula Disaster*, Chicago, Ill.: J. S. Goodman & Louis Lloyd & Co., 1877.

13. "The Ashtabula Bridge," *Railroad Gazette*, February 23, 1877, "every precaution had been taken to make the bridge safe."

14. D. A. Gasparini & Melissa Fields, "Collapse of Ashtabula Bridge on December 29, 1876," *Journal of Performance of Constructed Facilities*, 7 (2), May 1993.

15. "Ashtabula Disaster," *Harper's Weekly*, January 20, 1877.

16. *Iron Age*, 19 (2), January 11, 1877.

17. "The Ashtabula Accident," *Railway Gazette*, 26 (7898), January 5, 1877.

18. *The New York Times*, 26 (7941), February 24, 1877.

19. "Inspecting Railroad Accidents," *The New York Times*, 26 (7938), February 21, 1877.

20. *Iron Age*, 19 (3), January 18, 1877.

21. *New York Tribune*, January 13, 1877.

22. *Atlantic Monthly*, 1877.

23. In 1866, Charles F. Adams, Jr. began writing on railroads seeking for the broad principles that should apply to the development of railroad construction. These appeared in three books: *Chapters of Erie and Other Essays* (1871), *Railroads: Their Origin and Problems* (1878), and *Notes on Railroad Accidents* (1879), used in this chapter. When Massachusetts took the lead in establishing a Board of Railroad Commissioners in 1869, Adams was appointed one of the three members. The youngest and most active, he performed the labor, controlled the proceedings, and, in 1872, became the chairman. This position he held until 1879, producing a series of reports on railway accidents and policy that drew attention to the methods and utility of the board and led to the creation in other states of boards closely modeled after that of Massachusetts. He wrote this letter when he was 42.

24. "A Coroner's Verdict," *Railway Gazette*, March 16, 1877.

25. "The Ashtabula Disaster," *The New York Times*, 26 (7900), February 21, 1877; March 10, 1877.

26. MacDonald was president of Union Bridge Company and he supervised the design of the great cantilever bridge across the Hudson at Poughkeepsie [8, p. 156].

27. Albert H. Howland reported to both.

28. "The coroner's jury, with great courtesy, permitted your committee to examine a part of the testimony taken before it, and we submit of that evidence the statements of engineers A. Gottleib, of the Keystone Bridge Company, and John D. C Crehore, of Cleveland, Ohio, and Joseph Tomlinson, who made the original drawings for the bridge." Two or three other engineers also testified for the jury including A. Howland whose report was also included in the legislative report [11, pp. 1-2].

29. Before it lauded the coroner's jury's verdict, *The New York Times* took every opportunity to note in its stories that E. W. Richards was only an acting coroner.

30. The Ashtabula Railway Historical Foundation Web site: http://members.aol.com/ARHF/index.htm

31. *Ashtabula News Extra*, March 8, 1877.

32. This suspicion has been confirmed most recently in [14, p. 123].

33. Joseph Gies, *Bridges and Men,* Garden City, N.Y.: Doubleday & Company, 1963: One further contributing cause for the bridge failure was that the Lake Shore & Southern Michigan employed "compromise cars" whose wheels were built extra wide to handle the inch and a half discrepancies in track gauges between the Lake Shore & Southern Michigan and connecting roads. These cars were notorious for "track-jumping," and their derailment could have contributed greatly to the accident.

34. Charles MacDonald, "The Failure of the Ashtabula Bridge," *Transactions of American Civil Engineers,* 6 (418), 1877.

35. Tyler Dennett, *John Hay: From Poetry to Politics,* New York: Doods, Mead & Company, 1934. There have also been suspicions that this loss of life, which was then the greatest in railroad history, also hastened the death of Commodore Vanderbilt, who owned the line and died just days after the accident.

36. *The New York Times,* 20 (6232), September 11, 1871.

37. S. W. Robinson, *Railroad Economics, or Notes, With Comments, From a Tour over Ohio Railways Under the Hon. H. Sabine Commissioner of Railroads and Telegraphs,* New York: D. Van Nostrand Publisher, 1882.

38. *Daily Graphic,* March 21, 1877.

39. Bill to Provide for a More Thorough Investigation of Accidents Upon Railroads (H. R. No. 4538). Introduced by James A. Garfield, February 1877.

40. Be it enacted by the Senate and House of Representatives of the United States of America Congress assembled:
    - That the President of the United States is hereby authorized and requested to appoint a Board of three Commissioners, who Shall be Officers of Engineers of the Army, inquire into the number, causes and means of prevention of accidents on railroads in the United States, the number of persons killed or injured thereby, and the most approved means of preventing the occurrence of the same; and it shall be the duty of said Commissioners hereafter to investigate such accidents on railroads as may in their judgment be accompanied by circumstances of an unusual or unexplained character, and specially report upon the same.
    - That the Commissioners appointed under this Act shall, in addition to their pay as officers of Engineers of the Army, receive compensation for actual travel and other necessary expenses incurred in the duties herein designated.
    - That, in addition to all special reports from time to time made, the Commissioners herein provided for, shall, at the close of each year, forward to the Secretary of the Treasury a general report upon the subject of accidents upon railroads in the United States during that year, which report, together with any special reports which the Commissioners may have made during such year, shall be submitted to Congress.

41. Thomas C. Cochran, *Railroad Leaders: 1845-1890—The Business Mind in Action,* Cambridge, Mass.: Harvard University Press, 1953: March 1, 1875 letter to Garfield from Stone.

42. Wu Jie, "The Public Reaction to Railroad Accidents in the United States: 1850-1900," Master of Arts Thesis, History Department, University of Massachusetts, Boston, 1982.

43. Charles Francis Adams, *Notes on Railroad Accidents,* New York: G. P. Putnam's Sons, 1879.

CHAPTER 8

Notes on Railroad Accidents

It is but necessary to stand once on the platform of a way station and to look at an express train dashing by. There are few sights finer; few better calculated the quicken the pulses. It is most striking at night. The glare of the head-light, the rush and throb of the locomotive, the connecting rod and driving wheels of which seem instinct with nervous life, the flashing lamps in the cars, and the final whirl of dust in which the red lights vanish almost as soon as they are seen—all this is well calculated to excite our wonder.

Charles Francis Adams, Jr.
"The Railroad Death-Rate" [1, p. 1]

"Railways are dangers should be the earliest round-hand text:
and one of the first chapters in the spelling-book—
the Chapter of Accidents.

"The Railway Nursery Rhymer" [2, p. 1]

A RAILROAD PHILOSOPHER

A member of the Massachusetts Legislature once described the Massachusetts Railroad Commission as composed of

a merchant, an engineer and a philosopher. The last title was given in good-natured derision, but as Mr. Adams had pursued the "scientific method" in his study of the railroad problem, the title was not altogether inappropriate [4, p. 9].

In the Revere accident, Adams had gone beyond his official boundaries and had become directly involved with the local coroner's jury, a petitioning group, and a meeting of state railroad officers, as well as performing his duty to compose the commission's official report the following January [5, pp. xcv-cv].

Three years passed, during which Adams continued his Commission duties and endeavored to mold public support for additional safety on railroads. However, in 1875, Adams decided to try and enlist this public support by again going beyond his official duties and discussing the accidents in public lectures

Figure 55. Danger Ahead! [3, p. 189].

and articles expanding on his Commission's official accident reports. Adams presented "Railroad Accidents" [6, p. 1] in a February 5 lecture—part of twelve lectures on railroads in the famous Lowell Institute lecture series [7, p. 71; 8]. In this lecture Adams combined the Revere disaster with two other disasters, endeavoring to show that each was preventable. As a result, Adams suggested that what had been learned from such accidents helped the railroads become safer:

> Mr. Adams says that in few ways are lives lost with such great and immediate benefit to the rest of the world as by railroad accidents. That is to say, the world thereafter travels more safely for the lessons taught by the accident. Illustrating this statement, he says that since the Revere disaster one hundred and twenty millions of passengers have been carried by railroads within the limits of Massachusetts. During that time but one passenger was killed by any combination of circumstances over which the passenger had no control. But as travelers will not always exercise due care, the average of persons killed or injured on the rail in Massachusetts during that time was three hundred per year. Considering all things—considering the rashness of travelers, the seventy thousand miles of track in the State, and the curves, culverts, and bridges—this is not an excessive sum total of disaster by rail. . . . It was shown that the danger of being murdered in Massachusetts was greater than that of being killed in a railroad accident. Examples of the truth of this are numerous; but the speaker proved by statistics that the average journey resulting in injury is twenty million miles. If a person travel on Massachusetts's railroads eight hundred miles a day he would, by the doctrine of chances, be seventy years old before he received injury by railroad accident [9, p. 4; 10, pp. 106-107].

Later that year the *Railroad Gazette* reprinted some of his Lowell Institute lectures [11], and Adams himself presented them again in a lecture in Oshkosh, Wisconsin. Eventually he reworked them into a lengthy article in an October issue of the *New York Tribune*, "The Railroad Question." Adams also used some of the same information in a series of articles for the *Atlantic Monthly* in November to January 1876: "Of Some Railroad Accidents" in November [12, pp. 571-583]; "Of Some Railroad Accidents II" in December [13, pp. 736-748]; and "The Revere Catastrophe" in January 1876 [14, pp. 92-103].

In 1878, Adams collected these articles and lectures into a book, *Railroads: Their Origin and Problems*. It was very successful and went through six separate editions. The following year he dipped into this material and produced a second book, modestly entitled, *Notes on Railroad Accidents*. *Notes* was the highpoint for the use of rhetorical persuasion to improve safety on railroads, and it included descriptions and analysis of three of the accidents discussed in previous chapters, the Gasconade bridge collapse, the Ashtabula bridge collapse, and the Revere accident [15].

CONTEMPORARY REVIEWS OF
NOTES ON RAILROAD ACCIDENTS

The reviews of Adams's book ranged from the unquestioning reproduction of passages from *Notes* in the *Railroad Gazette*, suggesting that they accepted the book as indisputable fact [16, p. 376] to reviews that focused on the implications of the book for railroad safety, such as in *The New York Times:*

> In his recently-published "Notes on Railroad Accidents," Mr. Charles Francis Adams Jr., shows that the percentage of loss of life and of personal injuries on railroads is exceedingly small, when compared with the amount of travel, and the risks of railroad travelers are much less than they are popularly supposed to be. He cites statistics to prove that it is actually safer for a man or his family to travel by rail than to stay at home, thus collaborating the saying attributed to John Bright that the safest place in which a man could put himself was inside a first-class railroad carriage of a train in full motion [17, p. 4; 18, p. 421].

However, another group of reviews astutely described a two-pronged rhetorical presentation used by Adams in *Notes*. These reviewers pointed out that on the one hand, Adams had to attract general readers to what may have appeared to be a rather dry, abstract subject, and he did this by graphically presenting the stories of the accidents. On the other hand, Adams also wanted to lead readers beyond just a ghoulish fascination with the disasters to a scientific understanding of their causes and solutions so as to pressure railroad companies into using new safety devices and procedures. *Notes* had the same goal as Adams had in the original investigation reports of the Massachusetts Railroad Commission:

> Simply a medium, a species of lens by means of which the otherwise scattered and powerless rays of public opinion could be concentrated to a focus, and brought to bear upon any corporation [4, p. 11].

The reviewer in *The Nation* was one of those who observed the two-pronged rhetorical presentation that Adams gave in his book:

> The stories of railway accident are in themselves fascinating in a terrible way, and when they are not only graphically told but also grouped with reference to the causes and the cure, the reader feels that he is assisting at a scientific consultation on a subject which affects the safety of himself and his neighbors. The thrilling interest of the strange incidents of train disasters has added to it the zest of a worthy intellectual exercise of investigation, and what might the sensational reading if the narratives stood alone, is dignified by the clear purpose of humanity and progress with which the book is written, so that we have the attentiveness of a novel with the value of a work of science. It ought to be universally read, for its general reading would fix public sentiment so firmly in regard to the more necessary and feasible additions to the safety of railway travel that these would be hastened, and not have to await the lesson of human destruction which has uniformly been the inseparable antecedent of such progress hitherto [19, pp. 159-160].

The Literary World also picked up on this unique dual method of presentation:

> The lover of horrible and harrowing recital will find in these pages full and carefully sifted particulars of such terrible disasters as those at Abergele in Wales, Revere in Massachusetts, and Ashtabula in Ohio; and the student of science will be rewarded by an intelligent examination of systems of signals, competing brakes, and statistics of accident and death rates . . . [20, p. 312].

as did *The International Review:*

> This rather ghastly little volume is sure to be read by nearly every one beneath whose eye it happens to fall. The strange attraction exercised by a tale of a horrible railway disaster is simply irresistible; and here are narratives, each seeming to surpass all the rest in its aspect of terror, sufficient to satiate a coterie of Neros. One begins philosophically enough, but as he turns over page after page he comes to feel that his nerves are getting over-taxed; and yet he can no more escape from the hideous procession than could the wedding guest from the curdling recital of the Ancient Mariner. Such a collection would be simply brutal were it not made for a useful purpose, and that it was written for such a purpose is the reason for the existence of the volume. The moral follows the stories; and the last third of the book, it is to be sincerely hoped, will be carefully read by railway managers. Seldom does a disaster occur which does not teach its lesson, and Mr. Adams makes it his task to see that these lessons are duly comprehended. Many parts of the book, which are not horrible, are very interesting [21, p. 95].

and *Harper's:*

> The volume consists in large part of carefully prepared accounts of some of the most remarkable railway accidents that have occurred in this country and England, each of which is accompanied by an analysis of the causes, preventable or otherwise, that made them possible or inevitable, and by a statement of the obvious practical lessons suggested by them. Mr. Adams also gives, in connection with those accounts, very interesting sketches of the origin and perfection of the more important safety appliances which have now come into general use, and of the opposition they encountered from the avarice, stupidity, prejudice, and unconcern of officials [22, p. 465].

From these reviews, one can understand that Adams first had to attract readers through "thrilling incidents" that "are in themselves fascinating in a terrible way." To organize the incidents so that they can be "concentrated to a focus," Adams used taxonomy of accidents and remedies rather than a chronological order. Moreover, to endow his book with scientific creditability and to provide specific actions that can be brought to bear on corporations, Adams rendered the practical lessons in as scientific a manner as possible using statistics.

RHETORICAL ELEMENT ONE: "THRILLING INCIDENTS"

Graphic stories of railroad accidents had long been a staple of newspapers, especially the new illustrated weeklies (i.e., Figures 51 and 52). Later such stories had been collected in books like Howland's *Steamboat Disasters and Railroad Accidents* (1846). Howland had published a version of this book including only steamboat disasters in 1830, and, in his 1840 revision, once railroads had spread across the United States, he added fifteen railroad accidents to those of the steamboats [23, p. 40]. An example of such "thrilling incidents" can be seen in the following story and illustration from Howland's collection:

EXPLOSION ON THE HARLAEM RAILROAD,
In the city of New York, July 4, 1839

ABOUT 10 o'clock in the morning of July 4 the steam engine which comes into the city with the cars for Harlem, ran off the track opposite Union Park.

The steam was already generated to excess, but, unfortunately, the engineer neglected to blow it off. It is also supposed that water had not been taken in properly at the stopping place.

When the engine had thus run off the track, a number of the passengers, mostly mechanics, lent their services to get it on again. While thus surrounded, the boiler burst. The chief engineer was blown to pieces. His legs went into Union Park, his arms on a pile of lumber on the other side of the avenue, and his head was split in two parts. His abdomen was also burst, and his intestines scattered over the road.

The assistant engineer had both his legs broken and his head, face, and breast dreadfully scalded. He only lived a few moments. Another of the unfortunate persons employed, Philip W. Case, was dangerously wounded. The names of the other victims were Johnson and Spencer, and Roderick Matheson, the latter being severely scalded on his legs, and his face dreadfully lacerated by pebbles and sand being blown into it. Besides these, there were fifteen or sixteen other persons wounded or scalded. The fragments of the boiler were thrown in every direction, and the machinery of the engine was entirely destroyed.

Immediately after the accident, there was observed a disposition on the part of a number of Irishmen, who under the influence of liquor, to create a riot. Some were for marching in a body to destroy the company. Others insisted that the cars should be prevented from passing over the spot, and actually laid hold of the horses to carry out their purpose. Everything, in fact, that could be done, was done by a number of disorderly persons to make the results of this lamentable affair still more disastrous.

The foregoing particulars were extracted from the papers of the day. From other sources of the like nature we gather the following additional account:

"We cannot refrain, in this place, from awarding to Alderman Tieman the highest praise. But for coolness, forbearance, judgment, and firmness it is probable that a very serious riot would have occurred. So unreasonable a set of men we never before saw collected. Rum and excitement had destroyed the little self-command the low Irish at any time possess.

"From a passenger, we are sorry to learn, that the persons killed were both in a state of intoxication, and that, by the most common prudence all this might have been averted. It is even supposed that the engine was thrown off the track for a frolic. Surely this ought to be a lesson to the company, and compel them to employ trustworthy men in offices where not only the limbs, but the lives of our fellow-citizens are at stake, as well as the peace of the city placed in jeopardy."

In relation to the accident on the Harlem railroad the following are authentic particulars—

"1st. The locomotive engine was in charge of Spencer, one of the oldest and most experienced engineers in the country, who has been employed on the Long Island and other railroads, as engineer, for many years, and was thoroughly acquainted with the use of the locomotive engine.

"2d. The locomotive had brought up a trains cars from Harlem for the city, which was taken by the horses to the city hall and Walker street; after they had gone forward, the locomotive was crossing the switch to prepare to receive the return line of cars, so that it was quite alone, and wholly disconnected with the cars at the time it ran off the track.

"3d. As soon as the locomotive was off the track, Mr. Whigham, the superintendent of the company and several others in the employ of the company, set immediately at work to replace it upon the track. During this time the engineer was upon the engine, and constantly blowing off the steam. It had been stationary for about twenty minutes, while the men were at work to replace it; the superintendent giving repeated instructions to the engineer to take care of his steam. He was answered by Mr. Spencer that he was doing so; and he was constantly blowing off the steam. At this time the train of cars was approaching the spot from the city, as also the train from Harlem, and when the engine blew up, both trains were in sight; but, fortunately, so far distant as to escape any injury.

"4th. At the instant it blew up, Mr. Whigham and one of the collectors of the company were stooping down to place a stone under the frame, so as to get a lever by which to raise the engine about an inch higher, to get the wheels upon the track; and they both escaped with very slight injury, as the whole blew over their heads, while it killed Mr. Spencer, the engineer, and his brother-in-law—the only two persons who were killed on the spot. Five others were severely wounded by the fragments, and one of the collectors of the company scalded from head to foot.

"The limit by the corporation for the locomotive to come into the city, is at 14th street. It is only on the gala day of the fourth of July, that the engine comes below 32d street,—the horses of the company on that being insufficient to accommodate the public,—and it was solely to grant the greatest facility to the public, that the locomotive was brought to 15th street.

This, if we recollect aright, is the first explosion of the boiler of a locomotive, by which human life has sacrificed.

The modern construction of locomotive tubular boilers has rendered them liable to explosion only by gross mismanagement; and even in case of accidental explosion is generally only a partial one of a tube, or flue, so that no serious evil is to be anticipated. The wretched men whose recklessness produced this horrible catastrophe, have been victims to their own fault, and were sent to their account. But what shall atone for the agony caused to the families and friends of the innocent sufferers? [24, pp. 298-302].

No better example of Adams's ability to tell a thrilling incident as well as Howland can be seen in the following description of the Ashtabula bridge accident that seems even more vivid than the *Harper's Weekly* description reprinted in the last chapter:

There has been no recent disaster which combined more elements of horror or excited more widespread public emotion than that at Ashtabula Bridge. It was, indeed, so terrible in its character and so heartrending in its details, that for the time being it fairly divided the attention of the country with that dispute over the presidential succession, then the subject uppermost in the minds of all. A blinding northeasterly snowstorm, accompanied by a heavy wind, prevailed throughout the day which preceded the accident, greatly impeding the movement of trains. The Pacific express over the Michigan Southern & Lake Shore road had left Erie, going west, considerably behind its time, and had been started only with great difficulty and with the assistance of four locomotives. It was due at Ashtabula at about 5:30 o'clock P.M., but was three hours late, and, the days being then at their shortest, when it arrived at the bridge which was the scene of the accident the darkness was so great that nothing could be seen through the driving snow by those on the leading locomotive even for a distance of 50 feet ahead. The train was made up of two heavy locomotives, four baggage, mail and express cars, one smoking car, two ordinary coaches, a drawing-room car and three sleepers, being in all two locomotives and eleven cars, in the order named, containing, as nearly as can

Figure 56. Howland's locomotive explosion illustration (1846).

be ascertained, 190 human beings, of whom 170 were passengers. Ashtabula bridge is situated only about 1,000 feet east of the station of the same name, and spans a deep ravine, at the bottom of which flows a shallow stream, some two or three feet in depth, which empties into Lake Erie a mile or two away. The bridge was an iron Howe truss of 150 feet span, elevated 69 feet above the bottom of the ravine, and supported at either end by solid mason work abutments. It had been built some fourteen years. As the train approached the bridge it had to force its way through a heavy snow-drift, and, when it passed onto it, it was moving at a speed of some twelve or fourteen miles an hour. The entire length of the bridge afforded space only for two of the express cars at most in addition to the locomotives, so that when the wheels of the leading locomotive rested on the western abutment of the bridge nine of the eleven cars which made up the train, including all those in which there were passengers, had yet to reach its eastern end. At the instant when the train stood in this position, the engineer of the leading locomotive heard a sudden cracking sound apparently beneath him, and thought he felt the bridge giving way. Instantly pulling the throttle valve wide open, his locomotive gave a spring forward and, as it did so, the bridge fell, the rear wheels of his tender falling with it. The jerk and impetus of the locomotive, however, sufficed to tear out the coupling, and as his tender was dragged up out of the abyss onto the track, though its rear wheels did not get upon the rails, the frightened engineer caught a fearful glimpse of the second locomotive as it seemed to turn and then fall bottom upwards into the ravine. The bridge had given way, not at once but by a slowly sinking motion, which began at the point where the pressure was heaviest, under the two locomotives and at the west abutment. There being two tracks, and this train being on the southernmost of the two, the southern truss had first yielded, letting that side of the bridge down, and rolling, as it were, the second locomotive and the cars immediately behind it off to the left and quite clear of a straight line drawn between the two abutments; then almost immediately the other truss gave way and the whole bridge fell, but in doing so swung slightly to the right. Before this took place the entire train with the exception of the last two sleepers had reached the chasm, each car as it passed over falling nearer than the one which had preceded it to the east abutment, and finally the last two sleepers came, and, without being deflected from their course at all, plunged straight down and fell upon the wreck of the bridge at its east end. It was necessarily all the work of a few seconds.

At the bottom of the ravine the snow lay waist deep and the stream was covered with ice some eight inches in thickness. Upon this were piled up the fallen cars and engine, the latter on top of the former near the western abutment and upside down. All the passenger cars were heated by stoves. At first a dead silence seemed to follow the successive shocks of the falling mass. In less than two minutes, however, the fire began to show itself and within fifteen the holocaust was at its height. As usual, it was a mass of human beings, all more or less stunned, a few killed, many injured and helpless, and more yet simply pinned down to watch, in the possession as full as helpless of all their faculties, the rapid approach of the flames. The number of those killed outright seems to have been surprisingly small. In the last car, for instance, no one was lost. This was due to the energy and presence of mind of the porter, a Negro named Steward, who, when he felt the car resting firmly on its side, broke a window and crawled through it, and then passed along breaking the other windows and extricating the passengers until all were gotten out. Those in the other cars were far less fortunate. Though an immediate alarm had been given in the neighboring town, the storm was so violent and the snow so deep that assistance arrived but slowly. Nor when it did arrive could much be affected. The essential thing was to extinguish the flames. The means for so doing were close at hand in a steam pump belonging to the railroad company, while an abundance of hose could have been procured at another place but a short distance off. In the excitement and agitation of the moment contradictory orders were given, even to forbidding the use of the pump, and practically no effort to extinguish the fire was made. Within half an hour of the accident the flames were at their height, and when the next morning dawned nothing remained in the ravine but a charred and undistinguishable mass of car trucks, brake-rods, twisted rails and bent and tangled bridge iron, with the upturned locomotive close to the west abutment.

In this accident some eighty persons are supposed to have lost their lives, while over sixty others were injured. The exact number of those killed can never be known, however, as more than half of those reported were utterly consumed in the fire; indeed, even of the bodies recovered scarcely one half could be identified. Of the cause of the disaster much was said at the time in language most unnecessarily scientific; —but little was required to be said. It admitted of no extenuation [15, pp. 100-106].

This excerpt from *Notes* fits the observation from the *International Review* quite well: "The strange attraction exercised by a tale of a horrible railway disaster is simply irresistible; and here are narratives, each seeming to surpass all the rest in its aspect of terror, sufficient to satiate a coterie of Neros" [21, p. 95]. Dionysus Lardner, who investigated the 1844 *Richmond* explosion, wrote about such a strange attraction in his treatise on railroads:

The spectacle exhibited on the occasion of some great railway collisions would have been deemed by our forefathers too extravagant, even to be allowed a place in the wildest fictions. Colossal vehicles, weighing several tons, shivered to pieces, rods of iron, thick and strong enough to sustain a vast building, twisted and doubled as though they were rods of wax; massive bars of metal snapped and broken like glass; bodies of the killed dispersed here and there amongst the wrecks of vehicles and machinery, so mangled as to render identification impossible; limbs, and even heads severed from the trunks, and scattered right and left, so as to render impossible to recombine the disjecta membra of the same body; the countenances of the death, where countenances remain at all, having a ghastly expression of the mingled astonishment and horror with which the sufferer was filled, in the brief instants which elapsed between the catastrophe and death; the survivors, maimed and wounded, lying under the ponderous ruins, groaning in agony, and supplicating for relief and extrication! [25, p. 16].

However, Adams only used the attraction of these tales to draw a general audience who probably would not have read his official government reports. Adams had a salutary end, for as the review in the *International Review* observed, "Such a collection would be simply brutal were it not made for a useful purpose, and that it was written for such a purpose is the reason for the existence of the volume" [21, p. 95]. Professor George Vose, writing *Bridge Disasters in America: The Cause and the Remedy* [26] the year following Adams's *Notes*, also pointed out the need to draw in readers by a loss of life:

> It has been correctly remarked that in order to bring a disaster to the public notice it must be emphasized by loss of life. The Ashtabula bridge fell and killed over 80 persons, and a storm of indignation swept over the country from one end to the other. No language was severe enough to apply to the managers of the Lake Shore Railroad; but if that very bridge had fallen under a freight train, and no one had been injured, the occurrence would have been dismissed with a paragraph if indeed it even received that recognition. In February 1879, an iron bridge with a span 110 ft. on the Chicago & Alton Railroad, at Wilmington, Ill., fell as a train of empty coal cars was passing over it, and three cars were precipitated into the river, a distance of over 30 ft. No one was injured. Not a word of comment was ever made in regard to this occurrence. Suppose that in place of empty coal cars the train had consisted of loaded passengers cars, and that 100 persons had been killed. We know very well what the result would have been. Is not the company just as much to blame in one case as in the other? On the night of the 9th of November last, one span of the large bridge over the Missouri River, at St. Charles, upon the St. Louis, Kansas City & Northern Railway, gave way as a freight train was crossing it, and 17 loaded stock cars and the caboose fell, a distance of 80 ft. into the river. Two brakemen and two drovers, who were in the caboose, were killed. The bridge, says the only account that has appeared, did not break, apparently, for the whole span went down with the cars upon it. It could hardly make much difference, we should suppose, to the four men who were killed, whether the bridge broke down or went down. This disaster occurred early last November, and not a word has appeared in the papers since in regard to it [26, p. 4].

Vose also sadly noted that the public is fascinated by the effects, but bored with learning the causes of disasters:

> . . . as a business man, he [the editor] knew perfectly well that his patrons would read an account giving all of the sickening detail of a terrible catastrophe, while few, if any, would wade through a dry discussion of the means for protecting the public from such disasters. The public is very indignant with the effect, but does not care to trouble itself with the cause . . . [26, p. 5].

The method by which Adams moved the audience from thrilling stories to "fix public sentiment so firmly in regard to the more necessary and feasible additions to the safety of railway travel that these would be hastened" was by taxonomic organization and a scientific approach.

RHETORICAL ELEMENT TWO:
"ACCIDENT TAXONOMY"

Adams misdirects the reader in the first chapter, "The Death of Mr. Huskisson." This chapter is very much like the vivid incidents of Howland's book, and it announces:

> With a true dramatic propriety, the ghastly record, which has since grown so long, began with the opening of the first rail road—literally on the very morning which finally ushered the great system into existence as a successfully accomplished fact, the eventful 15th of September, 1830—the day upon which the Manchester & Liverpool railroad was formally opened [15, p. 3].

This opening strongly suggests to the reader that the book will be chronologically organized, perhaps proceeding from the British birthplace of the railroad to its progeny in the United States, France, etc. However, the book is organized taxonomically, with accidents "grouped with reference to the causes and the cure" as the reviewer in the *Nation* pointed out.

Adams may have received the taxonomy he employed from two international sources. Emile With's *Railroad Accidents: Their Causes and the Means of Preventing Them* [27] was published in France in 1854, then translated and published in English in Massachusetts in 1856. Adams most probably had a copy because With's "Preface" pointedly criticized the Massachusetts railroad accident reports in the era before Adams's work on the Commission:

> It is to be regretted that the returns of accidents in the railroad reports to the Massachusetts Legislature are so imperfect. They supply by scanty information as to causes, and any calculation based upon the number of cases reported to show the number of killed and wounded as compared with the number carried, would, we are persuaded, be altogether deceptive [27, p. 34].

With's taxonomy of eighteen types of railroad accidents was broken into the following categories:

- Explosion of locomotive boilers
- Carelessness of those in charge of engines
- Running off the tracks
- Faults in the construction of the railroads
- Bad state of track
- Wrong position of switches
- Instability of train
- Defects in the rolling stock
- Breaking of axles
- Faults in the rail
- Fires
- Inattention to Signals
- Collisions

• Irregularity in the Running of Trains
• Interruption of Communication by Snow
• Difficulties of Working a Single-Track Road
• Imprudence of Persons Traveling or Employed on the Train
• Want of Communication Between Conductor and Engine Driver [28].

Adams's taxonomic organization is similar, as can be seen in the following ten categories he used to organized his descriptions:

• Derailment over four years (15, Chapters 1, 2, 3)—"The four accidents which have been referred to, including that of April 17, 1836, upon the Manchester & Liverpool road, belong to one class. Though they covered a period of forty-two years they were all due to the same cause, the sudden derailment of a portion of the train, and its subsequent destruction because of the insufficient control of those in charge of it over its momentum" [15, p. 27].
• Telescoping and the Miller Platform (Chapter 5)—"Telescoping, however, was an incident of crushing, and a peculiarly American incident, which is not without a certain historical interest; for the particular feature in car construction which led directly to it and all its attendant train of grisly horrors furnishes a singular and instructive illustration of the gross violations of mechanical principles into which practical, as opposed to educated, mechanics are apt constantly to fall,—and in which, when once they have fallen, they steadily persist" [15, p. 47].
• Single line in which an excursion trains runs into a regularly scheduled train, (Chapter 6)—"it was one of that description the occurrence of which is most frequent. An excursion train, while running against time on a single-track road, came in collision with a regular train. The record is full of similar disasters, too numerous to admit of specific reference" [15, p. 62].
• Telegraphic Collisions
• Oil-Tank Accidents
• Draw-Bridge Disasters
• Bridge Accidents
• Car-Couplings in Derailments
• Rear-End Collisions
• Interlocking [15].

Not many technological solutions to safety problems were available when With's book was published in 1856, but a number were available in 1879 when Adams wrote *Notes*. Thus, immediately following the ten categories of railroad accidents, Adams included five categories/chapters of technological solutions: automatic block system, Westinghouse break, Miller platform, etc.

Another international source from which Adams drew his accident taxonomy was from the British Board of Trade's Railroad Inspectorate. The Board of Trade had the following taxonomy:

- Engines or vehicles meeting with or leaving the rails in consequence of obstructions or of defects in connection with the permanent way or works
- Defect in the rolling stock
- Accidents from trains entering stations at too high a speed
- Collision between trains and engines following one another on the same line except at junctions, sidings, or stations
- Collision between trains and engines at junctions
- Collision at sidings or stations
- Collisions on single lines from trains meeting from opposite directions
- Passenger trains wrongly turned into sidings or otherwise through facing points
- Accidents on inclines [9, p. 81].

Thus, while the readers of *Notes on Railroad Accidents* were thrilled by the stories, Adams's taxonomic organization moved readers from the specifics of a single accident to generalized conclusions: "Seldom does a disaster occur which does not teach its lesson, and Mr. Adams makes it his task to see that these lessons are duly comprehended" [21, p. 95].

RHETORICAL ELEMENT THREE: "STATISTICS"

In the last three sections of Adam's book, he moved from the description of accidents, their causes and their solutions to a statistical consideration of accidents:

The statistics of a long series of years enable us, however, to approximate with a tolerable degree of precision to an answer to these questions, and the answer is simply astounding;—so astounding, in fact, that, before undertaking to give it, the question itself ought to be stated with all possible precision. It is this:—Taking all persons who as passengers travel by rail,—and this includes all dwellers in civilized countries,—what number of journeys of the average length are safely accomplished, to each one which results in the death or injury of a passenger from some cause over which he had no control?—The cases of death or injury must be confined to passengers, and to those of them only who expose themselves to no unnecessary risk.

When approaching a question of this sort, statisticians are apt to assume for their answers an appearance of mathematical accuracy. It is needless to say that this is a mere affectation. The best results which can be arrived at are, after all, mere approximations, and they also vary greatly year by year. The body of facts from which conclusions are to be deduced must cover not only a definite area of space, but also a considerable lapse of time. Even Great Britain, with its 17,000 miles of track and its hundreds of millions of annual passenger journeys, shows results which, one year with another, vary [15, pp. 235-236].

The reviews of the book repeatedly pointed out this facet:

• *The New York Times:* "He cites statistics to prove . . ."
• *Literary World:* "the student of science will be rewarded by an intelligent examination of systems of signals, competing brakes, and statistics of accident and death rates . . ."

Moreover, three months after Adams's first presentation of the material at the Lowell Lectures, in May 1875, the editor of the *Manufacturer and Builder* used Adams's statistical information to attack the high premiums charged by life insurance companies to cover accidental deaths on trains which, in the magazine's words, were "based on false statistics, or having no base at all" [10, p. 106].

In 1879, the use of analytical statistics was a relative novelty for Adams's audiences; it wasn't really until the 1830s and 1840s that governments used analytical statistical approaches [30, p. 598; 31 pp. 125-126]. In With's book, he also concluded his presentation with "Statistics of Accidents," but his are largely tables with little analysis. Adams uses statistics at the end of his book to draw conclusions in the aggregate; he began with an extended description of an individual person, "The Death of Mr. Huskisson," and ended considering railroad deaths and injuries and accidents in the largest aggregate. He also used the statistics to draw conclusions that surprised the reader—especially after the long recital of accidents. For example, *The New York Times* observed in its review:

> . . . the percentage of loss of life and of personal injuries on railroads is exceedingly small, when compared with the amount of travel, and the risks of railroad travelers are much less than they are popularly supposed to be. He cites statistics to prove that it is actually safer for a man or his family to travel by rail than to stay at home . . . [17, p. 4].

Railroad World in November 1879 pointed out that Adams's statistical conclusions and recommendations were "well calculated to correct popular fallacies . . ." [32, pp. 8-9].

RHETORICAL ELEMENT FOUR: "SCIENTIFIC ANALYSIS"

To endow what the *Nation* recognized in the book as "the value of science," Adams again went overseas to the work of Sir Captain Henry Whatley Tyler (Figure 57) and the British Railroad Inspectorate, which had long been using science to solve railroad problems.

Both Tyler and Adams were the first in their nations to publish railroad accident reports for general readers. Tyler joined an Inspectorate that had been working for over a decade, and it was composed of three inspectors [33, p. 215]; Adams

Figure 57. Sir Captain Henry Whatley Tyler, Chief Inspector of the
British Railroad Inspectorate.

modeled his commission of three members on this British model. Neither the
British Inspectorate nor the Massachusetts commission had the power of law, but
both believed in the pressure of public opinion. In questioning before a parlia-
mentary committee, Tyler affirmed:

> Responsibility for safety on the railways . . . must remain with the individuals
> concerned. Any form of direct supervision or control by the Government
> would be harmful because it would inevitably divide responsibility and by
> doing so weaken it. There was only one right but harder way to bring about
> reform and that was by persuasion and by pressure of public opinion [34, p. 19].

Adams said much the same in an 1879 valedictory letter to the Massachusetts chairman of the Committee on Railroads, Charles S. Osgood, about the crucial role of communicating to the public about the accidents:

> The Commissioners have no power except to recommend and report. Their only appeal is to publicity. The Board is at once prosecuting officer, judge, and jury, but with no sheriff to enforce its process. This method of railroad supervision is peculiar to Massachusetts; but I do not hesitate to say that I believe that it is the best and the most effective method which has ever been devised,—the best for the community, and the best for the corporations.
>
> . . .
>
> Where, as in this case, a board depends for its power almost exclusively on the way it is able to present facts to the public, it can accomplish nothing unless it contains someone specially trained to do this effectively and understandingly.
>
> . . .
>
> The idea as respects railroads which this Board originated and now represents—the supervisory regulation through publicity and intelligent discussion—has just begun to be developed [35, pp. 3-4, 5-6; 45, p. 47].

Tyler's publicity of accident investigations worked in the long run. Simmons observed in 1994, "public opinion had been much influenced—to a large extent it had been molded—by the inspectors' comments on accidents" [33, p. 217]. Both hoped that the force of public opinion "concentrated to a focus" could be "brought to bear upon any corporation" and changes for the sake of safety would be made:

> Looking, therefore, to the great progress of improvement which has been made since the date of the first of the present series of annual reports on accidents, commencing with that for 1870, and to the continuance of that progress at the present time, it would appear that all that is necessary may probably best be obtained by giving greater prominence and increased circulation to the annual analyses of accidents and casualties to passengers, servants, and materials, which are contained in those reports, which might be freely circulated every year, and furnished to the companies for distribution among their superior officers. The moral inducement thus brought to bear would have a stronger effect, in a better way, under the influence of public opinion, in the future, as it has had in the past, than any system of compulsion by any tribunal, existing or to be created. At all events, until this experiment, which has so far proved to be highly successful, has been further tried, it would not be wise to run the risk which would be incurred by the establishment of a tribunal endowed with compulsory powers of an attempt at duplicate management of the railways of this country [35, p. 164; 36].

More specifically, we can see how the report process, format, and tone of the Railroad Inspectorate came to be transferred to the Interstate Commerce Commission (ICC) when it was later formalized by Congress. The process of writing the British investigation reports was standardized in the following way:

The company on whose line it had occurred reported it to the Board of Trade, which would—if it appeared sufficiently important—appoint one of the inspectors to investigate it. He communicated his findings to the Board, and it might send a copy of what he had said to the company, together with any questions it wished to ask arising from what had happened, or such admonitions as it thought necessary. Sometimes the company would reply, protesting against what the inspector had said and trying to controvert it, and that might elicit a rejoinder from the Board of Trade. In due course the report, together with any additional documents it had given rise to, was printed and laid before Parliament. At first the reports were, in theory at least, confidential, but in 1854 they began to be furnished to the press, and from 1860 onwards they were put on sale to the public. No considerable attention seems to have been paid to them in the country at large. 'The official reports go to the Board of Trade,' said one commentator, 'and so into Blue Books and oblivion.' However that may have been, the doings of the companies and their servants, scrutinized with care by the inspectors, were now no longer kept secret. From 1871 onwards it became the practice for the Board to issue a general report on all the accidents that had occurred in the previous year, analyzing their causes and surveying them as a whole [33, p. 216].

This is exactly what happened with Adams's reports on the Massachusetts Railroad Commission. Newspapers not only published summaries of the reports but "once the Chicago *Tribune* not only carried the entire report as an item of general interest but also reprinted and distributed 10,000 copies on its own initiative" [37, p. 23].

Even more specifically, the inspectorate accident reports were written in the following fashion:

The report of the inquiry is written up in standard, traditional style. It is formally addressed to the Permanent Under-Secretary of State for Transport. The language of the report is often stylized and reaffirms the role of the Inspecting Officer as civil servant. The content of the report is detailed and follows an established sequence. The first section is devoted to a description of the accident, including details of the site, the course of the accident, the train and track, if relevant, and the damage. The second part of the report concentrates on that of witnesses and the results of technical examinations. The final sections comprise the conclusions and the discussion and recommendations. Site plans are usually incorporated at the end of the report and there may be photographs, graphs or tables to help explain particular points [38, pp. 186-187; 39, p. 133].

Just before Tyler joined the inspectorate (early 1850s), their investigations changed from being primarily accusatorial in nature to being inquisitorial:

A crucial aspect of the railway inquiry is that it is inquisitorial not accusatorial, its task is not to apportion blame but merely to determine the cause of accidents. This point is emphasized and re-emphasized by Inspecting Officers at the time of the inquiry: to witnesses; to next of kin; and in the report.

Throughout the inquiry the purpose of determining the cause of the accident is paramount, and Inspecting Officers strictly adhere to this by only permitting questions and representations which are strictly relevant to the investigation of the accident's cause(s). The inquisitorial as opposed to accusatorial style pervades the subsequent report. Nevertheless, individuals are sometimes inevitably named as the partial or even major causes of accidents. To this extent, therefore, blame is apportioned. The crucial point is that the inquiry itself is not a trial which attributes legal liability [38, p. 189; 40, pp. 168-170; 41, p. 30].

An example of these reports can be seen in the report below written by Tyler on an accident in 1870 when the changes in process and tone had been achieved by him as Chief Inspector. It is quite interesting to compare his 1870 report to Adams's Railroad Commission Report on the Revere Accident, and those subsequently written by the ICC—especially the two in the Introduction.

LONDON AND NORTHWESTERN RAILWAY.
1, Whitehall, 12th May 1870

Sir,

Like the subsequent ICC reports, Tyler's used the format of a letter.

In compliance with the instructions contained in your minute of the 18th ultimo, I have now the honour to report, for the information of the Board of Trade, the result of my inquiry into the accident that occurred on the 10th ultimo, near Gray Rigg, on the London and North-western Railway.

The 12.47 a.m. mail train from Carlisle for London left Carlisle at 12.52, five minutes late, on the morning in question, consisting of an engine and tender, a guard's van, six composite and two third-class carriages, a Caledonian post-office (No.5), and a breakvan. The engine-driver ran for 42 miles, from Carlisle to Gray Rigg, at his usual speed, and passed Gray Rigg some three or four minutes hate, without stopping. He had received, a week previously, in a printed circular from the manager's office, instructions to slacken speed between the 25 and 26th mileposts from Lancaster, in consequence of the lifting of the road. He accordingly slackened his speed after passing the Gray Rigg station, from 36 to 25 miles an hour. It was a dark rainy morning, and the engine-driver perceived a little oscillation in his engine shortly after passing the 25 milepost. He thought that the road was "rather unusually rough," and, his steam having previously been shut off, he reversed his engine, and applied steam against the engine, with a view to stopping the train as quickly as possible. He did not whistle for the guard's breaks; but the fireman, feeling also the rough condition of the road, and seeing that the engine-driver was reversing the engine, applied the tender break, which was previously partly on. The train was now descending a gradient of 1 in 106, and the engine-driver perceived shortly after-wards that something was "dragging" behind him. He

Tyler and the ICC reports address the head commisssioners as their audience.

brought his engine to a stand as soon as he could, and fearing that the down line, as well as the up line, might be obstructed, he sent his fireman towards Oxenholme; and, after attending to his engine, he went northward to see what had happened.

The guard in the leading van perceived some unusual oscillation after leaving Gray Rigg, but did not think that anything was wrong until, after a few seconds, he felt a severe shock, which threw him down in the van. His brake was already applied to a slight extent, and he got up as soon as he could, and turned it tight on, and kept it so until the train came to a stand.

The conductor rode in a second-class compartment of a composite carriage, which was the ninth vehicle behind the tender, and immediately in front of the post-office. He felt a "succession of violent oscillations or swayings," so much so that he jumped up in his compartment, for the purpose of attempting to seize the communication cord; but before he could reach it he felt that his carriage was off the rails. He was much "thrown about," and after holding on by different parts of the carriage, and struggling as well as he could, he found his carriage come gradually to a stand across the line on which he had been traveling.

The guard in the hind van applied his break after passing Gray Rigg, according to his usual custom, and after passing a field gate near the 25 mile-post, he felt a good deal of oscillation. He gave his brake handle another turn or two, and while doing so he felt his van jump off the rails. He was stunned, and does not remember, either how his van came to a stand or how he got out of it; but he ran back as soon as he recovered himself, with his lamp and detonating signals, to protect the train.

Tyler and the ICC begin with a recitation of facts of the accident as provided by eyewitnesses.

An examination of the line after the accident showed the train to be somewhat in the condition sketched in the accompanying diagram. The engine and tender and the heading van were all on the rails, and coupled together, and they had come to a stand at the Lamb Rigg level crossing, between the 25 and 25 mile-posts (from Lancaster), with the engine about 132 yards inside the former mile-post. Next behind the leading van was a carriage off the rails to the right (or east) by about nine inches. There were then three carriages on the rails, which did not appear to have left them, and two carriages off the rails, about 12 inches to the right, and the whole of these vehicles were still coupled together. The three carriages which had left the rails were somewhat damaged the first had the bands on the top of both the near springs fractured, and some of the spring-plates cracked; and the other two had damaged or broken ends, springs, and step boards. At 280 yards behind the front portion of the train, which thus remained coupled together, there lay two carriages, standing in an A form, across the up line, but still on their wheels.

They remained coupled together by one side chain, the screw coupling having given way, and they were not much damaged except that the bands of the springs were fractured. Immediately behind the last-mentioned carriage, and coupled to it, was the post-office, on its side, entirely off the rails, and partially down the side of the embankment on which this part of the line runs. At 84 yards behind this post-office the hind van was lying partially on its side, and resting on its near wheels against the slope of a cutting on the near side of the line.

Tyler and the ICC have similar high percentages of passive voice verbs— 31 percent for Tyler and 23 percent and 36 percent for the ICC reports in 1911. (Adams' report on the Revere accident for the Raiload Commission had 26 percent.)

Strange to say, in spite of the serious nature of this accident, only two post-office clerks and one passenger, out of 40 or 50 who were traveling by the train, have complained of injury.

The most notable fracture connected with the rolling stock was that of the near leading wheel of the post-office. This was a wheel of the description known as Mansell's Patent, constructed with a cast-iron boss, wooden disc, and wrought-iron rings for the attachment of the tyre. The disc of the wheel was found to be partly pushed off its boss for a distance of about three-quarters of an inch towards the outside, while the boss remained firmly secured and keyed upon the axle. The outer cast-iron face-plate was cracked into three pieces, but the bolts which secured it to the inner plate forming part of the boss were all sound) and the nuts were tight upon them. The inner plate itself was broken into seven larger and one smaller pieces, and the fractures, though rusted in places, are still more or less bright where they have not been affected by water. The disc of the wheel appears, on examination, to have been previously used with the same boss, or with a different boss of the same description, inasmuch as it is doubly pierced, one set of holes, which have been much worn, having been plugged up; and another set of holes having been made for the boss which was on the wheel when the accident occurred. The disc had also been tightly packed with plates of iron to surround the boss, no doubt in consequence of its having become loose from previous wear. These and other points connected with the construction of the wheel and with its fracture are fully shown in the enclosed diagram, with which Mr. Bore, the carriage superintendent of the London and North-western Company, has been so good as to furnish me. The post-office to which this wheel belonged was the property of the Caledonian Railway Company.

All the reports have similar readability scores: Tyler on the Flesh Reading Index scored a 55.2, which is between the ICC's 56.1 and 47.3. (Adams's report on the Revere accident for the Railroad Commission had 40 percent.)

The permanent way on this part of the line is laid with double-headed rails, weighing 84 lb. to the yard, and fished at the joints with wrought-iron suspended plates, and bolts and nuts. The chairs weigh 40 lbs. each, and are attached to the sleepers, each by two treenails and one wrought-iron spike. The keys are outside. The sleepers are laid transversely, three feet apart, on the average, from centre to centre. The road was relaid thus, with the ordinary London and Northwestern permanent way, about nine years ago. The roadway was in process of being lifted, an operation which had been continued for upwards of a fortnight; and the repairs which were being made at the same time had been carried on northward to within 100 yards of the first mark on the rail at the scene of the accident; while the lifting itself had been carried forward about a quarter of a mile north of that spot before the accident occurred.

The first mark observable on the permanent way after the accident, to show where any vehicle hind left the rails, was 217 yards south of the 25 milepost. The outer rail of the curve which there occurs, with a radius of about 70 chains, showed a wheel mark, as of a flange of a wheel mounting it and crossing it obliquely; and the outer jaw of the chair in front of the end of that wheel-mark was slightly chipped and indented, indicating where the wheel had fallen on the outside of the rail. There were, a little in advance, corresponding marks on the ballast and sleepers, showing where, after the mounting of an off wheel on the outer rail, a near wheel had also dropped inside the inner rail; and these marks continued on the sleepers, and could be traced to the spot where the post-office lay, 196 yards in advance, on its side, on the edge of the embankment.

At a distance of 56 yards from time first mark on the rail, it was observed that a vehicle had left the rail on the opposite or inside of the curve; and these marks conducted plainly and directly to the spot where the van lay resting against the side of the embankment. The road was not much disturbed, though the sleepers were damaged, between the point where the first mark on the rail was observable and the point where the hind van lay, nor indeed for 50 yards beyond that point; but for 30 or 40 yards further in advance the rails, chairs, and sleepers were carried completely over towards the edge of the embankment; and this was evidently done by the wheels of the post-office, before that vehicle turned over and fell on its side. The sleepers were much damaged, and a number of chairs were broken, for 300 yards further, and to the point where the engine and leading carriages came to a stand, but the rails were not displaced on that part of the line.

On the Flesh-Kincaide Grade Level Index, Tyler was listed as 12th grade, as was one of the ICC reports (as was Adams's Revere report for the Railroad Commission.)

In considering the causes which have led to this accident, there would appear to be no doubt that the post-office was the first vehicle to leave the rails and that the principal damage to the permanent way was effected by the wheels of the post-office, about 150 yards in advance of the spot at which that vehicle had so left the rails. It appears plain also that the hind van was the second vehicle to leave the rails, and that it had nothing to do with the origin of the accident.

As regards the permanent way, the platelayers had lifted it for a quarter of a mile north of and past the site of the accident, and they had left the sleepers uncovered by ballast, and had no spare ballast about, or any more than was employed in packing up the sleepers during the lifting. As tried by the engineer of the line on the morning of Monday – the day following the accident – the superelevation of the outer rail on the curve was found to he 4 or more inches, and to be uniform at and near the point where the first heel mark was discoverable; and it was tested, with the same result, by the district engineer on the Sunday morning, five or six hours after the accident happened. The gauge between the rails is also said to have been correct to within a quarter of an inch. A number of new treenails now observable in the chairs are stated to have been inserted, some before, but more since, the accident; this remark applying specially to that part of the line where the post-office first left the rails; and two new sleepers have also been inserted since the accident, the one nine feet behind where tile first wheel-mark was visible, and the other opposite to that mark.

The wheel of the post office, though fractured as above described, was found to be nearly complete in all its parts; but there were missing certain iron bolts or nuts, and a small portion of the inner plate (forming part of the boss), in a triangular form, with sides about two inches long. This portion was found twelve days after the accident, on the outside of the outer rail of a siding at Gray Rigg station, about two miles north of the scene of the accident, after having been much searched for by all the platelayers who were employed in maintaining and lifting the line. If this portion of iron dropped out of the wheel before the post-office left the rails, it would be fair to conclude that the wheel was fractured previously to the accident, and that the accident was caused by its failure; but the evidence on this point is hardly conclusive, inasmuch as a number of broken chairs had been collected and taken from the site of the accident to the Gray Rigg siding two days before the finding of this piece of iron; and it is not impossible that the piece of iron might have been carried, with other pieces of iron, to Gray Rigg after the accident. It might, or might not, have been previously discovered if it had lain at Gray Rigg from the time of the accident.

All the reports draw inquisitorial, not accusatorial, conclusions.

The carriage examiner at Carlisle, under whose scrutiny this train passed before it left for Gray Rigg, states that he carefully examined it all over, and that he is confident there was nothing the matter with any of the wheels when the train started from Carlisle.

The condition of the surfaces of fracture in the portions of cast-iron which have come from the broken wheel, is stated to have been nearly the same when the wheel was first examined after the accident as when I saw them on the 3rd May. Parts of these surfaces of fracture were still bright. Other parts were more or less covered with rust; and it would appear that the rust was almost as extensive over the surfaces and as thick, five hours after the accident as on the 3rd May. There was no flaw in the material which would lead to weakness so as to cause those fractures, and it was impossible to say positively from their appearance whether there were any cracks in time wheel before the accident or not.

With a view to time further elucidation of this point I requested Mr. Worthington, the engineer, and Mr.Bore the carriage super-intendent of the London and North-western Company, who took *Like one of the* opposite views of the probable cause of this accident, to ascertain *ICC reports,* experimentally whether similar portions of metal, newly fractured and exposed under similar conditions to the action of water, would *outside experts* in five hours assume the appearances which were observed on *are called in to* the portion of the wheel in question five hours after the accident *provide* occurred. I enclose the letters which I have received reporting the *evidence.* results of these experiments; and taking into consideration all the circumstances of the case, I am forced to the conclusion that the permanent way having been lifted, and time repairs having been in progress, the post-office was thrown off the rails in consequence of the defective condition of the permanent way, rather than from any failure prior to the accident in its own wheel.

The Secretary,   I am, &c.

 Railway Department,   H. W. TYLER,

 Board of Trade.   *Captain, R.E.*

THE IMPACT OF
NOTES ON RAILROAD ACCIDENTS

The book had only one printing and pales in numbers beside those of Adams's other railroad books, such as his *Chapter of Erie* or his *Railroad Origins and Problems.* On the occasion of the 1878 presentation of his book, *Railroads: Their Origins and Problems* [42], to Secretary of Interior Carl Schurz, Adams stated that he "wished to shape national policy" [43]. He came closest in the aftermath of the Ashtabula accident in 1876, when, with Congressman James Garfield, he introduced national legislation for the government inspection of railroad accidents modeled on Tyler's British bureau [44, p. 74]. It did not pass for a decade until the passage of the Interstate Commerce Commission legislation in the mid-1880s.

Adams hoped that *Notes* would put public pressure on companies to add safety features, as he mentioned in the preface to *Notes:*

During my term of public service, also, there have been four appliances, either introduced into use or now struggling for American recognition, my sense of the value of which, in connection with the railroad system, to both the traveling and general public, I could not easily overstate. These appliances are the MILLER PLATFORM and BUFFER, the WESTINGHOUSE BRAKE, and the INTERLOCKING and ELECTRIC SIGNAL SYSTEMS. To bring these into more general use through reports on railroad accidents as they occurred was one great aim with me throughout my official life. I am now not without hopes that the printing of this volume may tend to still further familiarize the public with these inventions, and thus hasten their more general adoption [15, p. 2].

In this endeavor, he was more successful. Within a decade of the book's publication, the Westinghouse brakes were in general use in the industry, as were the other safety "appliances."

The publication of *Notes on Railroad Accidents* was the highpoint of persuasive rhetoric's involvement in the campaign to increase safety. Soon however, Adams's rhetorical approach and the power of public opinion would be displaced by government regulations of the Interstate Commerce Commission and the publication of "specifications" by professional engineers from such groups as the American Society of Civil Engineers. Since these two new groups focused on a much narrower audience than did Adams, only on lawmakers and engineers, the need for thrilling stories diminished, while the emphasis upon science and statistics increased. The role of newspapers also diminished. No longer would there be a Commodore Stockton dueling with critics in letters to the editor or corporate subterfuge of "Justice" articles promulgating the defendant company's case. The efforts of "disinterested" scientific experts such as Locke, Kayser, and MacDonald provided the sustaining model of how to investigate catastrophes.

ENDNOTES

1. Charles Francis Adams, Jr., "The Railroad Death-Rate," *Atlantic Monthly*, February 1876.
2. *Brooklyn Eagle*, November 15, 1852, p. 1.
3. *The Railways of America: Their Construction, Development, Management, and Appliances*, New York: Trow's Printing and Bookbinding Company, 1890.
4. William A. Craft, "Ten Years Working of the Massachusetts Railroad Commission," in *State Railroad Commissions*, New York: *The Railroad Gazette*, 1883.
5. *Massachusetts Commission Reports, Third Annual Report of the Board of Railroad Commissioners 1872*, Boston, Mass.: Wright & Potter, State Printers, 1873.
6. "Lectures," *Boston Evening Transcript*, 48 (14, 658), February 3, 1875.
7. Harriette Smith, *History of the Lowell Institute*, Boston, Mass., 1898. Professor Silliman, who investigated the explosion of the *New England* in 1833, had also given lectures in the inaugural year of the Lowell Institute, 1839-40, but also in 1842-3. In fact, he nearly held the record of having given the most Lowell Institute lectures, 24.
8. "Lectures Last Evening," *Boston Evening Transcript*, 48 (14, 652), January 27, 1875: he had a "fair audience."
9. "Death on the Rail," *The New York Times*, February 9, 1875.
10. "Imposition of Accident Insurance Companies," *Manufacturer and Builder*, May 1875. Three months later, in May 1875, the editor of the *Manufacturer and Builder* used Adams's twenty million miles statistic to attack the high premiums charged by life insurance companies to cover accident deaths on trains which in the magazine's words are "based on false statistics, or having no base at all except the desire to obtain great

gains by extortion from timid railroad travelers." This was continued in its February 1876 issue, pp. 26-27.

11. Charles Francis Adams, Jr., *The Railroad Problem*, New York: *The Railroad Gazette*, 1875.

12. *Atlantic Monthly*, 36 (217), November 1875.

13. *Atlantic Monthly*, 36 (218), December 1875.

14. *Atlantic Monthly*, 37 (219), January 1876.

15. *Notes on Railroad Accidents* (New York: G. P. Putnam's Sons, 1879) went through only one edition.

16. George Vose, "Safety in Railway Travel," *North American Review*, 135 (311), October 1882.

17. *The New York Times*, December 10, 1879.

18. *New England and Yale Review*, (156), May 1880, makes a quite similar observation: "This little volume on railway accidents by Mr. Charles Francis Adams, Jr., who has acquired so high a reputation as an acknowledged authority on all matters pertaining to railways, strange to say, leaves the reader quite reassured with regard to the safety of all ordinary railroad travel," p. 421.

19. "Adams's 'Railway Accidents," *The Nation: A Weekly Journal Devoted to Politics*, (30), February 26, 1880.

20. *The Literary World*, (10), December 6, 1879.

21. *The International Review*, (8), December 6, 1880.

22. *Harper's Weekly*, 60 (357), 465.

23. Robert B. Shaw, *A History of Railroad Accidents, Safety Precautions and Operating Practices*, Binghamton, N.Y.: Vail-Ballou Press, Inc. 1978.

24. S. A. Howland, *Steamboat Disasters and Railroad Accidents in the United States to which are appended Accounts of Recent shipwrecks, Fires at Sea, Thrilling Incidents, etc.*, Worcester, Mass.: Warren Lazell, 1846.

25. *Railroad Economy*, New York: Harper Brothers, 1850.

26. George L. Vose, *Bridge Disasters in America: Their Cause and the Remedy*, New York: The Railroad Gazette, 1880.

27. Emile With, *Railroad Accidents and the Means of Preventing Them*, Boston, Mass.: Little, Brown and Company, 1856.

28. Laurence Turnbull and William McRea, *Railroad Accidents and the Means by Which They May Be Prevented*, Philadelphia, Penna.: Parry and M'Millan, 1854. It is also interesting that this book, which came out about the same time as With's, also had a taxonomy of sorts for its organizational principle. Turnbull and McRea organized their discussions of accidents around the following categories: accidents by collisions of trains, accidents at drawbridges, and accidents at switches. However, if one can extrapolate from the presence of this book in current library catalogues (WORLDCAT), Turnbull's book exists in only six libraries, With's in 32, while Adams's is in 242.

29. Royal Commission on Railway Accidents, *Minutes of Evidence Taken Before the Commissioners*, London: Eyre and Spottswoode, 1877—Tuesday July 28's interrogation of Captain Tyler.

30. Stuart Woolf, "Statistics and the Modern State," *Comparative Studies in Society and History*, 31 (3), July 1989.

31. Christian H. Hewison, *Locomotive Boiler Explosions,* North Pomfret, Vt.: David & Charles, 1983.

32. Review of "Notes on Railroad Accidents," *Railroad World,* November 8, 1879.

33. Jack Simmons, *The Express Train and other Railway Studies,* Nairn, G.B.: David St. John Thomas Publisher, 1994.

34. L. T. C. Rolt, *Red for Danger: The Classic History of British Railway Disasters,* Phoenix Mill, Stroud, Gloucestershire, G.B.: Sutton Publishing, 1998.

35. *Massachusetts House of Representatives Document Number 225,* March 1879.

36. Adams and Tyler also ran parallel courses, in that once leaving the areas of public inspection of railroad safety, they both were hired by large railroads as their presidents, Adams, the Union Pacific, and Tyler, the Grand Trunk Railroad of Canada (also president of Westinghouse Brake Company in Great Britain, see Tyler's *How the Brake Question Is Being Manipulated in England,* Glasgow, Robert Anderson, 1877). Also, both were the first to publish their reports and to go beyond the confines of their boards or department and take the lead in public inquiries and questioning.

37. Thomas K. McCraw, *Prophets of Regulation,* Cambridge, Mass.: Belknap Press, 1984.

38. Bridget M. Hutter, "Public Accident Inquiries: The Case of the Railway Inspectorate," *Public Administration,* 70, Summer 1992.

39. Christian H Hewison (an inspector in the 1930s), *From Shedmaster to the Railway Inspectorate,* London: David & Charles, 1981: "Writing the Report is the Inspector's most difficult task. To those who have never yet attempted it, the production of an accident report on, perhaps, two sheets of A4 paper might appear to be easy, and everyone who joins the team of EIs (Employment Investigators) invariably thinks so. In fact, it takes years of pen work before an Inspector becomes competent to produce a good, concise and accurate account of an accident, leaving out all unnecessary or irrelevant details . . . ," p. 180.

40. Henry Parris, *Government and the Railways in Nineteenth-Century Britain,* London: Routledge & Kegan Paul, 1965: "Accident inquiries were of special importance in this way, as soon as the inspectors reduced their early obsession with personal responsibility to its proper proportion. Even where companies neglected the recommendations resulting from particular accidents, enquiries served 'to show the Inspecting Officers what additional precautions should be required from railway companies proposing to open new lines'," p. 246.

41. Bridget M. Hutter, *Regulation and Risk: Occupational Health and Safety on the Railways,* Oxford: Oxford University Press, 2001.

42. *Railroads: Their Origins and Problems,* New York: Putnam's Sons, 1878.

43. Letter of Adams to Schurtz, October 31, 1878, Schurz Papers, Manuscript Division, Library of Congress.

44. "Government Inspection of Railroad Accidents," *Railroad Gazette,* February 16, 1877.

Glossary

Cast iron: Early process of producing iron in which the iron was cast in a mold and was hard, brittle, and nonmalleable in comparison to wrought iron.

Damping: Closing air ducts to the boiler fire and thus effectively turning down the fire.

Doctor: Auxiliary engine that would supply water to the boiler separate from an engine used for propulsion.

Foaming: Bubbles created by the boiling of the water in a boiler, which would cause water to issue from a stop-cock—seeming to indicate that there was water at or above the stop-cock—even though it was foam carrying the water up to the stop-cock from several inches below.

Freeboard: Distance from the water line on the hull to the top of the deck.

Fusible plates (or plugs): Safety device allowing pressure above a specified level to intentionally blow out of a boiler. These plates or plugs would blow out, rather than the whole boiler exploding, because they were made of an alloy that melted at lower temperatures than did cast or wrought iron.

High-pressure steam power: Type of steam engine in which the boiler would create high pressure to push a piston out, and, in comparison with low-pressure engines, used less fuel and required less weight in the engine.

Low-pressure steam engine: Type of steam engine, in which steam during its condensation phase created a vacuum that would pull a piston. These engines were termed "low pressure" or "atmospheric" steam engines, and, for their large size and heavy weight, could develop only low levels of power. Moreover, these "low-pressure" engines required a vast amount of fuel and cold water to produce a low level of power.

Safety barge: Barge towed by lines behind a steamboat and on which there would be no engine and thus no possibility of explosion. Used primarily on the Hudson River.

Safety valves: Safety device that would allow excess pressure in a boiler to blow off harmlessly rather than explosively. It was basically a lever and fulcrum with a weight attached to a rod at one end that kept a valve shut at the other end until the pressure of the steam exceeded the weight on the rod, at which time the valve would open and the steam above the weight on the rod would be expelled.

Stop-cocks (a.k.a. gauge-cocks): Safety device in which two spigots on the side of a boiler, one above the other by some few inches, would measure the level of the water and steam in the boiler. They directly measured the levels because water or steam issued from them when they were opened would indicate the level of steam or water inside the boiler. If water issued, then the valve was below or at the water line; if only steam issued, then the water was below that stop-cock. The accuracy of this apparatus was confounded by the problem of foaming.

Wrought iron: Later development of iron production that produced an iron that was tough, malleable, and relatively soft in comparison to cast iron.

Index

For Product Safety Concerns and Information please contact our EU
representative GPSR@taylorandfrancis.com
Taylor & Francis Verlag GmbH, Kaufingerstraße 24, 80331 München, Germany